Summer Showers In Brindavan, 1972

Discourses by
BHAGAWAN SRI SATHYA SAI BABA

During the Summer Course
in Spirituality and Indian Culture
for College Students
at Brindavan, Whitefield, Bangalore

Publications Division
PRASANTHI NILAYAM

**SRI SATHYA SAI SADHANA TRUST,
PUBLICATIONS DIVISION**
Prasanthi Nilayam - 515 134
Anantapur District, Andhra Pradesh, INDIA
STD: 08555 ISD: 91-8555 Phone: 287375 Fax: 287236
E-mail: orders@sssbpt.org URL: www.sssbpt.org

© **Sri Sathya Sai Sadhana Trust,
Publications Division**
Prasanthi Nilayam P.O. 515134,
Anantapur District, A.P. India.

All Rights Reserved

The copyright and the rights of translation in any language are reserved by the Publishers. No part, passage, text or photograph or Artwork of this book should be reproduced, transmitted or utilised, in original language or by translation, in any form or by any means, electronic, mechanical, photo copying, recording or by any information, storage and retrieval system without with the express and prior permission, in writing from the Convener, Sri Sathya Sai Sadhana Trust, Publications Division, Prasanthi Nilayam, Andhra Pradesh India - Pin Code 515134, except for brief passages quoted in book review. This book can be exported from India only by the Publishers - Sri Sathya Sai Sadhana Trust, Publications Division, Prasanthi Nilayam, India.

ISBN:978-81-7208-974-0
978-81-7208-691-6 (Set)

First Edition: March, 2013

Published by
The Convener,
Sri Sathya Sai Sadhana Trust, Publications Division
Prasanthi Nilayam, India, Pin Code - 515134
STD : 08555 ISD: 91-8555 Phone: 287375 Fax: 287236

Printed at
Createspace

CONTENTS

1. Exhortation To Students	1
2. Vedic Truths Belong To The Whole World	11
3. Nature Of The Human Mind	29
4. What The Upanishads Teach Us	45
5. The Nature Of Truth	63
6. 'Kama' And 'Krodha'	79
7. 'Purusha' And 'Prakriti'	95
8. Lessons From The Gita	109
9. Meditation	133
10. Destiny And Divine Grace	159
11. Self-control And Detachment	173
12. Sankara Jayanti	189
13. Customs And Character	205
14. The Perishable And The Imperishable	215
15. Worship Your Parents	223
16. Anger - The Greatest Enemy	237
17. The Path Of Devotion	249
18. Dvaita, Advaita, And Vishishtadvaita	261
19. God's Love Is Like Sunshine	277
20. Pleasure And Pain	287
21. Learning And Humility	303

MESSAGE
From
Bhagawan Sri Sathya Sai Baba

Philosophy is the butter churned out of knowledge. But, since human aspirations and ideals, which change from place to place and time to time, decide which aspects of knowledge are included in the churning process, it is often incomplete or inadequate or contradictory. Generally speaking, religious beliefs and practices, folkways, customs and traditions, educational methods, art-forms, etc. help the formulation of the underlying philosophy.

Believing that the world as cognised during the waking stage is real and that the highest goal is the attainment of happiness in that world, man accumulates the instruments and symbols of that happiness; he fashions after his own taste and inclination, according to the dictates of his own reason, the laws, ideals, institutions, and principles that would bolster that happiness. This attempt leads to a philosophy, which can be named "Western".

But, can the goal of Life be just this – to struggle amidst the waves of joy and grief that rise and fall in this visible objective world, to be carried along the current of desire, gathering food, shelter, comfort and pleasure, and finally, to flounder into the jaws of death? Consider what is happening now: in the name of progress, art is degraded into immoral and sensuous entertainment; educational advance results not in the advance of humility and reverence, but in rampant indiscipline, arrogance, and irreverence. The emphasis long placed on the development of character and the promotion of virtue through education has now been dropped. In their place is enthroned as ideals worldly success, self-aggrandisement, and high living. Laws, rules, and regulations are multiplying fast; but, there is no sign of unrighteousness and injustice being diminished. Greed is growing beyond control; the advance of science is marked, not by a proportionate advance in peace and happiness, but by a phenomenal increase in terror, unrest, and anxiety. With his thousand-faced curiosity, man is analysing and utilising the outer world; but, the inner world, which is basic, is ignored and forgotten.

Human life is a composite of the secular and the spiritual. But, now, the flesh is coddled, while the spirit is consigned into oblivion. As a result, neither the individual, nor the society, nor the nation can hope to have peace and security. The framework of Creation is an amalgam of right and wrong, joy and grief, cold and warmth; so, it is against the Nature to expect only right, or only joy, only wrong or only grief. It is not possible to uproot right wholly from the world; nor is it possible to make the world wholly free from grief in any form. The burden of wrong and the agony of grief can be reduced, however, in proportion to the loyalty that man offers to sublime ideals and his efforts to put them into practice.

So long as man lives on the level of the beasts, concentrating all his talents in the task of securing food, shelter, and other physical and material needs, the unrest now rooted in his heart cannot be got rid of. Therefore, the path of Dharma or Righteousness, which ensures inner purification and harmony, should not be given up.

What is Dharma? It is the way of higher life, directed by the ideals one holds dear, by the level of attainment one has reached, by the status of the individual in society, and the individual's own awareness of himself and his status. Mere awareness of 'I am a human being' will not guide him into the path of Dharma; those, who are aware only of this, will be guided only into the path of feeding, sleeping, and avoidance of fear from danger. Awareness of 'I am a human being' is only half the truth. 'I am not a beast' is the other half. Always remind yourself of what you are, as well as what you are not; when this is done, when activities are in accordance with that awareness, man will be manifesting the full significance of the name he is known by.

When man has resolved to understand his reality by the method of inquiry, he must avoid the error of condemning the points of view held dear by others. It is not right to deny their validity. He has to give value to all aspects, consider all views, for there is no clear cut distinction between mine and thine, this and that other. Truth is Knowledge; Knowledge is Limitless. Truth has to be discovered by analysing the complex mass of facts and things.

Indian Culture is the product of the experience of generations in the field of this Truth, of Knowledge that is limitless, that is seen through the vision of the Wise. When students have the chance once to look upon the Culture, to contact its living embodiments and expressions, and to hold converse with its manifold manifestations, all doubts regarding it will vanish from their minds. It is a fact that persons, who are too lazy to learn, who have not grasped the validity of Vedanta, or the relative reality of the world, feel that Indian culture is at best a ruse to while away one's time. We are not concerned with such persons. They have such ideas, because they do not know that Vedanta is their own history. Animals are not conscious that they are alive; they live without being aware of life. If man, too, leads life in this manner, verily, he is no better than a mere animal.

Your forefathers were being fed from infancy on breast milk re-inforced by the mixture of sublime ideals and principles of righteousness. As a result, they stuck to the path of righteousness, steadily, in a commendable form. They strove to help each other; co-operated in all efforts to promote the welfare of others and sympathised when others suffered or incurred loss or injury. They did not allow feelings of hatred, revenge, or violence to tarnish their minds. They recognised that their chief duty was to devote themselves in activities conducive to general good.

Today, those, who pride themselves on the enormous advance achieved by man and prance about prattling the stories of their paltry victories, are only demonstrating by their behaviour that they are totally ignorant of the high principles followed in life by their forefathers. What is the reason for the disappearance from the present generation of the sublime virtues of those days, of sympathy and mutual aid, of the peace and happiness that prevailed then? No inquiry is probing into this problem.

Can a King, declaring himself the master of a state, fulfil all the wishes of his subjects? Why, he finds himself incompetent to fulfil even all his own wishes! If he decides to pursue his fancies on the plea that he is the lord and master, his subjects draw him down from the throne. How does this happen? However high a person's authority, he has to bow his head to some laws and limits that are laid down to ensure proper exercise of that power. They might have been laid down by the king himself, but once accepted and announced, he is bound to them as strongly as anyone else. If he acts in contravention of the covenant, the subjects, too, would break away from the laws and limits that regulate their activities and behaviours, and anarchy would result. For, the saying goes, "As the ruler, so is the ruled." Therefore, the law-maker should obey the law; he, who lays down the limit, should himself respect it. This is the precious lesson, the shining lamp of wisdom, that the Ramayana is holding forth for the benefit of man. This is the excellence of the culture and history of India.

Students have to be instructed on these monuments of Indian Culture and informed of the ideals, which they embody. Their intellects, thus charged and cleansed, have to be offered to the nations of the world as ideals to be emulated. They themselves will be saved thereby; they will serve as guides and leaders to others. Intending to place before them the Truth, to remove from their minds the ruinous beliefs that have sprouted there, as a result of the craze for novelty in recent times, to uproot the specious arguments and fantastic doubts that are clinging to their reasoning faculty, and resolving to imprint on the pure, steadfast, and conceitless hearts of the young the peace and joy that their forefathers were able to live in, we have arranged to invite elders of invaluable experience in these fields and instruct youth on moral, ethical, spiritual, physical, and secular truths.

When such a sacred Yajna is held every year, present-day Youth can easily understand and appreciate not only the Culture of India, but also the Wisdom garnered by people of other lands. Thus, they will be rid of all feelings of separation and difference; they will be equipped and made ready to demonstrate in their lives the Truth that has been revealed to them. This Summer Course on Indian Culture and Spirituality has been planned and arranged with this belief and in this faith.

May this attempt achieve Victory! May all beings derive therefrom Peace, Happiness, Prosperity, and Security.

Baba

PREFACE

It is well-known that there are many gaps in the equipment of the student, which the present system of education does not find it easy to fill. Quite a few Commissions and Study Groups have reported on the problems relating to pressure of numbers, the medium of instruction, examinational procedures, the status of teacher and students, and the reforms required in the constitution of university bodies. The University Grants Commission has appointed several committees that have produced modernised syllabuses for various subjects, reported on the scope and method of research on educational problems, directed the production of text-books with an Indian and World View, and discussed the possibility of a general course for undergraduates in the evolution of Indian culture.

The re-orientation of the very objectives of higher education is also engaging the attention of educationists. The Kothari Commission has stressed the need for value education, for a moral and spiritual impact on the evolving personality of the student. The problem of value education has to be urgently solved. Some countries have a system of education, which is compulsive, seeking to fit students into patterns predetermined by the State. In spite of its excellence, the ancient Indian system was exclusive, designed for a section of society, not for all. The Colonial system revived values like Science, Love of Freedom and Reason. But, it left the ego unchanged and was powerless to bring about the sublimation of character and attitude.

A National System of Education in India will not stop short of Reason. All subjects, the physical and social sciences and the humanities, will be so studied and developed that they will help the blossoming of the spirit. They are at present tied up to the apron strings of philosophies, which do not emphasise the value of spiritual life. Education in India has to envisage a society built on love and co-operation, integrating castes and communities and creeds into one, through the awareness of the immortality of the soul and the equality of all in the realm of the spirit.

The philosophy of Bhagawan Sri Sathya Sai Baba lays stress on the core of Love and Bliss in each human being. Cutting across all distinctions, it underlines the brotherhood of man and the fatherhood of God. It promotes Truth, Righteousness, Peace, and Love in the individual, the family, the society, the nation, and the world. As an instrument for the reconstruction of humanity on these pillars, Bhagawan has planned Summer Courses in Spirituality and Indian Culture, of a month's duration, to groups of College Students and Teachers gathered from all the states of India. Each Course includes lectures by eminent scholars, thinkers, administrators, and repositories of classical learning and exponents of art, on Hinduism and other Religions, Vedanta and other systems of philosophy, Science and its impact on cultural values, Mystics and Saints of all lands, and kindred subjects, which will foster the values so essential for an educated person today. As a practical supplement to these discourses, the students will have bhajan, meditation, yogasana training, self-help activities, social service programmes in the villages around the place, where the Course is held. Bhagawan Himself discourses every evening at the Camp, amplifying and clarifying the points raised during the lectures of the day and elaborating in His unique, sweet, and simple style, with plenty of parables and stories, His Message of Love. These Discourses are herewith offered for the edification of all, so that His Message to the Students might be studied and assimilated by all those, who are interested in the uplift of youth. The book will also serve as an Introduction to the Teachings of the Avatar of the Age, for the uplift of Humanity.

1.
Exhortation To Students

When clouds gather in the high skies, they are usually accompanied by lightning. In the same manner, wherever there is education, it should be accompanied by wisdom. We have to recognise such an association as an essential truth. Many things like the fullness of life and all that is purposeful in this world have been involved in problems of education. Because we do not see these things clearly and they appear to us tarnished to a large extent, whatever is good in education is being hidden from us. Every thinking individual concerned with education is today faced with a large number of problems; problems that have been agitating the minds of students and of teachers. It is the duty of everyone to see that these problems are solved and the right solutions are put into the hearts of young people and thereby, infuse a sense of the Divine in their minds. Because good qualities, like sacrifice, forbearance, truth, and love, have been somewhat pushed to the background, the society is suffering from various ills. It is the sacred duty of good education not only to rectify such ills and give proper shape and form to society, but also to rid the minds and hearts of people, as well, of all evils. In our educational methods of today, we are attaching great importance to giving voluminous books and the information contained in these voluminous books to the students. We are not making an effort to improve the ideas and ideologies of the students. By their acquaintance with these books, the students are filling their heads with the contents of such books to the fullest capacity and without any discrimination. They are not utilising properly the matter that is going into their heads. It has been mentioned earlier this morning that the present educational system in our country is resulting in our students taking in quite an amount of information and that they are not converting this information into useful knowledge and wisdom. But, I feel that our students lack in the discriminating capacity by which to selectively absorb only good information. If they do so, they can also convert it into useful knowledge. We are no doubt keeping in mind today the ideals and the goals of good education, but that is not enough. We should also make an effort to put them into practice.

Keeping aside for one moment the educational system itself, I have to state that in the name of education, many new habits, many new cultures, and many new ideas are being injected into the minds of our children. As a result, the parents are not able to lift their heads with honour in the society around them. Fathers and mothers, who have sons and daughters who are students and are part of the contemporary educational system, know that the children are behaving in such a manner as to create problems in the house. The parents often wonder how these problems can be tackled and how their children can be handled. These sons and daughters are not able to develop sufficient confidence in themselves. Their fathers and mothers wonder what their future is going to be. Today, man's ideas are taking an extraordinary and crooked shape, because there is a certain amount of distortion in their minds, caused by their running after western civilisation and western notions. As a result, they attach great importance to temporary gains and transient successes. Life is not that transient or that trivial, so as to be played with. It should not be sold to running after wrong and distorted aims. Students should attach more importance and sanctity to life than they do now. The minds and hearts of students are tender, sweet, soft, and gentle. If, at this age, when their hearts are still tender and gentle, they cannot take in the values of life, they will not be able to take them in later. The essential reason for this lies in the way fathers and mothers are looking after their children and in the ideas they are giving to their children. In the ambition and desire of the parents that their children should have freedom and that they should rise to high positions in their lives, they are giving them freedom without telling them how dangerous freedom could be, if not utilised properly.

The end of wisdom is freedom.

The end of culture is perfection.

The end of knowledge is love.

The end of education is character.

There is a desire on the part of all of us to acquire these four qualities, namely wisdom, culture, knowledge, and education and reach their ends, namely freedom, perfection, love, and character. But, students should realise that if these qualities are not properly utilised, then they cannot call themselves students. As students and future citizens of this country, you have the responsibility for shaping the future of this country. Put your hearts in the right path by listening attentively to the more experienced men. Then, you will be in a position to enlighten others and proclaim the ancient glory and culture of this land to the whole world. I have no doubt that after this summer course, you will be able to proclaim proudly the sacredness of the culture of this land of ours and of the values contained therein. You may be thinking that there are only about three hundred students from this vast country of India attending this course and you may be wondering how such a small number can do anything to rectify and alter the terrifying phases, which life in this country has assumed.

My dear students! There may be hundreds and thousands of sepoys and jawans to be trained, but there will be only a small number of teachers to train them. These are the commanders and leaders. Taking this example, even though there are thousands of students in this country, you as leaders must get the training you require to train the many thousands of others in the country. This is the idea, with which you must go through the summer course. This is the first summer course you are attending and I hope and bless you that, after you have gone through it, you will acquire the virtues of leadership. Those of you, who are here, have to acquire by going through these classes, a certain amount of strength and character. With this strength, you will be able to lead your country. In this world, most of you wish to do some noble and difficult work. All those, who wish to participate in such work, have to accept leadership and responsibility. Those students, who today feel that it is good to accept such a responsibility, are the ones, who will do well in the future.

If we cannot recognise our duties, we will not be able to rectify our methods. Take the example of a leader, who is very much addicted to drinking. How can he propagate the usefulness of keeping away from drink? How can he preach prohibition? In the same manner, how can such teachers and students, who succumb to evils, do good to and improve society? If we want to accept the responsibility of telling others to rectify their faults, then the first thing to do is to rectify our own faults and change our own lives, so that there are no more faults left in us. So, the right thing to do is to cleanse our own hearts and then, move to the area around you, say your own village. After purifying the people of the village, then you can move to the district; after purifying the district, you can move to the state and after purifying the state, you can become a leader in your country. If you want to become a leader without these prior acts, then you will be disappointed and you cannot be a leader. It is only when we understand and recognise the responsibility and the duty of a citizen, we will be able to change the methods of education and infuse into those methods love and peace, which are the essential qualities of a good citizen. For students and other members of society, education should be a kind of social ideal. It should constitute a bridge, on which you should walk to reach your goal. If this bridge of education is not built with sufficient strength, it will be harmful to the individual. The students should take the road of reorganisation and endow education with the strength it needs. By developing prejudicial attitudes and maintaining attachments, we are not going to derive happiness from our actions. It is only by developing a correct vision of things that we will be able to derive happiness. Today's education is aimed at giving those, who go through it, an amount of temporary happiness, temporary beauty, and temporary pleasure. The conduct of students of today is not controlled in any manner. Principles of education, which do not connect the students with their parents, will bring unhappiness to all of us in the future. One of the essential facets of Indian culture is to recognise the mother and father as equivalent to God. If we do not deserve the love of our mother and of our father, from who else can we ask for such affection? We should therefore develop attitudes, by which we can promote such love and respect. It is only when you are able to respect your parents, your children will respect you when you, in the future, become fathers and mothers. In every action of ours and in every thought of ours, there is a reflection and an echo. If in your future, you aspire to and want some happiness, pleasure, and peace; you must practise certain principles at the present time. You must practise these principles now to bring peace and contentment for yourself in the later stages of your life. Indian culture is constituted of certain rituals and certain practices, which have been handed down to us through the ages. Today, students regard these rituals, some of which are the essence of Indian culture, as being foolish. They think that they are very clever and that these rituals are meaningless.

Today, many scientists of great reputation are inventing gadgets and flying to the moon. They are spending so much money on such things, but they do not have peace of mind. Leaders and men, who are at the top of society, feel that they have everything. Alas! They do not have any peace of mind. Why is this so? We have to enquire and find an answer for this. One can count stars and fly to the moon. But, if one cannot look into the inside of one's self, how can he find happiness? Our culture and traditions are such that they enable you to know who you are and help you to understand yourself. The first thing to have is self-confidence, after which alone you will get self-satisfaction. Once you have got self-satisfaction, then you must acquire the virtue of self-sacrifice and after self-sacrifice alone, you come to self-realisation. Thus, to achieve self-realisation, self-confidence is the most important thing. In all these four attributes, namely self-confidence, self-satisfaction, self-sacrifice, and self-realisation, the one common word is self. To understand this self, you must find out from experienced people what they know about it. From today, for a whole period of one month, to enable you to find out the meaning of this self, we have invited a large number of people, who have experienced this self, to tell you what it means.

It is possible that during this one month, there may be certain inconveniences that you have to put up with. The food and comforts may not suit you. You have to bear up with all this and bear it up with happiness, because such a training is essential in your lives. This discipline is in fact the first step in self-realisation. The reason why I have called this the first step during your training is that, today, there are a large number of people, who cannot put up with difficulties and inconveniences and yet, wish to achieve bigger and more subtle things. This study and discipline, to which you will submit yourselves, will lead you to happiness and bliss. If you cannot put up with small difficulties, how will you be shaping into people, who are to rectify social evils? Some day or other, difficulties are going to come your way. So also, sorrow and great inconveniences are going to come your way. It is much better to stand firm and know what those difficulties are, when you are young. Then, you will be able to withstand such difficulties in your later lives with some ease. In this summer course, you must take various difficulties you come across as part of your education and put up with them cheerfully. Some people do physical exercises to keep their bodies strong. While doing such exercises, you feel tired and experience discomfort, but after the exercises are over, you get the strength for your muscles. There is no doubt that all the difficulties and obstacles you may come across will be the necessary exercises to give you happiness, in your later lives. Dear students! This is your house and in the one month you are going to spend in this house, you must acquire the necessary wisdom and knowledge and then, communicate this knowledge to your friends and to the society, in which you live and thereby, proclaim the greatness and glory of our culture.

There is one other matter. According to our rules, we give great importance to silence and cleanliness. If you should talk, you may do so softly and in a controlled manner. Do not go out of the campus and move freely. These are the tools, with which you should give shape to your future lives. We are used to regarding summer as a month of holidays. This is not correct. Those students, who are here, should not regard this as a month of holidays, but should regard it as one of holy days. The manner of spending our holy days is not by eating sweets, but by filling your minds and hearts with matters pertaining to the Divine. Try to imbibe all the things that various teachers are going to tell you. It is not enough to imbibe what is taught, but you must also put into practice the sayings of those teachers. With this advice, I would like to close My discourse of this morning.

2.

Vedic Truths Belong To The Whole World

Although born in the human race, born as human beings, and enveloped by human environment, alas! Men have forgotten the essential qualities of the human race. Amongst all the animals and amongst all the living things that are born, the birth of a human being is a very unique one. To be able to earn the gift of being born as a man is an extraordinarily difficult thing. Having attained that gift from the hands of God and having succeeded in being born as a man, if you do not make full use of such a gift, you will be committing a great sin. We must realise that being born as a man in this birth, is the result of having attained and acquired the 'punya' or the fruit of many good turns that we had done in several previous births.

This body is like a boat. Our life is like a river and we have to cross that river and reach our destination.

Our destination is the destination of Divinity. Our life, the present one, is one of living in the contemporary world. In this process of our trying to cross the river of life and reach the destination of Divinity, the boat that we have to use, namely our body has to be safeguarded and taken great care of. This boat should not develop leakages enroute. We should believe that all these students, who assembled here today are really good, strong, and new boats, which do not have any chance of developing leaks. If we do not make an attempt to use the boats as they are right now, good as they are and without leakages, or in the alternative we postpone and try to use these same boats after they have become older and developed leaks, then our lives are sure to be subjected to some kind of difficulties and harm. This body has got the name 'Deha', which it has acquired, because the name signifies that the body has been essentially made of elements, resulting in its going ultimately to be destroyed. The temporariness or the transient nature of this body is contained in the very name that has been given to it. Further, the indestructible Divine strength, which has come into this destructible body, has been called man's soul or the human spirit. Because the body contains this indestructible Divine spirit, the live body has also been called 'man'. In the very word 'Manava', which stands for man, we are able to see the Divinity that is present in man. Manava, the word which stands for man, has got three syllables. The first one, 'Ma', stands for 'ajnana' or ignorance, absence of knowledge. The second one, 'Na', stands for the desire that ignorance and absence of knowledge should disappear. The third one, 'Va', conveys the injunction that one should conduct oneself in a manner as to remove ignorance. Our ignorance is equivalent to or synonymous with death. Thus, there is no meaning in our attributing ignorance to man. Today, we do this, only forgetting the immortal soul in man, attaching importance to what is temporary and transient around us, and not giving the necessary attention to what is Divine in us. This is bringing some kind of shame and disrepute on human qualities themselves. That which proclaims the natural shape of man, that which makes evident to others the true nature of man, is called Vedanta.

Today, in the morning, some ideas about Indian culture and Indian traditions were given to you in the very first lecture. You were also told the meaning of spirituality. You learnt about essence of all the religions of the world. Two aspects of this essence were indicated to you. One is philosophy, the other is our having to go through the spiritual path. From what was said about these two aspects, namely, philosophy and spiritual path, I have got the impression that you have understood that philosophy, because it represents the qualities of the head, and spirituality, because it represents the qualities of the heart, are somewhat antagonistic and unrelated to each other. It is not possible that either of these things can dissociate itself from or ignore the other. If there is no heart, there is no use having the head. Even if one has the head, there is no use for it, if there is no heart. Therefore, if in our lives, we do not have either of these two, namely, the head or the heart, life will become completely useless.

Yes, it is the first essential requirement that through our head, we should make all the necessary enquiries relating to philosophy. After we have made the necessary enquiries with the head, we should attempt to reach the heart. That is our spiritual path. The first one concerns itself with the information and the second one with transformation. If we do not gather the information, it is not possible to achieve transformation.

Some people belonging to some regions of the world have been making attempts to gather the essence that is contained in all the religions of the world. They are not only attempting to gather the essence of all the religions, but also the essence that is contained in all the cultures of the different countries of the world. They are then attempting to reconcile them. When we make the necessary enquiries about the religions of other countries, it becomes evident to us that all those religions have been established by wise people as a result of their own experience. The fact is that those religions have been established by human beings, however wise and saintly they may have been. But, the religion of this country is not something that has been established by man. It has been established by God. The one religion or the essence of all religions of this country is not related to anything that has come out of the experience of man. It has not come as a result of any effort on the part of man. In essence, it has come out of God Himself and that is why it is called the religion of Vedas. He, Who established man's religion in this country, He, Who gave the guidelines for man's religion in this country, and He, Who had really been the source of religion in this country, is not man but He is the Man of all men, that is God Himself. Vedas are very old, have no describable origin, and are timeless. Vedas do not need support from any quarter, as they support themselves. In fact, Vedas are God's breath and the Vedic religion, which has been established in India, originated in God's breath. Thus it is, that God's religion is the religion of India. Of all the religions of the entire world, it appears to us that the Indian religion, the religion that has been at the back of the Indian mind, is the life breath and is the stream that is flowing through all the religions of this world. The religions of other countries are certainly as sacred and sanctified, but for only a certain limited time. On the other hand, the religion of this country is something, which had had no beginning and will have no end.

Although some of the religions of the rest of the world show us a slightly different path and differ from each other in the matter of detail and sometimes, seem to differ somewhat only apparently in the matter of their destination, we have to accept and believe that the essential content of all these religions is one and the same and that relates to the Divine Atma. Although the human body is made of many different organs, we do realise that heart is the essential basis and support for all these organs. It supplies the life blood to all other organs. In the same manner, we certainly see many different religions all round the world, but we have to accept that the Indian viewpoint is like the heart, which supplies the life blood to all other religions in the world. You may have some doubts, when

I describe the situation in this manner. The doubts are somewhat of this nature. Why is it that great saints, great men of religion were born only in India and the Vedas themselves were born in India? Why is it that these Vedas and the people, who expounded them, were not born in other countries? God is present everywhere. God is omnipresent. Therefore, Vedas, which simply constitute the breath of God, are also omnipresent and should therefore, be everywhere. The sound of Vedas, the essence of Vedas, the fragrance of Vedas is indeed to be found all over the world. Here is a small example. When did we find out that the Earth has got the power to attract? When a Western scientist by name Newton, through his experiment, through his intelligence, and through his work, discovered that there is an attracting power called gravitation, natural to the Earth. From that day, we started believing that Earth has the power to attract. But, did not Earth have the power to attract before Newton? The phenomenon of gravitation surely could not have had a separate beginning. In fact, ever since Earth came into existence, Earth should have had the power to attract. In the same manner, as one single Western individual named Newton, after his efforts and his research, has uncovered the existing fact that Earth has the power to attract, so also, the fact that the Vedas are the life breath, which were given to us by God, was something, which had been uncovered and found out by the efforts of Indian Saints. Just as there is an amount of truth in the statement that Newton, by his effort and by his researches, has discovered that Earth has the power to attract, exactly the same amount of truth is also contained in the statement that Indian Sages and citizens of India, by their efforts and by their researches, have discovered that the Vedas, sounds of the Vedas, and the inner meanings that are contained in the Vedas are God given. In the same manner, intelligent people, belonging to one particular country discovering something relating to Nature and people belonging to another country discovering again something else, relating to the external world, are on the same footing as intelligent people in this country discovering something spiritual. This practice of citizens of each country discovering something new and presenting their discoveries to the rest of the world has been a time honoured phenomenon all the world over. That is all what is to it and we should really not utilise this situation to regard either the philosophy of a particular country, or the spiritual path adopted by that particular country as being any distinctive and as being the monopoly of that particular country. Such truths really belong to the whole world.

The difference that man creates in the notions that we develop about philosophy and spiritual paths are only creations of his mind. They are, therefore, causing difficulties at times. Spirituality and philosophy are two things, which are closely related to each other and which follow each other. This is something, which we should accept and believe in. We should not look for differences between these two and regard one of them as the head and the other as the heart.

Here is a small example. On one tree, we see a large number of different fruits. Those fruits are not reaching out to us as soon as we see them. When we see them, our mind persuades us and prompts us to go near the fruits. As soon as we go near the fruits, there is a temptation to have those fruits. We then bend down and our hands pick up a stone. As soon as we take the stone in the hand, our shoulder will make us throw the stone at the fruits. Then, the fruit falls to the ground and the hand takes the fruit and hands it over to the mouth. This fruit gradually reaches the stomach. We now ask what is responsible for this act of the fruit having reached our digestive organs. Can we decide whether it is the hand or it is the shoulder that is responsible or is it the stone or is it the mind that is responsible or ultimately, is it the fruit itself that is responsible? It is the combination and the combined effort of all these various individual items that has resulted in the one final act of the fruit reaching your digestive organs. Thus, it is only when we are able to coordinate the essence of all the religions, the goals of all the religions, and also the contents of the various philosophies of different people and look at them as one containing the Divine spirit, that we can get rid of our doubts and satisfy our hunger for peace by grasping the one Divine truth. If one takes all these religions, whether it is Hinduism, or the Parsi religion, or Buddhism, or Christian religion, or Islam and if one takes parts of them and experiences those parts, there is no doubt that he derives a certain amount of joy. But, that does not mean that we have to give up any one of them or take any one only. You have to recognise that, in all of them, there is a common factor, which relates to the oneness of Divinity, the Atma, and that recognition alone will be the complete realisation and utilisation of these different religions.

Our ability to comprehend and acquire complete knowledge is defective and has in many cases disappeared. That is the reason why, when we look at a religion, we do not comprehend the whole of it, but we take a bit of it and form an opinion. Many of you may have heard the story of a number of blind men reaching an elephant and touching it. One blind man, who happens to touch the trunk of the elephant, gets the feeling that it is like a big root of a big tree and therefore, he thinks that the elephant is like the root of a tree. Another blind man just happens to touch one of the legs and he feels that it is like a pillar and concludes that an elephant is like a pillar. Another blind man happens to touch the ear of the elephant and he thinks that it is like a big fan and so, concludes that the elephant is in the shape of a big fan. Another blind man touches the stomach or the tummy of the elephant and thinks that it is a huge wall and concludes that an elephant looks like a big wall. Thus, each one of these people, having touched only a part of the elephant, comes to the conclusion based on the impression, which that part has created, that the elephant looks like that particular part. They, amongst themselves, are not able to realise that it is the combination of all these individual parts that really constitutes the elephant. Thus, when people of different countries look at the world religion, they see only parts of it and like what the blind people have thought of the elephant, each one, who looks only at a part of the world religion, thinks that the world religion is only that part. Each one for himself is not able to get a comprehensive picture. We have to realise that the world religion is a combination of all the individual components, which each one of them is getting at. We have to believe that this religion is in essence like sacred 'prema' or love. Yesterday, I told you that there is only one religion and that is the religion of LOVE.

In one of the talks this morning, the words 'knowledge' and 'wisdom' were mentioned. It was said that there is a great difference between knowledge and wisdom. Knowledge is something, which is related only to the head. It is possible that by conducting some enquiries and by working with some special types of machines, one can reach an important position in the matter of acquiring knowledge. One has to say that, to some extent, this is simply bookish knowledge. Just by such an acquisition, our capacity to comprehend truth is not going to improve. What we call knowledge is the essence of all sciences. Wisdom, on the other hand, is something, which we acquire as a result of practice. Knowledge acquired from books differs very much from knowledge acquired from experience. Wisdom is acquired by experience. This tells us something about the very sweet nature of our life. But, knowledge, which we have acquired from books, enables you only to experience and understand the phraseology, the grouping of the words, the subtle way, in which ideas are being conveyed by keeping words in different places. But, it cannot take you beyond that. In order that you may clearly understand these things, let us take the case of the very large ocean.

If we take water from that ocean and put it in our mouth, we will get the taste of its being very salty. If the same salt water is converted into water vapour by the heat of the sun, constituted into clouds and then, comes back as rain on the earth, that water will be very sweet. Whether it is the water that is flowing in the river after the rain, or the water that is taken directly from the ocean, it is the same water. But, we should ask where the change has taken place, as a result of which this sweetness has come. This is 'samskara' or purification. This can be compared to wisdom born out of experience. It is only when we take the matter that is contained in the ocean of books or scriptures and use our 'buddhi' or intelligence, which can be compared to the sun's heat, and convert it into clouds, which can be compared to 'prema' or love, then only, like the water that results after the rain, our knowledge will be sweet and this will be called wisdom. In every effort and in every thing that we do, cleansing or purification is very essential. From time immemorial, our Indian traditions have been attaching great importance to this practice of purification.

In no human endeavour can we bypass this process of purification. I wish to cite another small example. Every student has a watch on his hand. When you take this watch and put it in fire, you will find that the whole of it reduces to metal or metallic ash. All of it will fetch in the market only a few naya paise. But, so long as it remains as a watch, it will fetch you anything like a few hundred rupees. Are we paying this few hundred rupees for the metal that is contained in the watch? Or are we paying that amount for the purification and the transformation, which has been given to that metal before giving it the shape of a watch? The payment of a few hundred rupees is obviously towards the transformation, which has been given to the metal from which the bolts, nuts, wheels, the spring, and all the contents of the watch have been made. It is not being paid for the metal or the steel, which has gone into making these bolts and nuts. It is therefore, not possible to assign any high value to the many different individuals and different shapes that you see in the human beings. If you really want to assess the human beings and assign values, you have to see and assess how these different persons are behaving, what their character is, what changes have come about in them after birth, and what are the paths, which they are following. If, therefore, one wishes to change himself to being really a man, in other words, if he wishes to be like a human being, there is a need to take great care about the way, in which one behaves. The respect, which Indians are going to get for themselves as groups and as a Nation, is not going to come either through the wealth or the property, which they possess, or through the positions of authority, which they may be occupying. Such respect will come only through the character, which they develop, and the behaviour they exhibit.

Take the case of Ravana. We know from our mythology that at the time when Ravana lived, there was no other individual, who had access to property and wealth any more than Ravana had. Ravana had all the position, which one could command. He had all the authority that one could have. Inspite of that, the fact that Ravana was subjected to great difficulties towards the end and that he lost his life in battle is noteworthy. We should compare this with what happened to Rama. Rama intentionally and wilfully gave up all His property, He gave up His kingdom, and He went into the forest for several years. Ultimately, He was given the honour of having maintained dharma in this country. From this difference between Ravana, who had all the property, position, and authority, and Rama, Who willingly gave up all the property, position, and authority, we should conclude that we cannot attach any importance to either property, position, or authority. We can only attach importance to character and to the pursuit of right conduct. Thus, we conclude that money comes and goes, whereas morality comes and grows. It is only in this context that we often say, "Dharmo rakshati rakshitah." This simply means that those of us, who safeguard dharma, will be safeguarded in turn by dharma. This is the essence of Indian culture. But, how to know what is right? How to know what is righteous conduct? This is something, which you all will know later, as days go by.

The issues relating to the statements that God is omnipresent, that God is omniscient, that God knows everything, will have to be gone into in some detail. In this context, we should know that for human life, support essentially comes from the five senses. These five senses are called 'shabda, sparsha, rupa, rasa, gandha'. We have also the five material elements. They are the earth, water, fire, air, and sky. We have to enquire and ask where these five elements are and what is it that comes out of the combination of these five elements. We have further to ask how these material elements are connected with 'shabda, sparsha, rupa, rasa, gandha'. We have to note that these five sensations or senses of perception are present in their totality only in the earth. They are not present as all five in water, or in fire, or in the air, or in the sky. Because all these five sense perceptions are contained in the earth, that becomes rather heavy and that is the reason why the earth is able to stay as a massive body in one place. The second element is water. In water, you will find that one of these senses has disappeared and that is the smell. We do not smell water, but we have the shabda, sparsha, rupa, and rasa in it. Because out of the five qualities, one, namely the smell, has disappeared. We have the other four, that is the sound, the touch, the shape, and the taste. These four are contained in water. So, water is not so heavy and hard as the earth. It is able to move out a little more freely than the earth can. The third element is fire. In this, one more quality has disappeared. Neither rasa, nor gandha can be attributed to fire. We have only the sound, the touch, and the shape exhibited by fire. Therefore, it has become still lighter than either the earth, or the water and it is able to go higher and higher, and more freely. The fourth one is air. In air, there are only two qualities left and those are shabda and sparsha, the sound and the touch. The shape, taste, and smell have all disappeared and they are no longer qualities of air. So, it has become very light. Air is able to move more freely and go wherever it wants to go. The fifth element is the sky. The only quality, which the sky has, is shabda or sound. All the other four qualities have disappeared and this is the reason why we find that the sky is present everywhere. God is beyond and above all these five senses of perception. He has none of the five qualities or attributes of matter. Therefore, He is lighter than all these five elements and He is present everywhere. It does not matter whether you look at this description from a spiritual angle or from a scientific angle, the truth of the statement, which has now been made, will have to be accepted by everyone. That is why God is described as 'Anoraniyam, Mahato Mahiyam'. This statement means that God is like an infinitesimal being amongst the infinitely small ones. God is like an infinite being amongst the infinitely large ones. Gopikas, who have had considerable experience of Divinity, had at one time been singing the praise of the Lord, describing His qualities and His greatness in the following terms, "How can we find You? You are present in all the 84 lakhs of different kinds of living things and You are like an infinitesimally small One, when we think of infinitesimally small things. You are like an infinitely large One, when we think of infinitely large things. You are infinite and You have rendered us with minds, which cannot know and even get an estimate of Yourself, Who is present everywhere, in small things as well as in big things. Thus, You have given us this ignorance and we would like to call You a 'thief', a Person, Who has done something which has put us in difficulty."

He has also been described as One, Who has stolen their own 'chitta' or their heart. This is a matter, which is of extraordinary interest, in that the Gopikas, who had not any spiritual practice, who had not read any shastras, who had not undergone any sacrifice or experience of a Divine nature, had been able to bind down the Divine One to themselves. The one single effort involved related to 'prema' or love and that is all. To know the Lord of the Universe, to understand Him, and to be able to get closer to Him, there is no need to read all the text books. The one thing that you should practise and that you should have in your heart is 'prema'. But, because the ancient 'Rishis', who lived in this country, had handed over to us the sacred texts, which are full of meaning, it is our responsibility, it is the responsibility of all Indians, to read them, to try and understand them. We should also put into practice what is contained in them and hand over all the essence and the good things to the rest of the world.

There is a story about Sankara that after having read and understood all the Shastras, the Upanishads, and the Vedas, while going to Benares, he found that in one out of the way place, a poor man in a poor hut was reciting 'Vyakarana' or grammar. One young student of Sankara went to the hut and tried to peep through a hole in the wall and wanted to convey or teach something to this person, who was reciting grammar. He addressed this grammarian by calling him 'moodhamate' or an ignoramus and said, "You must realise that you should now perform 'bhajan' or the Name of the Lord should be repeated by you. Your time for that is right now. Do not wait till the end of your life." It is necessary for us to understand that it is very much more sacred and sanctifying to fill our hearts with 'prema' than to fill our heads with all kinds of books on spiritual matters. Today, India's culture is becoming weaker and weaker. For that reason, the students from various parts of this country, who are going to be our future citizens, are brought here into these classes, which we have organised. Through the experienced teachers and their lectures, we are giving you the contents of not simply one text, but all the Vedas, the Upanishads, and all our scriptures. So far as you are concerned, it is essential that you should develop the feeling of 'prema', which alone is the rich experience in the Vedas and the other texts, which the teachers are giving you. I bless you, after having the experience, to go back and to grow into good citizens of India and re-establish the glory and the shining, ancient path of this country.

3.
Nature Of The Human Mind

Just as one, who wants to live in this world, should first become human, one, who wants to learn 'Brahma Vidya', should first become a spiritualist. The human body is composed of all the five elements and the soul in it has no binding of any particular kind. If you introspect on this matter, you will find that the soul inside the body is the real essence of it. In common parlance, when we live in a rented house, we say that we pay a rent. We may query if we pay the rent to the house or to the owner of the house. The answer is obvious. But, in regard to spiritual matters, we do not seem to bother about such questions. The human body is like a rented house. An individual is living in that rented house. The individual has really to pay the rent to the owner of the house, namely, God. He should not pay the rent to the body. In truth, God is the Owner of the house, in which we live, as He owns the body.

This house of man should be regarded as something, through which we should acquire knowledge and wisdom. Spiritual knowledge tells us that the Divine dwells in this body, although we regard the body itself as a destructible thing. We also call it a 'kshetra', a place where something is living. These notions arise on account of the fact that something permanent is inside the destructible human body. This morning, two ideas have been dealt with, namely the destructibility and the indestructibility. We should know the connection that exists between these two concepts. All that you see in this world is destructible. In fact, all living beings that you see around you are destructible. The only indestructible thing is 'jiva' or the soul that is contained in the living beings that you see. If you want to understand this with ease, then you have to accept and believe that every thing that undergoes a change, everything that transforms from time to time is a destructible thing. The human body is associated with six stages of transformation. These six are birth, growth, change, evolution, death, and destruction. Because the body is passing through all these phases and because the body is not a permanent one, we are attributing to it the quality of destruction or destructibility.

The difference between destructibility and indestructibility is something, which is very fine, which is very small. If there is no destruction, then we will not be able to comprehend what it is that is permanent or indestructible. On the other hand, if there is no permanency or indestructibility, then we will not understand what it is that gets destroyed. Sometimes, these aspects will convey to you a lesson that they are related to each other, in fact related to each other so closely that one cannot be separated from the other. This is what is contained in the 13th chapter of the Bhagavad Gita, where the 'kshetra' and 'kshetrajna', that is the place and one who lives in the place, have been dealt with. In very clear language, the relationship between the abode and the one, who lives in the abode, has been explained. We have to make an enquiry and ask if the realisation of the self or the soul is the final achievement. That is not the end of the enquiry. Of course, by such an enquiry, we understand what is the destructible part of man and what is the indestructible part of him. But, there is something, which is neither the body, nor the soul. This something is what may be called the 'Purushottama' and it exceeds both these things. We can take it that we have reached the goal of our practice only when we have been able to realise this 'Purushottama'. There is a small example for this. A servant, in order to find out his master in a dark room, enters the house and goes in to the dark room. In the dark room, with his hand, he tries to touch and feel everything that is contained therein. As he moves about in the dark room and as he tries to feel and touch various objects, maybe on one occasion, he would touch a chair and then, he would say, "No, this is not my master." Then, he may touch a bench and he would say, "No, this is not my master." He may then touch some kind of a box. Then, he would say, "No, this is not my master." This kind of enquiry will lead him through various situations, by which he would say, "This is not my master, this is not my master," and he would exhaust all that he can feel inside the room. In this manner and while making such a search, he will go and touch a cot. After he has touched the cot, he will touch the feet and then, he will say, "Now, I have found my master." It is not right that he should feel happy, satisfied, and contented as soon as he touches the feet and as soon as he thought he found his master. His objective will be fully achieved only after he goes further, goes nearer the master, and is able to recognise and take himself closer to the master.

In this body, which can be compared to a house, all the desires, which come through the various organs which are parts of the body, may be compared to the darkness in the house. In this dark house, that aspect, which we may call the individual, is going around like the servant in a dark room, searching for the soul or the Lord. The first thing, which this individual does, is to touch and feel the organs of the body. After that, he feels the presence of the mind. After that, he feels the presence of intelligence. Through this intelligence, which can be compared to the cot which the servant touched as the first step to finding his master, he is able to find out the feet of his master. In this analogy and in this spiritual path, what we have to find is the existence of these four aspects, the soul, the intelligence, the mind, and the sense organs. The soul, the intelligence, the mind, and the sense organs have been mentioned this morning, but it has been made out that for the organs, the mind is the master, for the mind, intelligence is the master, and for the intelligence, soul is the master. Thus, if we want to reach that soul through the process of climbing from organs to intelligence, then to the mind, and then to the soul, it is going to be a very difficult task. If we make a deeper examination and go into the matter with some care, we will find that all that is related to these four different aspects is just one and that one aspect is the Atma or the soul. I may cite another example, which is slightly of a different kind. Let us take the case of milk. At first, we are looking at milk. After that, in order to satisfy our taste, we are changing milk into curds. After that, we are going to churn these curds and take some butter out of it. When we take the butter out of the curds, what is remaining is what we call buttermilk. So what is left after all these changes, which looks somewhat trivial, is the buttermilk. That should be compared to our sense organs. What is left is apparently useless, as all the essence has been removed by way of butter and so on, and that may be compared to the sensory organs. Mind can be compared to the curds. That, which we call butter, can be compared to intelligence. Because curds, butter, and buttermilk have all come from the first source, the milk, we would compare milk to the soul. Now, we should enquire into how important these sense organs or the buttermilk are and how far through these senses can we go in realising the original source, that is the soul or the milk. The mind and the intelligence are associated with various organs. We have to consider in detail what distorted picture we are getting of the source, namely the soul, as a result of such an association.

There is one other example. In a cup, we fill some very good fruit juice. The cup is only serving the function of containing the fruit juice, but the cup does not know the taste of the fruit juice. Then, we put a straw inside the cup and suck the fruit juice. The fruit juice is flowing freely through the straw. Even then, the straw does not get a taste of the fruit juice. But, when the fruit juice reaches the tongue, the tongue is able to realise its sweetness. But, the tongue also is not experiencing the taste of the fruit juice. The tongue, without experiencing the taste of the fruit juice, is handing it on to your digestive organs. In the same manner, we are putting the fruit juice of the Divine feeling in the body, which can be compared to the cup. Our sense are to be compared to the straws. Neither the body, which is the cup, is enjoying the taste of Divinity, nor are the straws, the senses, enjoying the taste of Divinity. But, the intelligence, which can be compared to the tongue, is able to make some kind of an enquiry and decide that this is like this and so on. But, like the tongue, which did not experience the taste of the fruit juice, the intelligence is also only to discriminate and know the taste, but it does not experience the taste. As the tongue has handed on the juice to the digestive organs, so also the intelligence hands on this feeling to the soul. It is in this context that we refer to intelligence as something, which cannot solve our problem any more than the sense organs can. That, which cannot be understood, which cannot be realised either with the sense organs, or with the intelligence, is the 'Atma Tatwa' or the nature of the soul.

It is only when we are able to put our sense organs, our mind, and our intelligence along the right path that we will be able to go somewhat closer to realising what this soul is and what the permanence inside the body is. However, in order to completely realise that, we have to go only through something, which is similar to Atma. Atma is something, which is beyond or which is above the sense perceptions. It follows that sense perceptions, because they are below Atma in status, can never reach or realise Atma. In that context, we talk of two different disciplines, one is physics and the other is philosophy. That is also the reason why where physics ends and is not able to move any further, philosophy starts. In order that you may understand and you may realise this aspect of Atma, you have to do some exercises and you have to undergo some practices. If you want to do that through your sense perceptions, through your mind, and through your intelligence or in this analogy, if you want to convert milk into curds, curds into butter, and butter into buttermilk, naturally, you have to adopt some accepted and standard procedures and you have to apply them in the proper manner. If you do not know the procedures of converting them or if you do not apply those procedures properly, you cannot convert milk into curds, curds into butter, or butter into buttermilk. In every act of ours, we should not forget the goal or what our destination is. In this analogy, the original source is milk and everything else, curds, butter, and buttermilk, are only things, which have come out of the source, namely the milk, by some kind of change that has been introduced. There is a saying, which says that mind is the mirror of one's inner being. So, what comes from within ourselves, what emanates from the inner being, is the mind itself, when it is reflected properly. That is also the intelligence and that also represents the aspect of actions, which we do. There cannot be anything either by way of mind, by way of intelligence, or by way of our actions, which comes from outside. All these come from within our body.

To those of you, who are new and who have come here for the first time, it is necessary to convey in a full manner what the significance of all this is and, therefore, I am going to give you another somewhat familiar example, which some of you may have heard earlier. This thing I have in my hand is a piece of cloth. All of you accept that it is a piece of cloth. But, in my view, this is not a piece of cloth. This is a bundle of threads. If you look at it from another point of view, this is not even a bundle of threads, but it is just some cotton. Cotton, thread, and cloth, all these three are same. So, in a similar manner, the sense organs, the mind, and the intelligence are all going to unite into one and we will have a situation, when we have to refer to just one and the same thing. Just as curd, butter, and buttermilk have all come from one and the same source, what you have in your mind as the basis, the foundation, or as the source is simply the original, from which all the transformations have come. If we now decide to do something, by which to make this cloth disappear, some of you may wish to set fire to it and the cloth will disappear. But, that process is not the right one. On the other hand, if we can pull out all the threads one by one, one thread after another, then the cloth will disappear. So, if we make a proper and detailed enquiry and ask ourselves what is like the cloth and what are like the threads, we get the answer that mind is like the cloth, desires are like the threads. By the desires, like the threads, coming together, we constitute the mind, which you may call the cloth. If you want to make the mind or the cloth disappear, then you have to pull out, as you had pulled out the threads one by one, all the desires, one desire after another. So, because we are filling the mind, in fact we are constituting the mind by putting together large number of desires, a variety of desires, that mind made up of so many desires is giving us a lot of trouble. On the other hand, if we do not harbour these desires, we do not constitute the mind. That is not going to trouble us at all.

Many of you have travelled in the railways and have seen in the railway compartments the saying that, "Less luggage makes travel more comfortable." In that sense, our life is a long journey. This long journey, because we are accumulating a lot of luggage in the form of many desires, becomes somewhat troublesome. When we can diminish this luggage consisting of desires, then to some extent, our journey of life is going to be less troublesome. This process of diminishing the luggage or shedding your desires as you go up in the journey of life is referred to in the language of Vedanta as 'Vairagya'. Vairagya does not mean abandoning the house, leaving your surroundings, leaving your wife, leaving your children, and living in a forest. That is not vairagya. When we stay in the house, stay in the midst of our duties, and perform our duties, which we have to perform, having our minds free from desires and attachments to those duties, regarding all that we do as our actions in God's pleasure, that would be called proper vairagya. This is what is referred to as performing all the duties, which you have to perform, as being performed for God's pleasure. These are not being performed for your pleasure. The realisation that whatever you do is in the name of God and for God's pleasure, will eliminate all losses, difficulties, and troubles to you during your life.

By definition, our Vedas give you knowledge about everything. This word has come from the root 'Vid', which means knowledge. Many persons, even amongst those belonging to this country, ask questions and have doubts about who has written these Vedas, what the significance of Vedas is, and about what they teach and what they contain. It is a pity that these doubts arise in the minds of many Indians as well. To get at the origin of these Vedas, it has to be said that sacred 'Rishis', the seers of this country, when they performed penance and when they made enquiries about God's nature, perceived them through various sounds that have reached them. These Vedas are the products solely of hearing by the seers of the various Divine sounds. They are not the result of either study, or of reading or writing books. Because these have been received through the act of hearing sounds, these are also called 'Sruti'. For such a thing like what is found by hearing, there is no other 'Pramana'. You cannot quote something else as an authority to prove the authenticity of Vedas, as they have been just heard through sounds. This is like the breath, the taking in and the giving out of the breath of God Himself. To regard such sacred gift or such sacred grace of God as some kind of text, which dictates to us procedures and conduct, is not correct. Today, if a scholar can write ten lines, then he would go all out to show his own name as the writer of those ten lines. He would use all kinds of devices like the copyright law and so on to be able to establish that he has been the author of those ten lines. But, in the case of the Vedas, which are endless and which have no limitation of time, their Author, God, has never exhibited Himself anywhere in the Vedas as the author thereof. A total personality and a complete individual, Who could hand over what the Vedas contain and also, give us the enormous amount of bliss that they have been able to give, has neither a name, nor a shape. What is the strength of One, Who has neither a name, nor a shape and yet, could give us such bliss as is contained in the Vedas? God has given us, in His grace, these Vedas in order to enable us to understand the significance of the world, to understand the significance of humanism and also, to understand the Spirit of the Divine.

At the time when they first came out, there was an endless number of Vedas, but over centuries and at the present time, we are finding only four different Vedas. In these four, the first one is Rigveda. Because small stanzas or small mantras have been put together, they constitute Rigveda. That is how it got its name. This Veda, in addition to giving us these small stanzas, important statements like 'Sathyam Vada' – speak the truth –

'Dharmam Chara' – act in a righteous manner – also contain various rituals and procedures, which ultimately go to keep the society intact. The second one is Yajurveda, which has been helping us to maintain our duties. It tells us how we have to conduct ourselves, in addition to some extent also looking after the security of the society. The third one, the Samaveda, is something, which is more important than any other one. In Samaveda, the main theme is music. In addition, in some places in Samaveda, the essence of Rigveda and Yajurveda has also been mentioned. The fourth and the last one is the Atharvana Veda. The Atharvana Veda has not only taken into account the three Vedas, which have been mentioned earlier, but has concentrated on telling us how man, during his daily life, should take care of the various things which he has to do, how he has to take care of his children, his family, his elders, and how he can make them survive and be happy. In addition, this has also taught us some special disciplines, like 'Gokarna' and 'Gajakarna'.

Such sacred texts and sacred scriptures, which are intended to turn man's life and man's outlook towards God, are being neglected by some of us in this country. We are giving up the rituals that have been told to us in the Vedas as necessary to perform. Moreover, we are also questioning the authenticity of those Vedas. We are asking, who is the author of these things and we are regarding them as useless and with no specific purpose for us. Even in the desperate feeling that there is no author for these Vedas, we should not give up our duties. Here is a small example. You may ask a question, looking at this electric current, as to who is its author or who found this electric current and from whom has it come. The answer to such questions is not something everyone will be able to give. Just because we do not know the author of this current, are we going to deny the usage of the current to ourselves? So also, although all of us do not know the authorship of the Vedas, it would be proper for us to follow the paths and the duties that have been prescribed in these Vedas. It is by such a process that we will deserve happiness.

The people, who teach and who convey the ideals and ideologies that are contained in the Vedas, are referred to as the 'Maharishis'. It is only when we are able to understand and accept the ideals that have been put forward by the Maharishis and incorporate them into our lives, that we can really see who these Maharishis are, what their thinking is, and what their views are. These experienced Maharishis are like the people, who are controlling and who own the electric current. If we can follow them, if we can accept what they have taught us, and if we can take to the paths that have been indicated by them, verily as we can get light out of the electric current, we will also get bliss and happiness from our conduct. Therefore, you young people, young students, boys and girls, should understand what Indian culture is, what is contained in our sacred texts, like Ramayana, like Mahabharata, and all the 'Puranas'. Not only should you understand, but also strive hard to put those things into practice and act up to them. It is only when you do that, that you will realise the sacredness of human life and then, you will derive the necessary happiness and pleasure. I am also hoping that you should prepare yourselves in future, to understand the contents of these Vedas, what they convey, and what the detailed principles involved in each one of them are. These will be taught to you in the classes that will come ahead, by very many experienced scholars. When they teach you these contents, I am hoping that you will listen to them with the necessary care and the necessary devotion. Young students, who spend their lives in a care-free manner and who try and fulfill various desires of theirs, will find it somewhat difficult to understand and follow Vedanta. This afternoon, there were some classes on Vedanta and in the report that was presented by one of the girls, it was stated that what was taught was somewhat above your heads. But, because you feel that there is something which has gone above your heads, which you have not been able to understand, you should not lose hope, you should not feel disheartened. You should make an attempt and with all humility, you should again approach the teacher, when he teaches you Vedanta, and try to understand with care and devotion what has been said. When you begin your education, you start with learning the alphabets 'A,B, C, D'. Naturally, at that time, there will be some difficulty and you feel that you are not able to understand more words. But, just for that reason, are you giving up education? So, by effort, by care, and by working hard, we must bring ourselves to a position, from where we can understand. That part of the education, which enables you to understand yourself and to realise yourself, is good education. That, which is mere learning for just making a living or getting a salary for the sake of your living, is not good education. If I have to tell you briefly what Vedanta is, I should say that it is that, which tells you about yourself. So, make an attempt to understand yourself and make an attempt to see who you are. Do not make an attempt to find out who the others are, or what they are. Do not also make an attempt, before knowing yourself, to find out what the world is. There is no use your trying to understand others or what the world is, without first knowing yourself.

During our life, we are always saying this is my body, this is my mind, this is my intelligence, and these are my organs. All the time you are saying so, have you ever at any time made an attempt to find out who you are, before saying this is mine and that is mine? Is it not that after you have found out who you are, that you get the capacity or the right to say that this body belongs to you? So long as you feel that all these things are yours, you are implying that you are something separate from the body, mind, and so on. If I call this My towel, then I give rise to an opportunity, by which I can throw the towel away and stay myself separately and apart from the towel. So, if you say this is your body, then you arrogate to yourself the power to throw away the body and remain separately and apart from the body. You are not the body. When you say that it is your mind, you are not the mind. So, what is in you, which is neither the body, nor the mind, nor the intelligence, nor the sense organs belonging to you? That, which exposes and expounds the true shape of yourself and furnishes the answer to this question, is Vedanta.

It is to find the true nature of self that a young boy, Nachiketa, went to Yama and asked him many questions. He was not deterred at all by the temptations, which Yama put before him by granting him several boons. He stuck and asked questions to find out what this real self is. In those days, this young boy, Nachiketa, with the intention of finding out the nature of his true self, put himself to several difficulties and was not content, until he got what he wanted. As against that, today, we have forgotten what the nature of that true self is and we are occupying ourselves in fulfilling various desires. We are involving ourselves in undesirable situations and bringing shame and disrepute on our country, which had such glorious traditions. No, it shall not be like that. You, young students, who have come here and who are participating in this summer school, must make up your minds to establish 'Sanatana Dharma', to follow the paths that have been shown by our texts and Vedas, to be disciplines, and to proclaim by your actions to the rest of the world, the greatness of your country and your own determination. You should demonstrate to the world that you are the soldiers and the torch bearers of bliss and of peace, of which we have been proud. You should behave in a manner, by which you will become the leaders in the areas, into which you go. You should never allow these ideas to go out of your minds or out of your hearts. I hope and I bless you that you will be able to do all this.

4.

What The Upanishads Teach Us

The juice that is contained in the fruits is not enjoyed by the tree, which bears the fruits. The honey that is contained in the flowers is not enjoyed by the creepers, which bear the flowers. Those beauitful sayings, which are contained in the text books and scriptures, are not enjoyed by the books themselves. The beauty that is contained in nature is not enjoyed by nature herself. How can the writer, who deals with the material world, enjoy the spiritual bliss that is contained therein?

In our society and in our civilisation, Indians have always described the Lord with great affection, love, and happiness, by the name 'Madhava'. The word Madhava contains three syllables in it. These are Ma, Dha, and Va. Ma can be interpreted to mean Maya or illusion. Ma can also be interpreted to mean 'Prakriti' or nature. Ma can also stand for 'Lakshmi' or the Goddess of Wealth. 'Dhava' means husband. One, who is the husband or the owner of 'Maya' or 'Prakriti' or 'Lakshmi', He is 'Madhava'. He is also the 'Paramatma'. Such 'Paramatma' is full of bliss. The 'Jivatma' or the 'jiva', who is subordinate to nature, cannot become one with bliss. 'Paramatma' is independent. He is free, whereas 'jiva' is dependent and depends on something else. Thus, if we want to enjoy surpeme bliss, this can be done only when we look at and identify ourselves with and understand the supreme attitude. We should subordinate ourselves and identify ourselves with 'Madhava' or the husband of Lakshmi. Otherwise, to imagine that we are having supreme bliss is only an illusion. It is a 'Bhranti'. So long as we are connected with nature, we cannot have supreme bliss. We should not really become despondent and give up hope, but have to make enquiries as to what are the paths, what are the methods, what is that we have to do in order to understand and reach this sacred and Divine Purusha or the Divine Atma. The answers to the questions, where can we find the supreme Atma? How can we get to the supreme Atma? And how can we understand the same? Are contained in the Bhagavad Gita and in all other texts of that kind. Once, Arjuna, while talking in affectionate terms and in a friendly manner to Lord Krishna, asked where the Lord was staying those days. He said, "I do wish to find You. I would like to get from You the permanent address, where You stay, the address of Your head-quarters. I do not require the address of Your branch offices, as it is possible that You will not stay in the branches all the time." The answer to this has been, "Yes, My permanent address is care of all the living things."

There is another example, which Draupadi has nicely handed to us. Draupadi, after she had gone through all her troubles and tribulations, was sitting and talking to Krishna on one occasion, with some happiness and ease, and at leisure. She addressed Krishna as her dear Brother and asked, "What is the matter? I remember having been in great difficulties and having called You with the fullness of my heart and begged You to come and save me. But, You came late. You never came in time. Can You now explain to me what stood in the way of Your coming in proper time?" Krishna then replied and asked Draupadi, "You say you addressed Me and called Me. May I know in what manner you called Me and how you addressed Me?" Then, she replied, "Yes, I said, 'Hai Krishna, hai Dwarakavasa.'" The Lord replied, "Yes, you addressed Me as Dwarakavasa. Where is Dwaraka and where is Hastinapura, to which place I had to come? That was a long distance. If only you had addressed Me as 'Hridayavasi' or as One, Who is living in your own heart, I would have appeared immediately. In the manner of your addressing, I had to travel all the way from Dwaraka to Hastinapura and how could I have come in time from such a long distance?"

In this way, all the utterances of God only demonstrate to us His closeness to us. The Upanishads also demonstrate exactly this closeness of God to us. What does it mean, close to whom? It implies our going close to God or Paramatma. What is the consequence of our going close to Paramatma? I will give you a small example and thereafter, go into the Upanishads. We have an air conditioner inside the house. When we are close to the air conditioner, naturally, it will exhilarate us to some extent. The external heat is at a distance from you and the air conditioner gives you some happiness and pleasure. In the same manner, in winter, we go and sit near a fire. Then, the heat of the fire will remove the cold, which is troubling you and will give you some amount of comfort and ease. So, what the air conditioner is doing is to remove the heat, which is in us and give us comfort. Similarly, what the fire is doing is to remove the troublesome cold that is near you and give you some comfort, by giving the heat. In the same manner, when we go close to God, what He is doing is to remove all the material desires, which are in us, make them go farther away from us and give us the comfort of getting rid of those material desires. The 'jiva', which is surrounded and encompassed by the five elements, is being retrieved from the bondage that is caused by the five elements. This can be referred to as the 'Kaivalya'. That, which establishes such a Kaivalya, that which gives you the Kaivalya and shows the path by which you can reach Kaivalya, is simply equivalent to getting relief from the bondage by the five elements. This is what the Upanishads do.

When an individual, whom we do not know, comes close to us and wants to get acquainted with us, the first questions that we generally ask of such a new individual are; Where are you coming from and who are you? What is the business you have with me? In the same way, those of you students, who have come here for the first time and who are not acquainted with the Upanishads, have to ask of the Upanishads the questions, who are you and where do you come from and what good can you do for us? What good can we do for you? If we ask such questions, the Upanishads will reply to us that they are such as have been repeated many times by the Maharshis and seers of this country and also, that they are the essence of what God's breath has given to us in the form of Vedas. In our Vedas, there are three parts: Upasana Kanda, Jnana Kanda, and Karma Kanda. The same three parts are also contained in the Upanishads. These Upanishads have been telling man what it is that he should do, what it is that he should not do, what paths, if adopted, will lead him to good, what paths, if adopted, will lead him to bad, and so on. When we go deeply into the contents of the Upanishads and when we understand their inner meaning, then our own life will look to us like a happy dream. It will lead you to a situation, when you will not again want to be attached to this life.

The Upanishads have come out of the Vedas. For example, out of the Yajur Veda has come the 'Eashavasya Upanishad'. This relates to the path, which has been termed as the Jnana Kanda. In this, there are 18 mantras. Out of these 18 mantras, the first two are concerned with 'moksha'. The other sixteen mantras teach us about various other matters, into which it would be possible for us to go a little later. The next upanishad is the 'Keno Upanishad' and it has arisen from the Sama Veda. There is an alternate name for the 'Keno Upanishad' and that is 'Talavakaro Upanishad'. These Upanishads have got names, which signify their meaning and those names are generally such that they commence with the first word of the Upanishad itself. All the Upanishads have come to us with the sole purpose of leading man to God. They have not come with the purpose of binding him with any specific rules or giving trouble to him in his life. It is only when every Indian is able to see the inner meaning and contents of these texts that they can give them real happiness.

This morning, the nature of Bhagavad Gita was explained to you in a very lucid manner. However, just by reading and repeating the text of Bhagavad Gita, you are not going to get any help. On the other hand, it is by assimilating the essence and enjoying it that you will be able to derive the much needed benefit. It is only when we are able to picture in our minds how Arjuna and Krishna were seated, when Bhagavad Gita was being preached by the latter, when we are able to picture other details, such as what kind of clothes they were wearing, what were the horses that were tied to the chariot, and how was the chariot made and so on, and when we are able to picture the details of the entire situation will we be able to get the essence of Bhagavad Gita. In this situation, there is a chariot, there is one, who is charioting it or the charioteer, there is one, who is sitting in the chariot and is being led, then there are the horses, which are leading the chariot, and then, there are the reins, which are controlling the horses. All these things together constitute one full picture of the chariot. But, where was this chariot taken? It was taken right into the midst of two fighting armies. When we make proper enquiry as to what this chariot is, where it has gone, what the two armies are, who the charioteer is, who the horses are, and what each detail is in the whole situation, it is only then, that we will be able to understand the fullness of this picture, which is only a picture of life and all the significance of every thing that is contained in life. This is what the Gita teaches us in a simple and easy way. The chariot is the body. The Jiva is Arjuna. The Atma is Krishna. The reins are the mind. Our sense organs are the horses. The whole picture has to be interpreted by saying that Krishna, Who represents the Atma, is leading the chariot, which represents the body, into the middle of two armies, the horses being our sense organs and the reins, which control the sense organs, simply standing for the mind. The body is being led into the midst of two armies by Atma, which is Krishna. The two fighting armies can be looked at as 'Iha' and 'Para', that is this world and the other world or good and bad, or Atma and Anatma, or what is temporary and what is indestructible, and so on. The body is being led to face these antagonistic situations, which represent the two armies. We should forget that the battle of Mahabharata was fought in Hastinapura. That may be a historical fact, but we should regard the battle of Mahabharata as something, which has been fought between the Kauravas and the Pandavas. Kauravas represent the bad qualities. Pandavas represent the good qualities. The fight that is said to have gone on in Hastinapura is actually going on every day, in our heart. The fight is between the bad qualities in us and the good qualities in us.

The citizens of Bharat should not simply regard themselves as belonging to a country, which was once ruled by Bharata, but the word Bharata simply means one, who takes his pleasure in Divinity. That means all the citizens of this country should have their pleasure and happiness fixed in God. Thus, it is no use our simply reading and taking into our own head the various good statements and the good rules that are contained in the Upanishads or in the Vedas. It is essential that, after reading those good principles, we have to correlate and co-ordinate them with our own life. The first stanza in the Bhagavad Gita begins by saying, "Dharma Kshetre Kurukshetre." Normally and in common parlance, we are interpreting these words as referring to the place 'Kurukshetra', which was the seat of the rulers Kauravas. Kauravas got that name, because they had descended from King 'Kuru'. We are also regarding it as the 'Dharmakshetra', where the Kauravas and the Pandavas fought with each other for establishing Dharma. If we examine carefully and take the proper meaning of the word 'kuru', it is not what has been said a little while ago. It simply means food. But, we have also a meaning, by which we can equate food to Brahma. What lives by food is the human body. The life in the human body depends upon food. There is another meaning here, which becomes evident, if we note that the life in the body depends upon food and that it should be utilised for the purpose of establishing and following Dharma or right conduct. Because we are using food merely to give growth to the body and in that process, neglecting the one that lives in the body, we are doing something quite wrong. We have been given this body by God, for the sole purpose of utilising it to recognise what is contained in this body, namely the soul. The body has not been given to us to let it grow and grow enormously on the food that is fed to it and all the time neglect and forget the soul. Today, ninety nine out of hundred people are only looking after the body and its happiness, looking after the growth of the body. All the time, they are considering what position this body can get in the surrounding environment. They are not devoting any part of their time to make some enquiry and understand and take care of the soul that resides inside this body. Like a tree, which does not bear fruit, like a fruit, which has no juice in it, like an animal, which has no intelligence, like a cow, which does not yield milk, what is the use of your being born without understanding the purpose, for which you are born? What is the purpose of the effort, which does not result in your knowing what you are and of the effort, which does not result in the recognition of the common element that is contained in the eighty four lakhs of the living species.

In this effort, some crooked qualities, which are contained in man's behaviour are sometimes leading us into peculiar results. If you forget God and if you do any work unmindful of Him, it is not going to give you happiness, nor is it going to give any prosperity to the country. It is in this context and against this background that you have been told this morning, that the many distortions and the many crooked ways, that have entered into the otherwise pure pursuit of science, have been leading us into peculiar results. We will have to make some effort, by which we can check and we can balance the way, in which we are going along such crooked paths. When this study of nature and acquisition of knowledge, which we call science, originally started, it did start with the belief in God. With such belief in God and by putting their faith in God, all the efforts, which they had made at that time in order to acquire knowledge about the world, were useful. They did, in fact, help in getting stability for the social structure, in giving some amount of prosperity to the world, and in giving happiness to the people. However, for some years in the past, these people, who have been following such distorted paths, began to develop individual aspirations in their own minds, were ambitious, and wanted to get a name for themselves or for the country, to which they belonged. Thus, they forget the real goal, the goal of acquiring knowledge. Such a personal ambition on their part, amounting to ego and greed, resulted in their forgetting the presence of God and the ultimate purpose of their enquiries. They have fallen into evil paths.

Science, today, has given up treading the paths, which are likely to yield results useful to people. On the other hand, scientists are taking to paths, which will be harmful to people. They have also been taking to paths, which create some difficulties and conflicts in the people. Because they have abandoned useful paths and have taken to harmful and dangerous paths, it has also resulted in their forgetting the presence of God. In whatever field it may be, if an individual is working so that ego gets hold of him, then it will not only land him into a dangerous position, but will also create considerable difficulties for him. Ego works on the stature of a man like the rays of the morning sun work on his shadow. In the morning, on account of the rays of the sun, our shadow will be a very long one. As the sun goes higher in the sky, the length of the shadow caused by the sun's rays will become smaller and smaller. In the same way, the stature of an egoist is something, which has to go down and down as time goes on. Humility, on the other hand, works on your stature in a manner that can be compared to the effect of the evening sun's rays on your shadow. The shadow in the afternoon will be small. As the sun goes down and down, as the evening comes on and on, the shadow that was quite small in the beginning becomes larger and larger. Therefore, humility is good and indicates the path, which is good for one's life. Humility and obedience, although they look as if they are tiny things, which do not confer on you any large powers, will really give you enriched and increased pleasure and happiness as time goes on. Young people should learn to be obedient to elders. You should also learn to have faith in good things. You should also learn to have humility. I wish you all to acquire these three qualities, obedience, faith, and humility.

Being students and coming to learn and acquire sacred knowledge, if in that process you do not adopt the right paths and the right methods, then it will be something, which is unacceptable. In additon to what these experienced persons are going to tell you about the contents of the Upanishads, you will learn as days go on, what the proper relationship, that should obtain between a teacher and the taught, is. Moreover, you will also realise that you as students should accept the position, that there is much that you do not know and you are sitting at the feet of a Guru. The relationship between the student and the teacher should be that the student does not know, the Guru knows, and what the Guru knows has to be communicated to the student, who does not know. This communication, which is the process of education, should be followed and gone through along the appropriate and accepted paths with great care, with great confidence in and respect for the teacher. In the olden days, when Vedas were being taught to the students by the teachers and when they have completed their studies and the students are about to be sent to their homes, the teachers used to bless them. They never blessed them in terms, such as you live long, you have plenty of wealth, you have plenty of prosperity, and so on. That was not the kind of blessing the Guru gave, when the student was sent home after completing the study of the Vedas. The blessing they gave consisted of only two injunctions: one was 'Sathyam Vada' – speak the truth, the second was 'Dharmam Chara' – conduct yourself according to righteous principles. But today, teachers after completing imparting education to their students, bless them by calling upon them not to forget to send them presents and so on.

For you students, it is a very important matter that you should introspect and ask yourselves from what high and noble pedestal and status our ancient education in this country has descended and at what low level and in what shameful situation it is today. Our education used to cover the most sacred paths, namely, knowing Atma and what was related to everything that is Divine. That was intended to fill your hearts with something that is sweet and take you to immortality. Today, as a result of the new education, which we are getting, we seem to think that there is no God; we do not seem to develop any respect for our parents; we do not seem to develop any respect for our teachers. Not only is it that we have no fear of God, we seem to be simply reducing our lives to the lives of animals, moving far away from the lives of human beings.

Today, we are all considering that what we see with our own eyes, 'pratyaksha', is the only thing we wish to accept as an authority. Anything that we do not directly see, we are not willing to accept as authentic. In the development of such a belief and in our insisting on wanting to see everything before we can accept it, there are several pitfalls. Accepting as evidence only the thing, which you can see, or that you can hear, or you can taste, or that you can generally experience through your senses of perception, is a very dangerous thing. In fact, that you will not be able to reach unhesitatingly the truth in this manner, has been established and has been explained to you in a very nice manner, when the Charvaka philosophy was expounded to you. The Charvakas have taken 'pratyaksha' as the authority. This cannot be a proper evidence. This is because a situation will come, when our five sense perceptions will not be so healthy as they are at the moment. They can acquire ill health. A situation can come, by which these sense organs can change. How can we, under such circumstances, say that whatever experiences you get through these sense organs, which will change and which can be unhealthy, is sure to be true? To give a sweet to a person, who is suffering from malaria, and ask him to put it into his mouth furnishes a small example. He thinks that it is bitter, because of his malaria fever, and he will proclaim that the sweet, which you have given him, is bitter. Is this truth? However much he may argue and quote the 'pratyaksha' as his authority, it cannot be the truth. He will go on saying, "I have tasted it, it is bitter." He can go on arguing, but simply the basis for this illusion is in him. It is the fever, which is in him. The fault is not in the sweet. It is only when you are able to remove all the fault in him, which in this case is the fever in him, the sweet will taste as sweet, as really it is.

Let us take another example. You take a healthy student, who has got good vision, and you ask him what are all the colours he sees around him. He will at once describe that he is seeing several colours and distinguish them. On the other hand, if you choose a student, who is suffering from jaundice, and if you ask him what are all the colours he sees around him, his reply will be, "I only see yellow colour all over." He will further argue that he is seeing only yellow colour. This is something, which is a direct experience of eyes and therefore, must be truth, because he is relying on an authority, which we call 'pratyaksha'. But, we have also enquired if these situations are going to last permanently or are there going to be some changes in them. These are only diseases and malfunctioning, which have come somewhere in between. They are not natural and will not last all the time.

So also, in the Charvaka philosophy, the saying, "There is no God," is like a temporary malnutrition or disease, which has come in between. Even in this, if we look at it with some care and enquire into it, you will see that what he is saying at first is 'there is'. 'No God' is coming later on. You cannot hide truth for too long a period. However much you may try to hide, truth will always come out. In fact, the Divine strength in man's heart will always be pushing him to proclaim truth. This is an inevitable thing irrespective of who the person is. As time goes on, he will have to recognise the Divine truth and in time, he will develop faith in God. Truth is not something, which will change. Truth is one and only one. If there is anything, which is dual, then that is untruth. But, when we try to put forward untruth as truth, we are only trying to change words and put them here and there. You may call this the magic of words. Let us take one sentence.

A disbeliever will say there is no God. If you get another man, who has gone a step further in his disbelief, he will say more emphatically, "God is no where." In this assertion, "God is no where," there are four words. By a small transposition of the letter 'w' from the beginning of the word 'where' to the end of the word 'no', you will change this into 'God is now here'. In this illustration, a little movement of the position of one letter to the left meant 'God is now here.' A movement of the same letter to the right meant, 'God is no where'. This is a small change in the position of one letter. No new words have come. Words, which were there, have not gone. It is because of our distorted ideas, helped by the bad environment and helped by our own ignorance, we are abandoning truth. We are disbelieving in God and we are bringing disrepute on our own sacred lives. Science does not take on itself the establishment of the 'pramana' or say that what we see alone is truth. It does not ask you not to believe in anything you do not see. Scientists, on account of some selfish aspirations and with a view to acquire certain advantages for themselves, have introduced into their methodology a disbelief in God. You should not accept such rules and say that nothing can be truth, unless you are able to have 'pratyaksha' as your authenticity.

In what you may regard as 'pratyaksha' or what you want to see in all those things, it is only an illusion to think that you actually and directly see the reality and the truth. Here is a small example for this. A son, whose age is 25 years, has been spending some time and living with his mother, who has attained the age of sixty years. For 25 years of his life, the son has been looking at his mother, has been addressing her as dear mother, and has been enjoying the presence of an affectionate mother. But, after sixty years of her age, her time was over. She abandoned her body and life had fled. The son has the body of the mother near him. Sitting next to the body, he was suffering agony and was saying, "Mother, have you gone away?" "Mother, have you left me alone?" "Mother, who is going to give me guidance hereafter?" There is something here, which we have to look into with great care. He says, "Mother, you have left me and gone away." Who is it that has left him and gone away? For 25 years, he has been addressing that body as 'mother' and speaking to her as 'mother'. If that body is the mother and if this man is saying, "Mother, you have left me and gone away," then there is an inconsistency. The body is still there. So, what has gone away is his real mother. The body that is still there is not his real mother. Thus, the true mother is the life, which has left and gone away. So long as the true mother, which was the life, was residing in that temporary and non-permanent body, he was calling the body as his mother. But, the moment the permanent life has left, he without any hesitation will cremate that body, which was till then being regarded by him as his mother. So long as life is present, we are to some extent enjoying and appreciating the bodily relationship of either a mother, or a father, or a brother, or a sister, or a wife, and so on. But, once life has fled, then we will realise that all the relationship, which we were enjoying, was only a bodily relationship and has no value. That anything that has been permanent was only in respect of the Divine soul that is contained in the body and not the body itself becomes very clear. Therefore, the one, who is a true relation to us, the one, who is a true friend to us, the one, who is a true guidance to us, that can only be God and none others. All other relationships are like passing clouds, which come and go. The permanent and eternal truth of God should be your ultimate aim. Other things, which look like truths, are not permanent truths. They are not eternal truths. You should give them up. You should fill your hearts with 'prema'. That is the only way, in which you can reach the eternal truth of God. You should work with a determination to fill your hearts with prema and reach this goal. Through the one month of courses that you will have here, you should acquire the capacity to recognise the permanent truth. I hope and bless you that you go back to your places and infuse this determination into others and thereby, generate a large number of people, who will establish Indian culture and who will bring glory to Indian beliefs.

5.

The Nature Of Truth

In the heart of every individual, there is the 'kalpa vriksha' or the tree that gives you all that you want. Around this kalpa vriksha, there is a growth of weeds and by your efforts, if you can remove all these weeds, then the kalpa vriksha or the sacred tree will become evident. The texts, which traditionally belong to Indians, are all intended to teach the inner meanings of all the sacred sayings, to put the outside world in its proper perspective and to make men realise their own individuality. God is not only capable of curing the ordinarily understood external diseases, but He also undertakes the setting right of all bad qualities that enter into the inner life of an individual. We generally make an attempt to cure various diseases by externally applying medicines. There are other kinds of diseases, to cure which we take medicines internally. There are still other kinds of diseases, which require not only external application of medicine, but also its internal administration. Today, you all have joined a hospital, which is connected with the Divine. For all your diseases, there is a necessity of not only applying medicines externally, but also of taking some medicines internally. Although, as the equivalent of external application of medicines, we undergo certain practices and certain sadhanas, we also have to realise the inner meaning of such sadhanas and such practices. It is the realisation of the inner meaning of such practices that constitutes the medicine that you take internally. The Gita, which is really the essence of all the Upanishads, teaches us how life has to be handled internally. It is in the 32nd stanza of the sixth chapter of the Gita that we are told how this internal cleansing or purification should be effected. Good qualities like kindness, like compassion, like prema, like sacrifice, make a man deserving of being called a devotee or a Jnani or one, who has attained Vairagya or detachment with the external world. But, till then, till the individual attains these good qualities, he remains a person only in the name and does not become one, who has had any experience of these things. That these good qualities should be observed only in limited circumstances with certain restrictions, while for example, you are engaged either in puja or in bhajan or in devotion, is not the right attitude. That when you come out of your puja, you may forget about these good qualities and begin to develop hatred instead of love, begin to develop lust and anger instead of compassion and forbearance are not the attitudes, which our devotees should develop. It is only when we can reconcile the observance of these good qualities both

The Nature Of Truth

outside and inside and put them constantly into practice, that we will feel some happiness. There is the necessity of your observing and accepting such qualities, like peace and forbearance always. By putting them into practice always, you will deserve the title 'Satatam yoginah' – you are always a yogi. Today, one does not become a yogi all the time. In the morning, you are like a yogi. In the afternoon, you are like a 'bhogi' – there is one, who eats and enjoys. In the evening, you are like a 'rogi' or a sick person, who gets the disease after eating. How can something, which changes in all the three parts of the day be of any lasting value? That is why our Upanishads, in the task of seeking truth, are telling us how we can get happiness throughout the day and every day. We have the story in our mythology that we did churn the ocean with the 'Manthara Parvata', a certain hill and got out of it many things like diamonds, like the 'kalpa vriksha' the tree that fulfils all your desires, like the 'kamadhenu' or the cow that gives you all that you want, the 'Amritam' the immortal nectar, and many gem stones, and so on and so on. In the same way, in modern times, we are churning the ocean of our life. By churning our life and by churning the bowels of the earth, on which we live, we get many qualities and many things which we require, such as food, gems, and so on and so on. If we look into the inner meaning of the parable or of our history, we note that there is a hill called 'Manthara' and by putting this hill inside the ocean, we churn it with the 'rakshasas' or the bad qualities on one side and the 'Devatas' or the good qualities on the other side. Out of the ocean have come some good things and some bad things. This is the meaning of the story. You may ask if this story has also got an inner meaning. You should know and you should understand that there is not one single story in the whole history of our culture, which has not got an inner meaning in addition to an outer meaning. They have decided that 'viveka' or wisdom is the source, from which these things come. The body has been established as the vessel. Our intelligence has been put into this body as the hill, with which you churn. We have decided that the essence of Vedanta is the essence in this churning. The essence of Vedanta has been taken as the milk in this story. In this churning, the right side and the left side have been equated to 'Ida' and 'Pingala'. 'Ida' and 'Pingala' are the two nerves and these have been taken as the ropes for churning. Taking the name of the Lord, the churning or the 'Sadhana' or the practice has to go on. Because of such churning, there has arisen in it what may be called the Divine butter. Therefore, if today we keep the good qualities on one side and the bad qualities on the other side, if we realise that our ideas are to be constituted into these churning nerves, the 'Ida' and the 'Pingala', if we regard our own body as the vessel in which the milk is contained and we apply the 'Sadhana' or the practice, then surely we will reach the Divine.

If I have to give you an illustration of what has been said in the modern context, I may refer you to the game of football, where some children are on one side and others are on the other side. There will be say, six children playing on one side and six on the other side. They have a ball put in the centre. This ball will be hit by the players,

The Nature Of Truth

who play on one side and the players, who play on the other side. Not only will they have two fixed boundaries, two limits, on either side, but also a regulation in the game that the ball should be maintained and hit only within the limits, which have been accepted on both sides. We will accept victory for that side that has succeeded in sending the ball through the goal of the other side. But, if the ball is hit in such a way that it goes outside the boundaries and not go through the goal, that would not be accepted as a victory, but that would be called a fault. Today, in the world, every man and every woman is continuously playing football during his life. When and after how long he will achieve a victory or send the ball through the goal, one does not understand. We may also ask a question as to what the game of football, which is said to be playing by us, is. Our heart is the football ground. It is not the physical heart, but it is the spiritual heart. In this playground of our spiritual heart, on one side are the 'Arishadvargas' or the six bad qualities. These six bad qualities are 'Kama', 'Krodha', 'Lobha', 'Moha', 'Mada', and 'Matsarya'. That is the lust, anger, greed, attachment, arrogance, and jealousy. On the other side are the six other players, Sathya, Dharma, Santhi, Prema, along with two others Ahimsa and Poornatwa, that is nonviolence and fullness. These two contestants are having the ball, which is the life, right between them. The good people are hitting the ball and the bad people are also hitting the ball. But, the situation now is that we are not able to decide who is going to get the victory. The bad people are having physical strength and the good people are having Divine strength.

We also have to ask ourselves, while this game of football is going on in the field of the heart, what the two limits are, the boundaries which we talked of beyond which the ball should not be hit? They are the 'Dharma Vidya' and the 'Brahma Vidya'. That is the education relating to our conduct in this world and the education relating to our conduct in the other world. These two are the limits within which the ball has to be kept. If during the play, we hit the ball as to go out of these two boundaries, which we have established, we would not be acquiring victory, but we would only be scoring a fault as we will send the ball outside the limits of the court. Thus, it is only when we understand the inner meaning of life and understand the circumstances, under which various things are happening in the outer world, that we can to some extent understand the reality of life.

But, the essence of all the Vedas, what is being taught by all the Vedas, come from within the man. It is not coming from anywhere outside. In the context of our believing that God is omnipresent, that God is present in front of you, inside you, and outside you, there is no need for you to give any special importance to what comes from outside. You will have to believe that everything is contained within yourself. On account of ignorance, on account of some illusion, and also due to some of the actions of yourself in the past births, you are thinking that there is something, which is coming from outside into yourself which has got some sanctity. This is not correct. It is only when we are able to overcome this ignorance, it is only when we are able to throw away this illusion, and it is only when we are able to put aside the idea that there is something sacred, which is coming from outside, then alone can you realise your own real form.

There is a small example for this. One dog caught hold of a dry bone and put it in its mouth and with the intention of eating it, had taken it to a place. However much the dog may have tried to eat the dry bone, it has not been able to get any essence or juice out of that. The dog, which was hungry, was unable to withstand the hunger any more and with the anxiety to get something out of that dry bone, it bites it hard with its teeth. The sharp portion of this dry bone pierces into the soft mouth of the dog. Immediately, blood started flowing out of the mouth of the dog. The dog then thought that, "Ah! Now, out of this bone is coming some juice, some blood," and it started sucking its own blood with great pleasure. That it is only an illusion for the dog is not clear to the dog. Really, the blood belongs to the dog and it has come from within itself. When you look at this story, you will realise that we are also more or less in the same position. So long as we remain in this ignorance, it means we are like dogs. If we succeed in throwing out this illusion or 'maya', then our view point will come from the other side and we become G O D. So, the one, who realises his true self, is God. The one, who does not realise his true self and who is in the illusion of believing that he is something else than his true self, that he has to get something sacred from the external world, will be entangled in great many difficulties. We will have to conclude that 'maya' or illusion is not something, which is our property. Maya is something, which belongs to God. It is not that maya is something, which you can get round by your effort. You have to get round maya only by the grace of God. Maya is something, which, by the consequences of your own 'Janma samskara' – what you have done in your previous births, can make itself look like a thing quite different from what it actually is. In fact, just by the result of an illusion on your part, it can create a considerable amount of fear and terror. There is a small example. After this discourse is over, you will be trying to go to the shed, in which you are staying. In the path, there is something like a crooked rope. As soon as one sees this rope, a fear comes that there is some snake there. The moment that there is a snake or the idea of the snake comes into his mind, his body goes far away from this particular rope. Not only does the body move as far as possible from that rope, but all the sense organs will start trembling. This will also give rise to a certain amount of desire in you, by which you begin to make an enquiry. This will show itself, as in the example, by his searching for a torch light. As soon as you bring a torch light and shine on the rope, then you will learn that it is not a snake. The moment he learns that it is not a snake, then a large amount of courage comes from nowhere and he will go very close to this rope. By, the snake, which was imagined to be there, has not gone away anywhere. The rope, which is really there, did not come there from anywhere else. The fact is that there is a rope and that it was mistaken for a snake. Later, when you had shone light, you realised that it was not a snake and that it was a rope. All these

The Nature Of Truth

changes are simply the result of the fear and the illusion that has been caused in your mind. So, it is the attitude of the mind, by which it can cause such an illusion. This is being referred to by the word maya. You may ask, how long will this trouble, this illusion that is being called maya, last? It will last only so long as you are not able to understand what the Divine nature is. So, if in the very first instance, we try to understand the meaning of the Divine, then we will not be subjected to either these troubles, or these doubts.

You may be getting some doubts as to whether we can get an answer to these questions through the study of either the Upanishads, or the Gita, or the Vedanta. By studying or reading these Upanishads, or the Gita, or the Vedanta, you will only understand and know the subject matter and what the substance of all these texts is. But, just by reading them, neither the maya, nor the ignorance is going to leave you, nor are you going to move any closer to Divine things. These books are all like guide posts. The guide posts only tell you that such and such a town is situated in such and such a direction, that another town is situated in another direction, and so on. The actual walking is got to be done by you, if you want to reach a particular town. So also, if you are only going to read the texts and if you feel that by reading texts, you have not been able to reach the destination, then that is also wrong. You should make an atempt to put into practice what you have learnt from the books. If you put into practice, there is no doubt whatsoever that you will reach the destination that has been indicated in those texts. By spreading the news of the existence of light in the world, is the darkness going to be dispelled? Will the poverty of an extremely poor man disappear by that man just thinking about money? Will the hunger of a hungry man be relieved, if he just hears about the sweets that have been prepared? Will the disease of a man, who has been struck by disease, be cured, if he just hears about some medicine, which can cure him? Our poverty is not going to be removed by simply learning that there is a large amount of money in a bank. Our hunger is not going to disappear by just being told that considerable amount of sweets have been prepared. So also, it is only when you put things that you have learnt from the texts into practice, is there a possibility of your enjoying and understanding the meaning of the Divine.

You are told that we have to recognise the existence of the three states, that is the waking state, the dreaming state, and the sleeping state. In the waking state, we are able to utilise the five sense perceptions. We are also able to acquire some results and put them into practice and enjoy something out of that. We also have learnt that in the dreaming state, there is only the mind that is functioning. The five sense perceptions are not functioning. In the waking state, it is not simply the five sense preceptions that are functioning, but as a result of the environment, of the time and of the individuals around us, we are able to understand something much more than these sense perceptions can tell us. There is a small example for this. We get an idea that we want to go from

The Nature Of Truth

here to Madras. Are we going to Madras immediately, when we get the idea? No, we have to fix the right time. At that time, we have to go to the Whitefield station. We have to purchase a ticket and reach the Bangalore City station. Then, buy a ticket to Madras and get into a train, travel all the night till the next morning, and it is only then, that you are reaching Madras. In this process, all the four elements, the idea, the time, the reason, and the act of going have all come together and this would be regarded as one unit. In the dream state, not only are all the five sense organs absent, but these additional things, namely the time, the reasoning, the person, who is doing, are all absent. Let us take another example. You are sleeping in the night in Brindavan. You are dreaming and your dream is like your having gone to witness a cinema in Delhi. In this dream, if you had felt that you had gone to Delhi and that you had witnessed a cinema and also witnessed a number of people in Delhi, we have to ask ourselves the questions, when did you travel to Delhi? How did you go? Did you go by a plane or did you go by a train? Where was the time? Where is the person, who is doing this act and where is the action itself? None of these exist in the dream state. Further, if you ask the persons, whom you had met in your dream, the next day and tell them that you had met them in Delhi, they would deny having had anything to do with you. They would say that they had not been to Delhi at all. This is not so in the waking state.

If you do something in the waking state, then all the other things, like the time, like travelling, like action, are all present there. But, they are not present in your dream state. In this description, we are thinking that what we see and that what we do in the waking state are true. On the other hand, in common parlance, we are thinking that what we see and what we do in the dream are not real, and that it is only an illusion. But, in Vedantic parlance, neither what you see in the waking state, nor what you see in the dream state is real. This is a matter, to which you should give some attention and about which you should find out and enquire with some care. Here, you will get a glimpse of the nature of truth. So long as you have the feeling in your mind that you are in a waking state and so long as you know that the five sense perceptions are working, then you get the belief that what you see is true.

Now, you are all sitting here, you are looking at Me, you are listening to Me. It means that your eyes are functioning and you are seeing Me. It means that your ears are functioning and you are listening to what I say. Not only that, but also the mind is able to take all that comes to you through the eyes and through the ears and the heart is able to enjoy all that you are seeing and listening. You can argue that this is not an untruth and say that you have seen it with your own eyes and you have heard with your own ears. You may say that you experienced it with your heart and you can thus argue and say that this is true. But, after you have had your dinner, after you have gone to your places and you have gone to sleep, then you get a dream. Then, where has all this awakening in the waking state gone? In that dream, you will go back to your village. What you had seen in the evening and in the day has nothing to do with what is

The Nature Of Truth

being seen by you during your dream. But, in that dream, you are feeling that you are really experiencing your village, your friends, your house in your village, and so on. When you get up in the morning, you do not remember either your village, or your house. You think all that was a dream and you do not attach any importance to it.

At the time of your dream, what you saw was true. When you were awake, what you saw when you were awake was true. Which of the two is really true? Is that, which you have seen in your waking state, true? The truth of what you have seen in the waking state does not exist in your dream. The truth of what you have seen in your dream does not exist in your waking state. What you have seen in the day is not contained in the night dream. What you have seen in the night is not contained in the day dream. Both are untrue. But, however, you are present in both. The truth is only yourself. What you saw in the day is the day dream and is not true. What you saw in the night is the night dream and is not true. Your self, which has been the witness in both places, is the truth. What is changing, namely what you have seen in the dream or what you have seen in the waking state, cannot be true. There is another supporting argument for this.

You may ask, how is it that what we see during the waking state is also being described as a kind of dream? How can it be? It is all right if it is on one day or on two days. We are living through several years, fifty years, sixty years, and all that we see during these fifty or sixty years in our waking state, cannot be a dream. I will give what you sometimes experience in your dreams as an answer to this question. One has had a dream. In that dream, he saw that he was just then born. In that dream, he found that after he was born, he had grown into a child, he had become an adult, he had entered the classes in Whitefield, he had gone through all the summer courses, gone back home, got married, got a child, the child had grown, and he got that child also married and that son, after his marriage, got another son, who becomes his grandson and all these were seen by him in the dream. So, in the waking state, if he was to have been born and if he was to have reached a stage, when he could have claimed a grandson, he must at least have spent 40 to 50 years. In the dream, the events that he was born, that he had grown, that he had a grandson, and that he could play with his grandson, which would have taken at least an experience of 50 years in the waking state, had all been handed to you in that one dream. Experience relates to 50 years, but if you see the actual time of the dream, it was only two minutes. If we make an enquiry and ask, where is this experience of 50 years and where is this time of two minutes, we will get the answer that the time of two minutes relates to the scale, which is applicable to the waking state, whereas the experience of 50 years relates to the time that is applicable to the scale of dreaming state. So, what was equivalent to two minutes of time in the waking state was 50 years of experience in the dream state. What prevents us to accept 50 years of experience in the waking state as equivalent to two minutes of experience in the dream state? We should not think, therefore, that because we are experiencing all this over a long period of 50 years in the waking state, this is not a dream. Thus, in the scale of time, which belongs to God or in the circumstances and environment, which is of the Divine, the standards and the scales of time, which we are used to in our ordinary life, do not apply. There is no point in taking the prescriptions, which we are accustomed to in the matter of time and space in our normal life, and carrying them into the Divine world. All that becomes irrelevant.

You may get another doubt. You may ask a question that, if what we are seeing is all a dream and if all our waking state actions are to be treated as a dream, then why should we do these things at all? Why should we do any sadhana, or bhajan, etc. in order to attain moksha, if all this pertains to the dream state? Even in the dream state, some kinds of dreams have the capacity to wake you up immediately and push you into the waking state. For example, if, in a dream, you see a lion chasing you, because of such a dreadful dream, you are suddenly forced to get up and you are in the waking state. Thus, what has happened in the dream state has enabled you to get into the waking state. In the same manner, in the waking state also, if you regard it as one dream, then a situation may arise, when, by the grace of God, you are quickly pushed from the waking state into the state of Jnana. Just as for the dreaming state, this is a waking state; if you believe the waking state also to be a kind of a dreaming state, then the Jnana state is a waking state for this dreaming state. That is why all the seers and rishis have told us to Awake and Arise and come to the state of realisation. The Upanishads are also preaching that we should Awake and Arise and approach a state of realisation.

We should now ask ourselves what is this sleep, from which we should awake. This sleep is not the ordinary kind of sleep. This is the sleep of ignorance.

Therefore, the things that are contained in our Upanishads and the pathways, which the Upanishads have been indicating to us, are to be well understood by you and you have to put them into practice. The contents of the Mandokya Upanishad tell you that OM is just one word. This is by its appearance a small word, but it contains very deep and important ideas. In the text of Mandokya Upanishad, there are only 12 mantras. These 12 mantras contain the essence of all the Vedas. Although they do not tell the way in which you have to do your Karma Kanda, they tell you in an excellent manner the aspects of Brahman. This Upanishad, more than any other, contains all the important issues and these will be taught to you in future classes. Even if we are not able to read the Vedas, this Upanishad alone shows us the path of liberation. Thus, the one and only Upanishad, which can hand to us the knowledge of oneness or Advaita, is the Mandokya Upanishad.

6.

'Kama' And 'Krodha'

The Jiva resides in the world. God resides in the heart. There is always an interplay, which goes on between one and another. People cry when they are born. People cry when they die. People cry even between birth and death for various things. We have, however, to ask, do people cry for obtaining real knowledge about the ultimate? Do they cry for the grace of God? Do they cry for understanding and realising God? In life, it is the desire of every human being to enjoy peace and happiness. But, have we made an effort to know the real reason for lack of peace and happiness in our lives? Such lack of peace and lack of happiness can only be relieved, when we know what we ought to know, when we forget what we ought to forget, when we reach the destination we ought to reach. In this, there are three main steps, which will lead us to the knowledge of what should be known. There is a necessity for asking once more the questions, what is it that we should forget? What is it that we should know? What is it that we should reach? The answers are, we have to forget the aspect of Jiva. We should know what our true self is. We have to reach Godhood. It is these three aspects that are being described to us by the three words Jiva, Ishwara, and Prakriti. It is to enable us and to let us know and understand the aspects and attributes of these three that the Upanishads exist. What has been called the 'Bhautika' refers to the aspect of the body, what has been called the 'Daivika' refers to the aspect of Atma or the soul and what has been referred to as the 'Adhyatmika' refers to the aspect of Jiva. What relates to the Jiva is responsible for bondage. What relates to the Atma is for releasing everything that is in the nature of a bondage. The Jiva Tatwa binds itself, whereas the Atma Tatwa releases everything. Atma Tatwa should be our basis.

You are not one person, but three, namely the one you think you are, the one others think you are, and the one you really are. If we are able to guide our lives, bearing these three aspects in mind, then it will be possible, to some extent, to get the Atma Tatwa into our lives. From time immemorial, such idealists, such torch bearers, and such seers have been teaching in our sacred country. It is because of the strength of 'Kali', who is now the ruling deity, such people, who have been able to show us good paths, are becoming more and more distant to us. We, in our turn, are getting outselves attached to the material notions and pushing ourselves away from the spiritual path. It is easy to drive away people, but it is very hard to lead and make them follow you. Today, those, who can lead, and those, who can show the way, are becoming fewer and fewer. By your good fortune and by your good deeds, you are getting these excellent opportunities of listening to experienced people, who have lived good lives. They will be handing to you good ideas and that you are able to secure them firmly in your hearts with devotion, indicates that in the future, there is going to be very considerable improvement in you.

It is known to every individual that it is the way of the world, that people are after riches, after foodgrains, after precious metals, like silver and gold, and so on. But truly, these are not our wealth, these are not our happiness, and these are not the things, which should be regarded as signifying our prosperity. Our good conduct is our true wealth. The Divine knowledge is the true riches that we should have. Proper action and proper conduct are our prosperity. It is only when we realise that these good qualities are what we should acquire as our riches and not the worldly pleasures, that we will be justifying what has been told to you in the morning, that 'Jantoonam Narajanma Durlabham'. That means that amongst all the animals, to be born as a man is extraordinarily difficult. Therefore, you should give great attention to cultivating good conduct and good behaviour throughout your life. To be able to sleep, to be able to eat, and to be afraid whenever there is fear are all common to man and to animals. These qualities do not distinguish a man from an animal. The only distinguishing feature, which marks out man, is that he has intelligence or 'buddhi' and if man does not use his intelligence properly, he is just like an animal.

Some of you may be wondering why man has also been included amongst the category of animals. We should not understand the word animal as referring only to non-human animals. This word has its root in 'Jan'. Whatever is born is a 'Jantu'. Everything that is born from a mother's womb is called a 'jan' or a 'jantu'. Since man is also born from a mother, it is appropriate from the point of classification, that he should be regarded as one of the animals. Man should be taken as having got that name, because he has been born from a mother, like all the animals.

In what you have been hearing, the philosophy of non-dualism, or Advaita, is one of the most important things. Sankara stated that what is truth is 'Brahman' and that the world is a 'mithya'. If we take this statement consisting of two halves and try to prove that what you see in the world is all unreal, you will be wasting your time. On the other hand, we should also take the statement that the entire world is covered or is contained by 'Vishnu'. If we put these two statements together, then the enquiry will proceed on proper lines. But, these two statements look as if they are contradicting each other. On the one side, we say that the world is unreal and on the other side, we say that the entire world is only a manifestation of the Lord. You should note here that when Sankara said 'Brahma Sathyam', he did not say that the world is 'Asathya' or untrue. He used a special word 'mithya'. So, we have to know the meaning of the word mithya. The word mithya should be explained by saying that it means neither 'true', nor 'untrue'. It is something between truth and untruth. It is really true-untrue, 'sadasat'. What we are seeing around us with our own eyes gives us the impression that they are all true. But, what we think is true, in the next moment vanishes and we don't see it, and when we don't see it, the same thing that we thought was true, we now think is untrue. What was not seen sometime ago comes back. Then, what we thought was untrue appears to us as true. Thus, you see that some of it appears as true and when that disappears, the same thing appears as untrue. Therefore, we have to describe this world neither as true, nor as untrue, but both as true and untrue. The appropriate Sanskrit word is 'sadasat'. In these manifestations, which are partly true and partly untrue, there is one, which is of a permanent nature and which we should recognise. There may be many amongst those, who have assembled here, who are used to going to cinemas. When you go there, the first thing you see is a screen. We cannot see or look at that blank screen for any length of time with pleasure. We will become impatient and we will be looking back at the projector and at all other places, from where the pictures have to come. After sometime, some of the pictures come and they exhibit themselves on the screen. They are moving away from the screen. Some of those, which have gone away from the screen, are not just going away permanently. They are coming back again and again to the screen. Therefore, the coming and going of these pictures in a repetitive manner is a sort of manifestation. When we say that the world is mithya, you have to take the world not as the inanimate part of it, but as the whole of it representing the conglomeration of all the living beings. They are all undergoing the cycle of being born and then, dying and going out. At any instant of time, a large number of people are coming in by being born and going out by dying. Therefore, this coming in and going out into this world should be compared with the pictures coming in and going out on the screen. That is the mithya, which we have to understand as the characteristic of the world.

But, we have to make an enquiry as to what it is that supports these pictures, which come and go. On the screen, they come and from the screen, they go. If the screen is not there, it is not possible for you to see any of this coming and going. When the pictures actually come there, where is the screen? You don't see it separately. It is a part and parcel of the picture. So, you should realise that the permanently existing screen, the true screen gets mixed up and combines with the transient or coming and going pictures. Then only will you understand that what is true is the screen and what is not true are the pictures. The screen is not coming and going. Here, the permanent screen should be compared to the permanent basis or the support for the entire world and that is the 'Brahman'. That permanent basis Brahman, when it gets mixed up and combines with these impermanent or transient people, who come and go, then you get the picture of the world like you got the picture of the cinema. That is why we say, "Sarvam Vishnu mayam jagat." This process, by which the untrue or transient pictures and the true and somewhat permanent screen are together combining and giving you an impression of permanence, may be called the 'Vishnu maya' of the 'Jagat'. The word 'Vishnu' here should not be understood as an individual, wearing his insignia like the 'Sankha', 'Chakra', and so on. The word 'Vishnu' here stands for omnipresence.

Sankara recognised that in this 'mithya' or in this mixture of truth and untruth, there is truth. That is how, when he said, "Brahma sathyam, jagat mithya," he recognised that there is truth in this world and that aspect of truth has to be conveyed and has to be taught to people. That is the reason why he made an effort to establish four 'Peethas' all round this country, the main purpose of which was to convey the truthful contents of this statement and to give knowledge and wisdom to all the people concerned. By Divine grace, these four 'peethas' have been serving as a fort-like wall round our country. Unfortunately, as time went on, we have allowed this fort to become dilapidated. Through the walls have come what are called the methods of 'western civilisation'. As a result of that, we have neglected our own culture and we have forgotten our ancient traditions and today, we are behaving like animals. Thus, it is very essential that we should recall to our mind the sacredness of the Indian culture, the way of life, which Indian culture has taught us, and recognise that there is a oneness in all the manifold teachings of life. We should put them into practice and teach it to others. But, in our culture, we have been taught to examine and enquire and say, "Oh, this is not what I am seeking, this is not what I am seeking." Thereby, we give up all that is transient in the world and fix our attention ultimately on that permanent Divine soul. And this is what our Vedanta has been teaching us as the right path. The same Vedantic path, when we begin to follow it, at the elementary stages, we ask ourselves the questions, "Am I the body? Am I the mind? Am I the Antahkarana?" There is no better process of realising ourselves than to make this kind of enquiry. If you have the belief that you are the body, then what is the meaning of the statement we generally make, namely 'my body'? Who is the 'my' and who is the 'body'? When you say 'my body', it means that 'my' is something separate and distinct from the 'body'. Again, when you say 'my mind', it means that 'my' is separate from the 'mind'. In the same manner, we are enjoying and we are experiencing all these things by saying, "These are mine". We are not saying separately 'I'. It is only when you make a proper enquiry about this 'I' and realise that the 'I' is neither the body, nor the mind, you would have steadfastly put yourself in the philosophy of non-dualism. Indian culture and the teachings of Vedanta take you through making the statements 'this is not I', 'this is not I', 'this is not I', and so on, until you are able to realise what 'I' is.

When Rama, along with Lakshmana and Sita, were moving in the forest and talking to several Rishis and meeting them, there used to be congregations where women used to sit on one side and the Rishis used to sit on the other side and discussions used to take place. In the place, where all the women were sitting, Sita also joined them. Rama and Lakshmana, because they were living in the forest and because they were wearing clothes appropriate to the forest, were also looking like the Rishis. However, amongst them both, Rama was showing a certain amount of Divine light. In the place where Sita was sitting, some of the women went to her and asked, "How is it? Have you come alone or have you come along with your husband as well?" She replied that her husband, too, has come. With the desire amongst the women wanting to see and find out who her husband is, they were asking her many questions and wanting to find out who amongst the men her husband is. Sita, a sacred woman given to righteous conduct all her life, would not get up when all the Rishis were present and say, "Here is my husband," by way of introduction. She would not do that and knowing what was passing through Sita's mind and recognising her reluctance to get up and point to her husband, one of the women asked Sita by pointing at one of the men, "Is that person your husband?" She then replied in the negative by just nodding her head. Another woman came and asked her, "Is that person, whose hair is tied up in knots, your husband?" She again nodded her head in the negative. In this way, when many women came and asked Sita, pointing at the wrong person and asking the question, "Is that your husband?" she was nodding her head to indicate a negative reply. When Rama, who was sitting there, was actually pointed out, Sita neither said, "Yes," nor said, "No." She simply exhibited a significant, happy, and pleasant smile. Our Vedanta teaches us something, which is exactly similar to this story. If you point at the wrong thing and if that is not the supreme reality, then you say, "No." Anything that is shown and is not the right thing should call forth the comment, "This is not that," "This is not that," and so on. When you put your finger at the surpeme reality, the Brahman, then you are in supreme bliss and happiness. Such is the nature of Vedanta of ours that we are able to give today, to you the young students, with pure and unwavering hearts, which you have. I am glad that you are attempting to acquire the good things of our culture and the teachings we are giving you. I hope and believe that this will constitute the security of our future.

You are also being told a few things about maya. Just as our own shadow will always accompany us and will not separate from us, so also, maya will always accompany God and will not separate from Him. There is a very good illustration of this fact in Ramayana. At the time, Rama, accompanied by Lakshmana and Sita, was moving in the forest, because the forest was a thick one and there were no wide roads and they could only make narrow walks, the way they were walking was such that Rama was heading at first, immediately behind him was Sita and immediately behind her was Lakshmana. In this way, all the three, Rama, Sita, and Lakshmana, were moving forward along a narrow path. In order to be able to recognise and understand this situation, you hold up your three fingers. The first finger represents Rama, God or 'Paramatma'. The second finger immediately behind represents Sita, or 'Maya'. The last finger in this row of three represents Lakshmana or the 'Jiva'. Paramatma, Maya, and Jiva, these three are going along in a narrow path in the wild forest of life. After a little while, Lakshmana, whom we have symbolised as Jiva, has got the desire and the ambition to have a look at God or

Paramatma. What is it that he has to do in order to fulfil his desire? There are only two ways of looking at Rama or getting His darshan. One is that Sita, who is in between, has to move away a little and let Lakshmana have the darshan of Rama. Alternatively, if Sita insists on staying where she is, Lakshmana has to move aside a little. To get Sita to move away, he may push her out from the place where she is standing, but then, he will be offending Rama. Rama will be angry, if such an attempt is made. So, what Lakshmana did was to pray to Sita in all humility and ask her to give him a chance of having darshan of Rama. Sita, in all her graciousness and in all her kindness, said, "Yes, certainly you can have the darshan of Rama," and just stepped out a little. So, if you get angry with maya, if you hate maya, and if you want to use force and your own strength on maya and push her out of her place and then, have the darshan of the Lord, you will not succeed. Maya, then, will become angry and will play tricks with you. Not only that, God will not allow such a thing to be done. The only way, therefore, to fulfil your ambition is to recognise that maya is the inseparable shadow of God Himself and pray in all humility and ask for an opportunity, by which Maya will stand aside.

You have been told by some of the lecturers that we are being born, we are getting entangled in this cycle of birth and death on account of some actions we may have done or out of ignorance. Moreover, after we are born, we get all kinds of desires. The getting of these desires and harbouring them has been called 'kama' and when these desires are not fulfiled to the extent you want them to be fulfiled, then you become angry. That has been called 'krodha'. These two qualities, 'kama' and 'krodha', the desire and the anger are responsible for all your troubles and sorrows. In these aspects, Ramayana has given us a very good lesson. When we read Ramayana, we should ask ourselves the questions, what is the reason and who is responsible for sending Rama into exile in the forest? In replying to such a question, some people put the blame on Kaika, some people put the blame on the foolish father, Dasaratha, some people put the blame on Manthara, who was the attendant, and so on. But, when we read the appropriate sections of Ramayana and try to secure the basis for this particular act in Ramayana, we will find that in some sections, it has been said that Rama, when He was a very young child, was playing with a ball and that ball fell on this ugly looking attendant, Manthara, who accompanied Kaika. From that day, Manthara has entertained some hatred and jealousy towards Rama. In addition to this, because Manthara was an attendant, who came with Kaika from the Kingdom of Kekaya, from where Kaika came, it so happened that she was not very happy with or friendly to the sons of the other queens. She was only attached to the son of Kaika. Because she could not do anything when the ball, which was hit by Rama, came and hit her on the back, which was an ugly hunch back, she was letting the hatred grow inside herself. She was waiting to take revenge at an appropriate time. This is the normal worldly explanation of things, but for all these things to happen, the original root cause is Rama's own wish. When the time came for putting Rama on the throne, then she found the opportunity and she schemed and she did everything, by which circumstances were so brought about and she had achieved what she wanted to achieve by sending Rama to the forest.

When Rama, along with Lakshmana and Sita, was spending His time in exile on the Chitrakuta mountain, it so happened that Surpanakha came and saw Rama and wanted to marry Him and have Him as her husband. For this bad desire of hers, Lakshmana gave her an appropriate punishment. Then, she went back to Ravana and did all that was necessary, by which to excite Ravana to go and get hold of Sita, who was leading a life of devotion to her husband. Although Ramayana is a very large book, is an extensive epic, you will find that these two names, Manthara and Surpanakha, who really have a considerable responsibility, have not been shown in any extensive manner anywhere in Ramayana. They appear only in one or two insignificant places. But, these two, although they appear very insignificant in the totality of the story, move the whole story of Ramayana through. For Rama, Who used to live in Ayodhya, to go to the forest, for Sita, who used to live in the forest with her husband Rama, to go to Lanka, Ravana's place; the responsibility for both these happenings is on Manthara and Surpanakha. Having stated that for the whole of Ramayana, Manthara and Surpanakha are responsible, we have to recognise that these two are not just individuals. Surpanakha signifies desire with attachment. Manthara signifies anger with vengeance. These two are the 'Kama' and 'Krodha'. These two, the Kama and Krodha or lust and anger are responsible for all kinds of difficult experiences, which we have in our lives. But, how are we to conquer these desires? How are we to get the upper hand over these desires? So long as we live in this world, there are bound to be desires, but you should not really become so despondent that we give up the attempt to conquer these desires. You may desire many things. You may experience many things you had desired, but if you are able to treat your desires as well as your experiences to be such as arising in the name of God, then there will be some amount of happiness. When we only worship nature and when we want to enjoy that we see in nature around us in the world and do not think of God and forget about the existence of the Divine, we are not going to be happy at all. For the path where you should sacrifice all these desires, Ramayana also contains an illustration of such a sacrifice. Because Rama started to go to the forest, Sita prayed in many different ways using many arguments, to be able to get His consent to go with Him to the forest. She sacrificed all her happiness, she sacrificed her bodily comfort, and she gave up everything by way of worldly pleasures. Thus, she sought, by giving up all desires or Kama, her being with Rama. For Sita, who sacrificed everything, all her happiness and all her riches and all her worldly pleasures, unhappily there came an instant when she began to be attracted by a golden deer. The moment her sacrifice had turned into her attraction to this golden deer, then Rama became distant from her. It was only when she sacrificed all her Kama, she could get Rama. But, the moment her mind turned to a desire or to Kama,

Rama became distant from her. Ramayana is a text, which teaches us such sacred inner meanings for every little content of it. But Ramayana, at times, got to be misinterpreted by various people, as an ordinary story where some bad man has taken away the wife of another person and that this person tried to get back his wife and that it is the story of a family quarrel involving women and so on. That kind of feeling about Ramayana is not only wrong, but is also born out of ignorance. When we realise that Ramayana is sacred text, which contains several lessons for us and shows us the way to reach the Divine, then only will we understand its full significance. Whether it be the Upanishads, or Ramayana, or Bharata, or Bhagavata, you find in them such stories, which have invaluable and sacred inner meanings. Just by reading the words and getting a superficial meaning, you are not realising the inner meanings contained in these sacred texts. In order that you may understand the inner meaning, you should come in contact with the experienced people, who are now teaching you and know from them, from their experience, or from their scholarship. You should then put into practice what you learn. You will then know the value of our traditions. You students should not feel tired, should not feel vexed, should not feel that you are here by compulsion to sit through the day. You must come here with the fullness of your heart.

7.

'Purusha' And 'Prakriti'

Who are the friends? Who are the enemies? Who is God? Who is the devotee? Who is the writer? Who is the author? Who is the Guru and who is the student? What is it that we have known? What is that we have not known? Is what we have not known less or more than what we have known? If it is that what we do not know is considerable, is there anything wrong in calling man a 'Vanara' or a monkey? Dear students, while in the entire creation, there are so many things which man has to know, any learned man to whom you may go or any of the Shastras or the Upanishads, which you wish to consult, will tell you that the first thing amongst all that you should know is about yourself. The substance of all our learning is to enable you to know your true self. We know that all shastras only teach us matters relating in some way or other to the soul. None of them teach things, which have no concern whatsoever with the soul. When we go into this question, "Who am I?" with some care, we find that the same question is coming up in the Bhagavad Gita. Everywhere, Bhagavad Gita points out the significance of this question, "Who am I?" In every place, Krishna has been preaching that in everything, it is He that is present. Every individual, each one of you may say, "I am Rama. I am Krishna. I am Ranganna, I am Anil, I am Sunil," and so on and so on. When you say these things, you are putting the letter 'I' right in front and after stating that, then you add the name that has been given to you. It may be Rama or Krishna. Thus, this 'I' is so broad and so widespread like the sky. It is demonstrating to us the infinite quality of this 'I'. If we can understand the aspect and the real meaning of this 'I', then we will have understood the contents of all the shastras. When we say, "Ekam Eva Advitiyam," the reference is to this one and only one without a second. So also is 'OM'. This one sound 'OM' is telling us that it is identical with Brahman. The sound of 'OM', the 'pranava', represents the entire content of the Brahman. This sound 'OM' is a combination of three syllables, 'AH, OO, and MA'. The isolated sound 'AH' cannot be the 'OM'. The isolated sound 'OO' cannot be the 'OM'. Similarly, the isolated sound 'MA' cannot be the 'OM'. AH is something, which is connected with the awareness. The same is also being called 'Visva'. The next sound 'OO' is somewhat a subtle one and is connected with the idea. This has some inner significance and is being considered as 'Taijasa'. One will have to say that this is not only subtle, but has some relationship with the dream state. Now, the sound 'MA' is causal. It is connected with the cause and effect is related in some way with deep sleep. This is also being called by another name 'Prajna'. 'Pranava' or 'Omkara' is in the place, where these three names 'Visva', 'Taijasa', and 'Prajna', all of them come together and combine. If we are anxious and if we are desirous of getting close and getting to know what is behind this 'Pranava' or 'Omkara', then we will have to make an attempt to get 'Visva' into 'Taijasa' and to get 'Taijasa' into 'Prajna'. It is only by combining these three in that manner can we really get a darshan of Atma, the soul, the Divine part of the human being. When the sound 'Ah' joins the sound 'Oo' and when the sound 'Oo' joins the sound 'Ma', then we can get the complete sound of 'OM'. If 'Ah' does not join 'Oo' and 'Oo' does not join 'Ma', we do not get the complete sound of the 'pranava' or 'OM' at all. In the same way, it is only when we are able to combine the three states, the waking state, the dream-state, and the deep sleep state, or combine the gross aspect, the subtle aspect, and the causal aspect of the body into one, we have a chance of getting a glimpse of the Divine soul.

For the creation of this entire world, the main roots are sounds. If there is no sound, there is no world. If there is no sound, there is no creation. Thus, if the young people, who belong to the modern world, raise a succession of questions like, "Where is God? Is there God? Where is He to be seen?" I get the feeling that they are only displaying a large amount of ignorance. Does this young man, who asks a question like that, not realise that the answer for his question is contained in the question itself? What is the question? The question is, "Is there God or is there no God?" The fact that the word God is contained in the question asked, namely "Is there God?", is proof that there is God. If there is no God, then the word 'God' would not have come into existence. Can any of you give a name of something, which does not exist? You can try. Something, which has no shape and existence, cannot get a name. Some people make a statement 'Gagana Pushpa', that is the flower of the sky. You may ask if actually, there is a flower of the sky. If not, how do these words come? But, remember that this is not a single word. It is a combination of two words. One is the sky, the other is flower. Taking the individual words sky and flower, yes, there is a sky and there is a flower. Therefore, you cannot quote this as an example of giving a name of something, which does not exist. Thus, some people, without going deeply into the meaning of these words, spend their time only in asking questions. They drive themselves into being atheistic and they do not believe in realities. To such people, there is no way of demonstrating truth.

In the context of this, we should recall that this morning, some explanation of the two words 'Purusha' and 'Prakriti' was given to you. Purusha stands for a large number of different persons. Prakriti stands for a wide variety of manifestations of the world. You have been taught that just as manifestations of the material world are very many, so also the manifestations of the Purusha or the soul are many fold. But, if we really enquire into this from the point of view of the meaning, which we are aiming at, then Purusha can be only one. He cannot be many. The Purusha or the soul is simply the manifestation of the Divine. On the other hand, the manifestation of matter, of the material things, is this world. This Prakriti or the world is something, which is filled with all the five elements. All these are destructible. They are not permanent. But, what is clear, what is clean, what is indestructible, and what is effulgent and shining, is only one and that is the soul or Purusha. Our srutis have described this soul as something, which has no attributes, as something which is superior, as something which is eternal and permanent, as something which does not change at all. All these have come from one, the self. In the questions that were formulated yesterday, by the students, there was one question, "How does creation go on?" In that context, there is one question, which I want to ask and that is, "How do you get a dream?" Can anyone give a reply to this question? For getting a dream, the cause if your sleep. If there is no sleep, you won't get a dream. Just as for a dream, the sleep is the cause, so also for creation, what is called maya is the cause. For maya, there is no beginning and there is no end. Thus, this creation or the world you see around you is something, which is related to maya. Maya always loves the soul, loves the purusha. It wants to be with Him, wants to reach God. So also, the creation wants to reach God all the time. So, sometimes, in some Puranas, it is said that Purusha has attached Himself to the world. In the material world, although many shapes come about and although we may make a distinction between men, women with many different names, while this distinction can be made in Prakriti, so far as Purusha is concerned, there can be no such distinction. Here is an example. In Anantapur, we have established a college for girls. Its name itself is girls' college. Will there be any boys in that college? In that college, on an occasion such as a college day, they will be having a drama. On that day, when they enact a drama, the girls are putting on the appearance of a Maharaja. They are also putting on the part of a Maharani. The one, who puts on the part of a Maharaja, puts on a moustache, she puts on a dhoti, she puts on a crown, she puts on all the insignia, which make up the Maharaja and she comes on the stage. While the audience are forming the idea that one girl is looking like a Maharaja and that another girl is looking like a Maharani, so far as the particular girl, who has put on the part of the Maharaja, is concerned, she will always think that she is a girl and that she belongs to the girls' college. She will never think that she is a Maharaja. In the same manner, this world is like a girls' college. Here, in this world, in the drama of our life, on the stage of this world, we are putting on the part of many appearances. Just because you have put on a part, you cannot become man. In the aspects of either these five elements, or the five 'koshas', or the five 'tatwas', all these people are equal and there is no difference. Therefore, it is not the body, but when you talk of manhood, what you have to regard as man, as Purusha, is the strength, the energy of Purusha that is contained in him. Thus, it is by the co-existence and by the combination of these two, the soul, or the Purusha and the Prakriti, or the world of matter, that creation is going on.

For such creation, there will have to be someone, who is responsible. We have seen the mud in the tank. We are also seeing the water in the river. Water alone from the river will not enable you to make a pot or a pan. The mud alone from the tank will not enable you to make a pot or a pan. It is the combination of water and mud that will enable you to create either a pot, or a pan. Simply by the combination of water and mud, the pot or the pan is not going to be ready. There has to be a potter, who will prepare the pots and pans. Such a potter is God. The energy or the power is the water. Prakriti or nature is the mud. The combination of these two things are the human bodies. These pots and pans of human beings some day or other will have to fall down and have to break. Because these human bodies are pots and pans and have been constructed, have been created in time, therefore, they must be destroyed also in time. The transformation or the changes that will come about for such pots and pans should not disturb us to any extent. But, by merging ourselves into the ignorance, into the darkness of ignorance, we are simply feeling that these pots are ours, these pans are yours and so on. We are not really able to understand what the significance of these pots or pans is.

I will give a small example to show you the amount of ignorance we are going in for, when we look at this natural world. A blind man has got a child. But, this blind man has not got the fortune to see that child with his eyes. Even if the blind man is not able to see his child, he knows that it is his child and he will be spending a lot of effort in making the child happy. In the same way, like the blind man, we think and get into an illusion that this Prakriti or the natural world has come out of us. Although we are not able to see the reality of the Prakriti, we develop some kind of affection, like the blind man, who although he is unable to see the child and recognise the child, is calling her his child. To establish and to know the true shape of God, there are eight different paths. The first one is concerned with Shabda or sound. The second one is concerned with the motion or movement. The third one is concerned with brightness or light and so on. In this manner, there are eight different paths. That is the reason why we have created what is called an 'Ashtanga yoga', which means the eightfold paths or practices. These eight ways, by eight different kinds of practices, can take one to the destination of the Divine. They have been named to you as Yama, Niyama, Asana, and so on. These things refer to various kinds of practices.

In another example, there is a light. By the breeze, you will find that the light moves a little, hither and thither. It will also have some smoke. If some water falls on the light, then it makes a noise of twinkling. If there is a lot of breeze, then the light itself will be extinguished. There are so many changes in the lamp. But, there is no change at all in the light that is coming from the lamp. To any one whosoever comes here, the lamp is handing on its brightness. In the same manner, God, Who has no

'Purusha' And 'Prakriti'

attributes, is handing His pure effulgence to everyone, irrespective of who he is. Because this aspect of God, which has no attributes, that goes and enters some other abode like the body, or Divinity gets joined to something else, there the differences appear. But, the original Divine thing is one and the same and does not change at all.

Although I have mentioned this many times to various people in the past, because this gathering contains some new comers, I must tell you the difference between these three aspects, the bodily aspect, the soul aspect, and the Divine aspect. A potter, in order that he may make his pots and pans, goes to a tank and takes the mud out of the tank, thereby creating a big, deep pit. He would take the mud by creating the pit and cutting out of the tank. He takes hold of that mud and brings it in a cart to his house. In this way, because every day he is bringing mud from the tank and putting it in front of his house, there is a big mound of elevation that has been formed. It means one has to go down the ditch or the depression in the tank. In front of the house, one has to climb up the elevation or the mound. The mud from the pit in the tank is the same as the mud in the mound in front of the house. The mound is consisting of mud and the pit has given the mud. The mud is the same in both. Afterwards, this potter takes some mud and goes on preparing every day some pots, some vessels, some pans, and so on. Gradually, as he makes the pots, the mud, which is making up the mound, is going on slowly diminishing in volume. The potter is preparing pots and he is putting them in fire and hardening them and he is selling them to various people.

Before the pots have been made and sold, when he has put water on the mud, which is in the mound in front of his house, that is being absorbed and is getting into the mud and mixing with it. On the other hand, after making the pot, if you put water into the pot, which consists of the mud, that water is not being absorbed. It is remaining as water inside the pot. Where from has this change or has this transformation come? But, the mud, which is either got from the tank, or the mud, which is either constituting the mound, or making up the pot, is all the same. But, it has taken the shape in one case of the pot, in another case of the mound, and in another case of the pit. For the depression, for the mound, and for the pot, the root cause is mud. But, in course of time, this pot is going to break. In course of time, the mound in front of the potter's house will become smaller and smaller. But, the mud is remaining all the time as mud. By some desires and by some actions of our parents and also, by the 'Sankalpa' or the wish of God, this body, the human body, which we may call the pot, is coming into existence. This life, 'Jiva' can be compared to the mud in the mound, which goes on diminishing time after time. The body is the 'Dehatma'. This is going to be destroyed. This mud or the basic constituent of the human body is the 'Paramatma'. All these human bodies in time are going to be destroyed. They will all be destroyed and converted back into mud. When they die, all that is going to go to its original place, from which it has emanated. Like the pots and pans, which have come from mud and as in course of time and after usage, they break and go back as mud, so also we have to accept that the contents of all these human bodies, which have come from the principles of soul, after the bodies have been used and destroyed, will again return to the source.

At this stage, we have to make an enquiry and ask, "What is it that is born?" What do you mean by 'I' was born? What was born was the body. If we make the enquiry, "What existed before we were born?" then if it did exist, there is no question of its being born. Suppose we take the view that it did not exist at all. If it did not exist, where is the question of something, which did not exist and does not exist, being born? How are we to find this out? How do we get the knowledge of what is this 'I'? "What is the way, by which I can understand this question also?" we should ask ourselves. Those texts, which tell us and teach us answers to these questions, are called Upanishads and shastras. To know myself, why should I go and hanker after what is contained in the Upanishads? To know myself, why should I go and seek knowledge from those, who are experienced elders? Such ego is not desirable and you should give it up. It is not possible to understand yourself, without seeking it from experienced people and without seeking it from Upanishads and without practising what these texts teach. If you have the cup, if you have the oil and also, if you have the wick, then are you going to get the brightness of a lamp? Somebody has to light up this wick. You have the flowers, you have the needle, you have the thread. Will it become a garland of its own accord? There must be someone, who will put these flowers together. You have gold. You have diamonds. Will ornaments come into existence on their own? Someone has to make them. You have intelligence. You have education. But, are you going to realise the nature of self? There is a small example. We write all the letters A, B, C, D on the board. We do not know how those letters sound. If the teacher simply writes those letters on the board, even if your intelligence is very high, if you are not told what sound is to be associated with each one of those letters, it will remain something, which you cannot learn by yourself. However intelligent you may be, someone, who is a teacher, has to tell you what sound has to be associated with each one of those letters. Only then can you learn the sound appropriate to each letter. Of course, in this world, we are seeing the five organs, the five 'koshas', the five elements, and even the Atma or the soul, we are able to realise and see. But, those that have to tell you what the paths are, which you have to adopt in order that you may realise fully the meaning of these things, are our shastras. So, we say that shastras are time honoured, old, and ancient. God is One, Who had no beginning and will have no end. Thus, if the newcomer wants to know what the One without an end and without a beginning is, you have to go and ask the shastras to tell you the method of knowing. If you go to a new place, you generally meet people called guides, whose duty is to tell you all about that new place. If you have gone there for the first time, you are a new person to that place. That place has been there all the time. The one, who tells you about the place, which has been there for all time, that guide will be referred to as the 'Puratana' or the ancient. How long will this new man, who has gone there, remain new? So long as the ancient person, who is there, who is telling the newcomer all the things, is needed and so long as you do not know them, you remain a new man. But, when you have learnt through the guide, who has been there for quite a long time, then you also join those, who have been there for a long time. Then, you become experienced and you become one, who has been there for a long time. Then, you can understand the nature of 'Sanathana' or this eternity. This understanding has also been called the understanding of 'Brahman', the eternal. He himself becomes the 'Brahman'. So, if you want to understand the full significance of this 'Sanathana' or the eternal truth, the way to do it is to join these 'Puratanas', those who have been there for some time, like the shastras, and through them and with their help you understand the nature of the Divine and you yourself join the Divine by that process. When you are witnessing, in the very place which is moving, also the person, who is responsible for that movement, then you yourself become stationary and lose all movement. For such a quest to begin, an essential thing is good company. For instance, if you have a lot of pieces of wood, you can get fire out of them, when those pieces come together. When fire comes out of these pieces of wood, which have come together, that fire is destroying not only the pieces of wood, which are together, but it can destroy everything around the pieces of wood. From this fire, sometimes you get also smoke, which is going to cover your eyes and your vision. Through such an act of setting fire to wood, you are also getting some difficulties and trouble. Alternatively, we can also light up two or three pieces of incense. The smoke, which comes out from the incense, is giving you happiness, is giving you fragrance. The incense, when set fire to, not only consumes itself, but it also hands in the fragrance to others, who are sitting nearby. A good man is like incense set fire to. A good man not only sacrifices himself, but he hands in the good qualities, like sacrifice, in him to people, who are nearby and he thus gives them pleasure.

8.
Lessons From The Gita

Bhakti or devotion is the only path for reaching the Divine destination. Bhakti is the only panacea for all the ills of this world. Bhakti is the only method for making you realise the truth. Students, who are 'Premaswaroopas' or who are essentially embodiments of Prema, I believe that there will be scarcely any Indian, who has not read through the text of Bhagavad Gita; that there would be none, who has not heard and is not aware of Bhagavad Gita. Bhagavad Gita means 'The song of God', words which have come to us as His flowers, as His 'prasad'. Vyasa has woven these flowers, the words of God, into a beautiful garland and has gifted it to us. God is the basis for this world. Bhagavad Gita consists essentially of three parts, namely Karma Kanda, Upasana Kanda, and Jnana Kanda. These are also being referred to as the six-chapter contents in each case. People say that through these three parts, Bhagavad Gita has been teaching us various spiritual aspects, such as Bhakti or devotion, Jnana or knowledge, and Yoga or meditation, and so on and so forth. But, Bhagavad Gita, in addition to these, has really also given us the great saying, "TAT TWAM ASI," meaning 'That Thou Art'. This is the essence or the key-note of Bhagavad Gita. The first six chapters teach us about the Jiva or the Soul that resides in this body and, through that, the nature of Jiva. The next six chapters, while teaching us the path of Bhakti, also show us the nature and content of what we call 'Tat' or 'THAT'. The last six chapters, while giving us the content and the meaning of the third word 'Asi', also tell us about how to realise the identity of the self, the Jivatma with 'THAT', the Paramatma and also teach us how to give up things, how to sacrifice and reach 'Moksha' or liberation. If we study Bhagavad Gita in the proper way and enquire into its contents, then we will understand the true nature of the saying 'TAT TWAM ASI'.

This morning, the concept of surrender or 'Sharanagati' and how the concept of surrender has been described in Bhagavad Gita has been conveyed to you. It appears to me that the real meaning of the word Sharanagati or surrender has not been properly understood. Our elders, by the study of many scriptures and texts, have conveyed to us the meaning. Despite this, we get the impression that the word surrender means putting at the disposal of God our body, our mind, all our powers, and all that we have. We take it that 'placing these before God' as the true meaning of the word surrender. This is not the correct and proper meaning of the word surrender. Our body is not in our control at all. Our body, under some circumstances, is posing to us several problems. Under such circumstances, when the body is not under our control, it is not understandable how we say that we will take such a body and surrender it to God. When we look at the mind, it is even worse. It leads us to many distorted meanings. While we are not only not in control of our mind even for one moment, we are even slaves to our mind and we foolishly enjoy the mind's wanderings. Under such circumstances, to say that you are surrendering your mind to God is something quite un-understandable. When you have to struggle so much to control your own mind even for a short while and when your attempts in that direction are often futile, to take such a mind and to put it at the feet of God and say that, "I am surrendering my mind to you," seems to Me to be ridiculous. Let us take the case of your various organs. When the situation is that the mind, which is the ruler, which is the controller of all your organs, is in such a condition, what is the point in talking about the organs and surrendering all your organs to God? So, when you say that you are surrendering to God, your thought, your word, your deed, it is simply a kind of trivial satisfaction to yourself. This cannot represent the truth and the meaning of the word surrender. God also never wants you to surrender and hand over to Him everything that you own. In fact, God has never asked for such a thing. If you make a proper enquiry to understand the true meaning of the word Sharanagati or surrender, you will understand that Sharanagati really relates to another aspect and it should be interpreted in the background and context of Divinity only. It is only when you accept and when you believe that the Divine is present in every human being and in every living thing that Divinity is omnipresent, then only can you understand the meaning of saying surrendering in thought, in word, and in deed and you will also become one with God. There is some justification in your talking of Sharanagati or surrender, when you are fully in control of your mind, fully in control of your word, and fully in control of your body. As soon as you are able to recognise the aspect of omnipresence of God and the aspect of omnipotence of God, then the feeling of ego, the feeling that there is an 'I', which is a distinct thing, will disappear. In other words, when we enquire and try to understand this teaching of Bhagavad Gita, the aspect which explains to you the meaning of the word Sharanagati or surrender, you will note that in the beginning, Arjuna started asking questions of Lord Krishna, thinking that he is using his own intelligence, his own capacity of enquiry, and his own ability of distinguishing right from wrong. He is thinking that he is using his own strength. Because he has relied heavily upon his powers and thought, felt that his own powers are capable of excelling and exceeding God's powers, he landed himself into a difficulty and he was not in a position to decide what he should do and what he should not do. As soon as Arjuna found it not possible to go ahead or even to go back, in fact when all his actions came to a stop, to a standstill; it was then that he turned to Lord Krishna and said, "I will take Your orders, I am not in a position to decide what I should do. I am ready to obey You and carry out whatever You want me to do and I will do so with my full heart." Thus, he surrendered his thought, word, action, and all entirely to God. Such surrender is the lesson of Bhagavad Gita.

It is not correct to say that even this is complete surrender. A situation has arisen when he is ready to take whatever order God gives and obey it implicitly. In this situation, the position is that God gives orders and another individual is willing to execute them. In other words, there is a duality here, in that the One, Who gives the orders, is God and the one, who wishes to execute them, is man. So long as there is this distinction in the mind of the individual, between God on the one hand and 'I' of the individual on the other hand, this cannot be accepted as complete surrender. So long as this duality is evident, one cannot accept the situation as complete Sharanagati or surrender. There is bliss and happiness in unity. There is no bliss and happiness in duality. So, when we are looking at the word surrender or Sharanagati in common parlance, in the ordinary way of doing routine things and interpret it by telling yourself that God has given you the order, God has told you what to do and you will accept that and will follow that, this meaning of surrender is alright only in a limited sense.

Of course, there is one other thing, which we have to recognise and take note of. We know that Krishna and Arjuna were living together for well over eighty years, were meeting each other very often, and talking to each other like friends. But, at no time in those eighty and odd years did Lord Krishna ever try to teach anything of Bhagavad Gita to Arjuna. It was only after eighty years of their living together and that too in the battlefield, and that again under some special circumstances, that the Lord wanted to give him the contents of Bhagavad Gita and give Arjuna a position of authority and competence, from where he could do something. We have to enquire into the meaning of all these things. In Bhagavad Gita, He has also taught that we have to recognise what is called 'Adhikara', or worthy of being entrusted with a task. He has also taught us that unless one acquires the qualification, merit, and worth, there is no point in teaching Bhagavad Gita to him. Conveying the contents of Gita to someone, who does not deserve it and who has not yet acquired that merit, has no meaning. We know that it is only the hungry man, who has the right to ask for food. It is only the man, who has the money, who has the right to spend that money. It is only the man that is poor and needy and deserving of charity, that is to be given such help. In this way, each individual gets the right to do something. The recognition of this right or qualification before action is initiated is an aspect, which is contained in Bhagavad Gita. The Lord has shown in the Gita that you could preach only after recognising the merit or qualification and worthiness of the recipient. It is explicit that there is no point in teaching such a good thing to one, who has no belief. You must see whether he has faith and belief or not. You must also see that the recipient has fear of sin and reverence for God. Unless he has these qualities, the recipient has no right to receive the good and great teaching that is contained in Bhagavad Gita. Not only that, your teaching may become irrelevant, if you go and teach one, who has not got these qualities.

Lessons From The Gita

It is God's word that if you have devotion to God, He will look after all your future. He will look after all the welfare that is due to you. Yes, so did the Lord say in the Gita. But, when would this be? He said that this would be done, provided the devotee spends all his time in the thought of God, provided he accepts God to be all pervading and as present in everything. But, the Lord never said that He will look after the welfare of a devotee all the time, inspite of the devotee spending only a little while, now and then, in the thought of God and if he goes on doing all kinds of evil and harmful things in the name of God and so on. There are three things, which one should keep in mind, namely, I will not think of anything else except God, I will not do anything else without the permission of God, and I will have my attention completely fixed in God. It is only when you accept and put into practice these three things, that the Lord said, He will look after your welfare. God has told us that if you respect and observe these three conditions and show your acceptance thereof by practice in your life, He will bear the entire burden of your welfare. Today, we are not bothering about the injunctions, which God has given us, but instead, we are arguing with God and asking Him why He is not looking after our welfare and our safety. It is true that God said, "If you want to deserve My love and you want to get My affection, then you should think of Me, you should do obeisance to Me, you should put your faith in Me, and you should trust in Me. Then, of course, you can claim and will get in full measure My love and affection." By simply reading and repeating the text of Bhagavad Gita, by merely thinking about the contents of the text, we are not going to get any benefit out of it. It is only by understanding the meaning of the text, by ruminating over the meaning in your mind, and digesting it completely and making It part and parcel of your life, only can you get the benefits out of it.

You have been told about the path of a monkey and the path of a cat. The relationship between the baby monkey and its mother monkey is such that no matter where the mother goes, no matter even if the mother is jumping hither and thither, the baby holds fast and clings safely to the mother, going wherever the mother goes. The child has implicit faith in the mother. In this way, just like the young monkey clinging to the mother under all conditions and under all circumstances, we should attach ourselves to God under all conditions and under all circumstances. That is the kind of behaviour we should accept. In this, there is no responsibility of any kind on the part of the mother monkey. The entire responsibility for this conduct rests on the young one. On the other hand, when we come to see the life of a cat and the kitten, the mother cat takes the entire responsibility of taking the kitten from place to place and looking after it. This was explained to you with a view to convey to you the meaning of Sharanagati. There is a significance here, which we can see; that if you stay where you are, then God Himself will take the responsibility of looking after you.

While the two paths, the path that has been described in the context of a monkey and the path that has been described in the context of a cat, seem to the alright in common parlance and so far as ordinary persons are concerned and in their daily life, they are not so in the case of a person, who is devoted and who wants to know the real inner meaning of Atma or the Soul. For that person, he will have to find a path, which is different from these two and superior to these two. To give you the meaning and the character of this devotion, Vivekananda had a good example. Every person wants and desires that he should get 'Moksha' or liberation, that he should attain that place of Moksha. We may say that liberation is synonymous with Freedom. When we desire Freedom, it implies that at the moment, we are in some kind of bondage. What is that bondage? The bondage is in our own family, in our own home, in which we are tied up and entangled. Your own affection and your people is the bondage. That is the chain, which has bound you. This is what you may call affection with some kind of an attachment. When you are tied up with the chain, the chain of affection and attachment in the family, there are two ways, by which you can free yourself from this chain. One way is to get the strength, by which to break the chain. There is a second way and that is to make yourself tiny, smaller and smaller that you can just slip and get out of the chian, which is binding you.

With the exception of these two alternatives, if you want to reach freedom and if you want to get out of the chain, there is no way of doing it. These two can be described as 'Bhakti' or devotional path and 'Jnana' or the path of knowledge. Bhakti or devotion means you recognise that there is a master, that you have to put yourself in a humble position and be subservient to the master. You also recognise that your conduct should be such that you please Him and get His grace. This is the procedure for Bhakti. This is referred to as an attitude of 'DASOHAM' or behaviour, which by implication proclaims 'I am your servant'. When you are bound by a chain, within that chain if you can tell yourself 'DASOHAM', 'DASOHAM', that means you are humble, you are developing humility, your ego is becoming less and less, it shrinks you so much that your humility grows, that you can slip and get out of the chain. The other path, which is the path of Jnana, is the way of getting out of the chain by telling yourself 'SIVOHAM', 'SIVOHAM'; I am Siva, I am Siva – that means you are expanding, becoming bigger, finally you become so big that you can break the chain and get out. So, to break the chain and free yourself, one is the path of Jnana and the other is the path of Bhakti.

The word Bhakti is sometimes also known as 'Prema' or love. To this word Prema, we are attributing many different meanings. We are also inferring for ourselves many different meanings. Sometimes, a meaning for the word Prema is given by describing it as synonymous with Kama. This creates an impression in your minds that Prema and Kama to some extent mean the same thing. Although Prema and Kama may look synonymous, we have to recognise that the experience of the path, the ways and methods of Prema on the one hand, and the experience of the path, the ways and methods of Kama on the other hand are different from each other. Kama is tying you up in bondage. Prema is bestowing on you happiness. Prema is a pure quality, whereas Kama is an impure quality. We should make an enquiry as to what the reason is for Kama becoming impure and what the reason is for Prema remaining pure. The water that flows and keeps flowing remains pure. The water that is stagnant and does not flow becomes impure. A stage will come when even worms can breed and thrive in stagnant water. In the same manner, prema, which moves, flows from one heart to another, from one place to another, from one person to another, ultimately reaches the destination which is called the Grace of God; such prema is pure. But, the kind of prema or love, which gets tied up to one individual by saying, "Oh! He belongs to me, he is mine," does not flow, but gets tied up to one individual. Such prema will be called Kama or will be prema with an attachment to that particular individual. That kind of prema, which has a limitation, which is narrow and is confined to one place, cannot be called prema in the real sense.

Although both prema and kama look synonymous in a limited sense, they are being experienced in different ways and by differenet processes. Prema, which has got this feature or which is confined to one or a few persons, will land you in difficulties, sometime or other. For instance, we have a rose plant. On the plant, there are some rose flowers, but right below the rose flowers, you also have got some thorns. When you are seeking only the roses, then you do not have to touch the thorns. But, because there are thorns, you are not going to give up asking for the roses. Our life is like a rose plant. On one side, there are flowers, there are roses, which give us the happiness and which give us the fragrance. On the other side, immediately below the roses, there are also the difficulties, the thorns. It is the same relationship that exists between the roses and the thorns. This is also the relationship, which exists between prema and kama. Love is a flower; Lust is a thorn. Prema can be truly called prema, only when it recognises the Divinity and only when it realises that we should love the Divine. That kind of prema alone can deserve to be described as true prema.

What is the special quality or what is the position of authority or merit, by which Arjuna deserved to be taught the Gita by the Lord? Arjuna's brother Dharmaraja had all the good qualities, in fact he had many more good qualities than Arjuna. Then, how did Arjuna get the right to get the teachings from the Lord? Why did not Dharmaraja get the right to get that teaching? If we are taking into consideration the physical strength, then we should remember that there is another brother Bhima, who had much greater physical strength than Arjuna. While on one side, there is a brother Dharmaraja, who is intellectually far superior and while on the other side, there is another brother Bhima far superior in physical strength, how did Arjuna acquire this right, inspite of the fact that he was arguing and himself raising questions? Even if we wish to ignore these two brothers, assuming that they do not deserve it inspite of their strength and power, then what about Bhishma, who can be regarded as one, who has no equal in the matter of his spiritual knowledge? Bhishma was a great person, highly mature and vastly experienced. Why is it that Bhishma also did not have the right to get the Lord's teachings? Arjuna himself had this doubt.

At one time, when the battle was all over, Arjuna himself asked the question to Krishna. Krishna replied in a very quiet and casual way, in a very soft tone to this question and said, "Let us take your elder brother Dharmaraja, yes, he is a very good person, he has got many good qualities, but look at him, he never had any forethought. He is having an afterthought, he is feeling now after the whole thing is over and asking himself why he entered this battle. He is asking himself why we killed so many people. This is a kind of feeling, which has come to him as an afterthought. This afterthought, by which to feel the guilt of some action after it is over, is the nature of man. Everybody will feel guilty and sorry after the thing is over. Such human quality is characteristic of Dharmaraja and therefore, he does not deserve to be taught the Gita." If we consider the case of Bhishma, the great experienced scholar, valiant son of Ganga, he is in a very different situation. On the one hand, he realises and states that righteousness or Dharma is on the side of Pandavas. On the other hand, contrary to what he has been saying, he is the head and the chief of the Army of Kauravas. This is a contradiction and a paradox in his life. Thus, in Bhishma's case, what he says is one thing and what he does is a different thing. Thus, he is riding a chariot with horses running in different directions. He does not deserve to be taught Gita.

Let us take the case of Arjuna. He had the forethought; all the suffering and all the miseries that are likely to accrue if he fought this war, were thought of even before he commenced the war. He asked the question, why do I kill all my relations and all my elders? He said that he would rather go out and beg for his food, rather than ask for the kingdom after killing all these people. He further said that not only does the kingdom, which he would get if he won this war, but even if he is promised the heaven if he won the war, he would not be willing to enter the war and kill all his relations. He would rather give up both. Thus, he prayed to Krishna to get him out of this mess. Thus, Arjuna gave up all desires, was prepared to sacrifice all the pleasures of this world, was also prepared to give up all desires for the pleasures of the other world, and he surrendered completely to the Lord. Thus, we can recognise in him a person, who deserves to be taught the Gita.

In other words, we have to understand that what earned for Arjuna the right to be taught by the Lord, is the fact that he stood in complete and total surrender and was prepared to take whatever instructions the Lord would give. It is to such a person and under such circumstances that one can give the sacred meaning of the Shastras or the sacred significance of the Divine. Every one will have to deserve this, earn this by good conduct, by good behaviour, and by doing good things. Whether you are in difficulties or in joyous circumstances, whether you are in pain or in pleasure, it is only when you have faith in God and accept Him as your very life-breath, you will be in a position to derive real peace and happiness. Our own conduct is responsible for and is the root cause of all our pleasures and pains. We cannot say that God is causing us either pleasures or pains. He is only a witness. For our pains and for our pleasures, for our sorrows and for our joys, our own actions are responsible. If we spend our life with good ideas, with good conduct and good deeds, then we do not have to ask anybody, in fact, we have not to ask God to give us happiness. That will come of its own accord as a result of our good deeds.

I will give you another example, which is coming out of the good qualities and virtues, which the Pandavas had. The two armies were standing poised against each other in the battlefield. In the centre, Arjuna was standing; on both sides, these armies are ready for battle. In a few minutes, each one will raise his own individual war cry. In this circumstance and in such a perilous situation, Dharmaraja, who was standing on his chariot, removed his armour, removed all the protection, removed his shoes, and got down the chariot, and was attempting to walk right into the centre of the enemy's army. The people, who were in the Kaurava army, looked at Dharmaraja, who was removing his armour and who was walking towards them in this unprotected manner, and all raised a cry of joy, thinking that Dharmaraja was walking to them already in a spirit of weakness and defeat and wanting to surrender to them. No one understood why Dharmaraja took this course of walking barefooted into the army of the enemy. There was one person, who understood it, and it was Krishna. On one side, Bhima was very much upset with the behaviour of his brother. He was wondering why his brother is doing like this at this critical moment and he got very angry and excited. On the other hand, Arjuna was also feeling very much upset. He was looking at Lord Krishna in his chariot and his eyes were like two balls of fire. But, Krishna just signalled to both these people and told them, "Look here! You have been following your brother in everything all your life; it is good for you to follow him and accept what he does even at this moment."

The eldest brother Dharmaraja was showing this path, which they could not understand. He has given up his armour and when they turned to Krishna, the latter gave them the advice that they, too, should follow their brother. Though they could not make anything out of it, but with a view to follow the brother, every one of them had laid aside their armour and began to walk barefooted behind Dharmaraja. Looking at this sight, the Pandava army also lost heart and they began to feel despondent. But, there was confidence and there was faith in the Pandava army that Dharmaraja is not the man, who will do something without an appropriate reason for it. When all were looking at Dharmaraja, he straight went to Bhishma, the old warrior. He touched his feet, made obeisance to him, and addressed him and said, "We, who have not had our father, had been looked after by you like your own children. It was your love and care that nourished, nurtured, and brought us up. You, a person who has been everything to us and who has been a father to us! Please give us the permission to enter the war today. You are in the place of our father, you are equal to our father. It is not possible to fight with one, who is in the place of our father, unless you yourself give us permission. Unless you bless us, we cannot fight with you."

Bhishma, who listened to these words of Dharmaraja, was very much moved and was astonished that even at such a critical time, even under such difficult conditions, Dharmaraja was not swerving from the righteous path and was behaving in the most faultless manner. Bhishma was so much moved by the situation that he lovingly patted Dharmaraja all over the body and praised his strict adherence to righteous behaviour and said, "Yes, you will be victorious."

Then, Dharmaraja went to his guru, Drona. He touched Drona's feet and said, "It is the greatest sin to fight against one's own guru. However, if I have to fight, it is only after getting your permission. Then only can I fight with you. Please give us permission to enter the battlefield." At the conduct of Dharmaraja, Drona's heart melted away. He was deeply touched. Drona felt so much that he even revealed the secret of his life to Dharmaraja and told him how he could be put to death.

The moral of it all is that if we shape our conduct and choose our path in consonance with propriety and truth, then they in turn will not only protect us, but will even show us ways of winning victory. Just because it so happens to be that the time was critical or that the time was one with difficulties or you happen to be in the midst of sorrows, by that reason you should not deviate from the moral path, you should not swerve from truth. Even if it is going to lead you to defeat, you must adhere to the correct path. Just because you want to avoid defeat and get victory, you should not deviate from the right path and take the wrong path. Even if we are doing a small thing, we must enquire into whether it is right or wrong. It need not be a big thing to call for such an enquiry. Leaving the right path and resorting to wrong path will put you completely out of the game. Even if you are going to be defeated, provided you have accepted and followed the right path, then you will have a chance of joining the game once again. If you swerve from the correct course and if you play a foul game, then you will create a situation by which you will have no place in future in any of the games.

You may have committed, knowingly or unknowingly, some wrong. Having committed a wrong, if you now go and tell the untruth, that would not be the right thing. On the other hand, having committed a wrong, if you go and tell the truth to your father or to your mother, or to your guru, then you will be getting their grace. On the other hand, with a view to cover up the wrong that you have done either knowingly or unknowingly, you tell untruth and if you want to hide it away from your father or mother or guru, then you will simply harm yourself for all the future.

The first thing, therefore, to do is to promote self-confidence in yourself. Today, a situation has arisen when self-confidence has completely disappeared amongst the students. An individual, who has no self-confidence, cannot achieve victory in anything whatsoever. It is only when you have self-confidence that you will attain self-satisfaction. Today, we do not find any individual having self-satisfaction. When a small bird goes and perches on a small plant or a small branch of a tree, then on account of the weight of the bird, that branch moves up and down.

But, the bird is not going to be upset by such a movement. What is the reason? The bird, which is sitting on the branch, is not depending for its safety on the branch. It is depending on its own wings. Even if the branch moves up and down or even if the branch breaks, because the bird is depending on its own wings, it can fly away. It does not worry at all. Even that small bird, which is sitting on the branch, has got so much confidence in its own wings and in itself that it is fearless.

On the other hand, a youth of today, who claims that he is very well educated, who claims that he is highly clever, who claims that he has got all the good qualities, is having no confidence at all in his own capacity. When he wants to do something, he gets into terrible doubt whether he should do it this way or that way. One, who has no confidence in himself, whom is he going to trust? His whole life will become a bundle of doubts. He is not going to blossom into a complete, integrated, and sound personality. Therefore, we should enter the path, by which we can clear the doubts and not enter the path, by which we accumulate all the doubts in our hearts. So that you may get rid of all these doubts, you should have cleansed your mind and your heart.

In order to cleanse and achieve the purification of yourself, you have to control your sight, you have to control your tongue, you have to control your senses to some extent. As a prelude to your doing something wrong or something unworthy, there will have been an initial action, by which your eyes must have seen something bad, or you must have heard some words, which had excited you to do something bad, or you must have gone through an experience, which will have made your mind wander and excited. This is the way, by which one becomes mad all through one's life. If you, the youth of today, take great care that your sight does not become impure, that your hearing does not become impure, that your words do not become impure, then you will be able to attain the purity of mind and the purity of your thought.

Today, we know that there is a material world and in that material world, there are all kinds of material attractions. We think that because of the existence of those material attractions, we are having pleasure and happiness. It is not so. So long as these material desires and material attractions do not reach your eyes, do not reach your ears, and you do not participate in them, they cannot affect you in the least. I will give you a small example and bring this discourse to a close. Now, you are standing here. Your ears are with you. Somebody behind the gate is talking about you in a good way and praising you. Thus, some good talk about you is outside the gate; your ears are here. So long as the ears are away and not listening to what is being talked about you, there is no pleasure. In the same manner, if behind the gate, somebody is talking about you in a bad way and you are not hearing, there is no reaction, either elation or depression. It is only when this particular talk falls on your ears, or when somebody comes and tells you that so and so had spoken ill of you that it is possible that you may have some reaction; you may become angry or you may be hurt to some extent. It is only when the contact is established between the appropriate sensory organ and the action, which we have been talking about, that there can be any reaction and experience in our mind.

The distortion that follows your thought is even more fearful. Many people may be raising doubts and may be saying, "Oh! Swami is calling a large number of experienced people and experienced scholars here and a large number of students are sitting and these experienced people are talking to them. Just by talking of their experiences and of their scholarship and the students merely listening to all these, are the students going to improve? Are they going to change?" This kind of talk will go on, these kinds of doubts are raised by many people. There are 99 out of 100 persons, who have such doubts. Of course by talking, the mind can be changed to a great extent. Because the whole world is filled with sound, sound can achieve many wonderful things. There is nothing in this world, which cannot be achieved through sound.

Here is a small example. One teacher, having about 10 students, is teaching them some good things. To such an ashram came one, who had some position and power. This teacher did not go to the door to welcome and receive him. This man, who came there, because he had some position and authority, felt somewhat hurt and he went right into the class and asked the teacher, "Why is it you didn't care for me? You have not come and received me. What are you doing?" The teacher said, "I am busy teaching the children some good things." The person, who came in, asked, "Just because you are teaching them some good things, are the hearts of these children going to be changed and become more sacred?" The teacher took some courage and said, "Yes, of course, there is every opportunity of their mind changing by my teaching." The intruder said, "No, I cannot believe it," and the teacher replied, "When you cannot believe it, it simply means that you have no faith in it. Because of that, I cannot give up teaching these boys some good things." Then, this person, who felt somewhat important, started arguing and said there is no possibility of changing a mind merely by words. The teacher, who is clever and who has known these things, asked one of the youngest boys to stand up. To the hearing of this visitor, the teacher told the young boy, "Look here, my dear boy! You just get hold of the neck of this visitor and throw him out of the door." Immediately on hearing these words, the visitor became completely excited and his eyes were red and he was very angry and he came to beat the teacher. Then, the teacher asked, "Sir, what is the reason for your becoming so angry? We did not beat you, we did not throw you out. The only thing that has excited you to this stage of anger are the words, which I conveyed to this young boy. You, who said that you do not believe in changing the mind by mere words, what is the reason by which these mere words, which I have uttered to this young boy, have changed your mind so much that you are so excited? So, it is very wrong to say that with mere words, you cannot change the mind. With mere words, you can cause any excitement. With mere words, you can cause any amount of affection. With mere words, you can earn the grace of anyone else."

So, if in this world, you want to promote friendship, you can do so by using sweet words, by talking in a very sweet manner, and by speaking about sacred things. On the other hand, if you use harsh words, if you use painful words, you are not going to promote friendship in this world. I am hoping that you will be able to follow this path and use sweet words, in all your conversations with others. You will notice that the eyes have only one capacity and that is to see, the ears have only one capacity and that is to hear. Similarly, the nose has only one capacity and that is to smell, the skin has only one capacity and that is to touch and feel. But, the tongue has got two capacities; this is very different – one is to feel the taste and the second one is to utter the words. This double capacity of the tongue should enjoin on you, that you should take great care by which to control your tongue. With words alone, by using sweet words, you can melt the Divine and you can earn the grace of the Divine. Therefore, you should not have in your life any feeling of hatred and take to things, which are bad. Bad sight should be avoided. All evil has to be avoided. By doing this, I am sure you will be able to earn the grace of the Lord and you will develop ideally in such a way that you will reach the goal of victory and that you will be worthy citizens of this country. I am hoping that you will be able to do that and I bless you.

9.

Meditation

The Muslims pray in the name of Allah, the Jews pray in the name of Jehova, the Vaishnavites pray in the name of Phullabjaksha, the Saivites pray in the name of Sambho. That One, to Whom prayers are offered in this manner, He is God and may He grant happiness and prosperity to everyone. God is One, though He is addressed and prayed to by different groups of people in different names.

Many of us use our education to earn a pittance of living and just to fill a tiny little stomach. What is the use of such education, when it cannot give full and complete happiness to man? If man cannot show his fellow-beings the way to reach the Divine, how shall he justify himself? Every rise will be followed by a fall. Elation will be followed by depression. You cannot avoid such antitheses in life. Affection that follows attachment leads to pain that follows separation. Affection and pain are the two things, between which man is being tossed about. In order to escape from this tossing between affection and pain, the only way is to believe in and surrender to God. When man looks at the sun rising, he is elated and feels very happy. The same man, when he looks at the sun setting, will be looking forward to the next day and will cheer up with hope. But, with this process of sunrise and sunset, man does not quite realise that his life span itself is continuously diminishing day by day. Every man wants only good. Every man is wanting to experience good, but he is not considering how he can improve himself, how he can change his heart so as to reach and acquire this experience of goodness. From the early days of one's life and till the very end, every person is only asking questions like, what is the profit that I can get out of this life?, what is the pleasure that I can get out of this life?, what is it that helps me?, and what is the benefit that I can derive out of all these? But, he is not giving any thought to another aspect of these questions, such as in what way can I be of use to the world?, in what way can I be of use to the society?, what good can I do to people, with whom I come in contact? These questions, he does not ask. He is engaging himself and using his time only for his own pleasure and his own profit. If we make a proper enquiry into this situation and try to understand it, we will come to the conclusion that man is always ready to take and receive things for himself. It is the selfish attitude of life. He is not willing to give, hand-over, or contribute something to others. Life is not a one way traffic. Man should be prepared to give and take.

Bearing such sacred duties and obligations of man in view, our shastras have established and given to us

Meditation

four 'Purusharthas' or goals of life. These four duties of man are 'Dharma', 'Artha', 'Kama', and 'Moksha'. Almost every experienced and learned scholar will tell us that among these four Purusharthas, the most important aim of our life, the ultimate goal of our life, in fact the object, on which we should concentrate, is Moksha or liberation. Then, we ask ourselves the question – if Moksha is the supreme and ultimate objective, why mention Artha and Kama also? There is an inner meaning and it is not as if there is no meaning for these two words Artha and Kama. Moksha is the highest or exalted position. That is our destination. In order that we may reach that exalted position, which is our destination, we have to take recourse to something that should serve as a ladder. Since we want to go and climb up to that exalted place, this ladder will be of much help to us in that process. This ladder, which consists of various steps, must also have some support. This support is the earth. That is sometimes also called Nature. Thus, we are making an attempt to have this ladder, consisting of two sides and the steps, Artha and Kama, supported on the earth, which we have called Nature or Dharma. By the help of this ladder, we want to climb up and reach this exalted position of Moksha. Support is the earth; destination is Moksha; the earth, which is the support, is like Dharma or our conduct. It is only when we take the support and our destination, Dharma and Moksha, as our primary objectives, the two intermediary steps – Artha and Kama – will be meaningful and will have some significance to us. But, if we neglect Dharma and Moksha, the basis and the goal, then Artha and Kama will become useless.

Every individual, who is born on this earth, who is born into this world, should to some extent understand the nature of this world and the meaning of this world. Dharma upholds this entire creation and we should also follow Dharma or righteousness in our conduct. You have been told about the life story of Rama in a very lucid way. What is life? What is it that we understand by it? We are accepting that man's breath, what he breathes in and out is his life breath, and we regard that as his life. But, what kind of sound does this air, which is being breathed in and which is being breathed out, make? What is the inner meaning that is contained in the subtle sound we hear? Although we are breathing in and breathing out many times every day, we are not stopping and trying to understand the meaning of this breathing in and breathing out, nor even the significance of the number of times we breathe in and breathe out. 'Soham' that is the way we take the breath in and we leave it out. 'SO' stands for the word 'THAT'. 'THAT' means God or Brahman. 'SO' therefore stands for 'GOD'. 'HAM' means 'I' or 'ME'. Thus, when we breathe in and when we breathe out, the sound that comes out means 'SOHAM' – 'I AM GOD', 'I AM GOD'. In the sound, the one that is all important is called Pranava. From this one single sound called Pranava, all other sounds are emanating. This situation is referred to by saying 'EKOHAM BAHUSYAM'–'Out of the ONE come many'.

In our Bhajan, we use a musical instrument called Harmonium. Sometimes, other people also use other instruments like the Piano. What is it that we do with the Harmonium? We fill air into the Harmonium, that is all.

But, when we press one reed, we get one sound. When we press another reed, we get another sound. So, out of one substance, namely air, by pressing different reeds, we get different sounds. The air that has been filled is only one. However, we are hearing a large number of different sounds. Wherefrom are all these different sounds coming? They are coming from one and the same air, which has been filled into the instrument. The basis or the origin is air and that basis is like the sound Omkara. Out of this basic sound Omkara, we get so many different sounds. Those sounds are mere transformations of the shape of Omkara. It is only in this context that the Maharshis have addressed Rama by saying, "Ramo Vigrahavan Dharmaha" – which means Rama is the embodiment of Dharma or Righteousness. Just as for this Omkara, there are three principal sounds, which go to make it up, namely A, U, M – Rama, Who is the embodiment of Dharma, also has three supporting characters, who are Lakshmana, Bharata, and Sathrughna. The analogy is that Lakshmana, Bharata, and Sathrughna together make up Rama, the Embodiment of Dharma. The sound A can be compared to Lakshmana, U can be compared to Bharata, and M can be compared to Sathrughna. The combination of all these three is the Omkara and that is Rama Himself. So, we have to recognise the inner meaning that Rama, Who is no other than Omkara and in order to establish Dharma or righteousness on the surface of the Earth, has taken birth on this Earth.

When we try and understand the teaching of our Upanishads, then we will learn that OM is 'Ekaksharam

Brahma' or OM is the one thing, which is the same as Brahman. 'EKAM EVA ADVITIYAM BRAHMA' – Brahman is One and only One and there is no second to that One. When we think of our great Seers and these great Mahavakyas or great sayings, which have been taught by them, we will realise that the entire world is Advaita, one in which there is no dualism. It is just One and only One. Even though those, who follow the dualistic philosophy, do not accept and agree with the truth of non-dualism or Advaita, the philosophy of non-dualism does not suffer from any special drawback therefore. Some day or other, after some time, when proper enquiry has been made, the dualistic philosopher as well as everyone in fact, whether he is a believer or a non-believer, whether he is a yogi or whether he is one, who is steeped in earthly wealth and pleasures, no matter who he is, all will have to accept Advaita as the truest philosophy. When we go deep and make proper enquiries about the world, you will realise that it really is one, there is no duality and the non-dual one will make itself evident to you ultimately in this world. The appearance of plurality is something, which is only a reflection of your own illusion. This is also being referred to by the word ignorance. The differences, the distinctions, and this plurality have started in fact from one-ness. It has not started from the basis of plurality.

In our Upanishads, we have the story of one individual, who was a very learned man and who was himself a guru. His name is Uddalaka. He had a son by name Swetaketu. This son, Swetaketu, made several attempts to get his education at the feet of his own father, Uddalaka. But, the father did not agree to such a procedure. The reason for this is, for a son, who moves freely with his father, it is rather difficult for both himself and the father to deal with and abide by the right disciple and guru relationship. The son will always be in the idea that the teacher is his father and the concept of father and son will persist. This is because of the affection that obtains between the father and son. Here, you will also have the justification for calling the son a 'Kama Putra', a son who was born out of affection. Where there is attachment, where there is affection, and where there is a feeling of belonging to, then there will be lenience and it is not possible to impart education in its fullest measure and with the right discipline. Because Uddalaka understood and realised the situation that education cannot be complete and proper, when there is a relationship of attachment, he sent his son Swetaketu to another guru and desired that his son be taught and given proper education.

Looking at this situation, Swetaketu being young and inexperienced, mistook and interpreted it to himself wrongly and got the feeling that perhaps his father is not quite learned and hence, has no competence to teach him and hence, he is being sent to another guru for studies. For some years, Swetaketu stayed in the Guru's house and completed all his education and came back to his father's house with some conceit of high learning. Noticing this, the father asked the son, "What is it all that you have learnt? What are the various systems that you have learnt?

Have you learnt about Brahman? Have you learnt that particular branch of education, which if one has learnt, one need not have to learn anything else and will be knowing all?" Such were the questions asked by the father. While the father was asking these questions, the son was behaving in a rather queer and funny way. He was still showing superior airs and conceit as if he was far more educated and learned than his father and that the latter would not understand at all, if he started telling what all he had learnt over those few years. The father could easily understand the false vanity and the immature state of his son. The son was trying to show off, replying to his father that God is like this, God is like that, and so on.

Uddalaka felt that his son will not be able to grasp anything at all, if he tried to tell him the Truth about Brahman in words. He thought it better to teach him by example. So, he brought a pot filled with water. He brought also some sugar in his hand and he showed the sugar to the son. After showing him the sugar, he put all that sugar into the water in the pot. Then, he stirred the sugar till it was completely dissolved in the water and then, looked at the son and asked him, "I have brought the sugar with me and you have seen the sugar yourself. I have put it into the vessel. Can you tell me where in this vessel does that sugar lie now?" The son looked into the vessel and of course, did not find any sugar remaining as such in the vessel. The father put a few drops of the contents of the vessel from the bottom, on the tongue of the son and asked, "How do you find the taste? You can take a drop from anywhere within the vessel and taste it." The son had to agree that sugar was there now, in every drop of the contents of the vessel and that it was present everywhere in that vessel. Then, the father explained, saying, "Just as you have now seen this sugar being present everywhere, so also Brahman assumes the form of a 'Saguna' or one, who has attributes and comes into this world and resides in every being, in everything, in every thing that you see around you in this world. It is not possible to see Him separately with your eyes, it is not possible to get hold of Him separately with your hands, but it is only possible to cognise Him by experiencing Him in the state of the world. You cannot do anything more with your gross body than to experience Brahman, Who is omnipresent and all pervading."

It is only after you have attained this rich experience that you will be in a position to talk of Advaita and give expression to the nature of God, His omnipresence, etc. It is only after such an experience that you will have any claim, right, and authority to talk about the omnipresence of God. Otherwise, just with mere book-knowledge and prattling like a parrot about God and His omnipresence, as if you truly know all, is all untruth. Only after the non-dual experience of Divinity can you talk of Advaita or non-dualism. It is not possible in common parlance, in ordinary work that you do around yourself in the material world, to teach or to expound Advaita. When you put your finger in your mouth and when you take out the finger from the mouth, you want to wash it with water. If there is so much difference between the limbs and the organs of one individual, how is it that we are going to expound unity and oneness of the entire world? That there is only one God in all the beings of the world, in all the living things in the entire world, is something which you learn, which you can believe, in which you can build your faith, by listening to experienced people or by reading texts or by listening to our Shastras and so on. But, unless you yourself have experienced it, you cannot truly convey this to others.

Taking the one truth that God is present in all the living things in the entire world and if we examine it, we will find an ocean of difference between one Jeeva and another in our experience and in their external appearance. Take the case of an ant. If the ant comes near you, you just push it away. Take the case of a snake. If the snake comes near you, you get terribly afraid about it and you run away from it. The fact that you behave in so different a manner towards these two living things, shows that you are not able to experience the feeling that God is present and is the same in all living beings. How can we expound what we do not practise in our daily life? You should, therefore, not be merely content by using words and quotations to understand and explain Advaita or non-dualism. You must make an attempt to experience this feeling. Otherwise, there will sometimes be danger too. It may land us in a situation, which is totally contrary to what we are understanding by the term Advaita.

One individual, who was always talking of Advaita, once went into a village. He went near a house and asked for alms. The lady of the house came and told this individual, the scholar who was asking for alms, "What is the point in my giving you uncooked rice? Why don't you go and have a bath and come back? I can then give you cooked food, which you can eat." This Pandit, who was well versed only in dialectics, in talking and in describing Advaita in words, said, "Govindeti Sada Snanam," which means mere utterance of the name Govinda is equivalent to having a bath. He said that he did not have to go and have a bath. The lady of the house then replied, "Ramanamamritam Sada Bhojanam," which means that just the thought of Rama and repeating the name is equivalent to having taken food always. So, she asked him to please go away. If in truth the utterance of the name Govinda is equivalent to having his bath, why should that be not also equivalent to his having food? Thus, to depend only on these words, to be argumentative with these words, and to understand only the word meaning of what Advaita is, may lead you into very difficult situations. The proper thing to do is, at the beginning, to accept a Saguna Brahman, that is a Form with some attributes, and so on, and through practice and through sadhana, gradually get over the situation and reach and attain the Advaitic experience. For the Saguna, that is one with attributes, and for Sakara, that is one with a Form, there is always a pre-determined place. So, at first, in that pre-determined place and at that fixed time, you will have to take to it and derive the pleasure and benefit.

It is possible that you may be getting a doubt that while God is present everywhere and anywhere, why should one go to a specific place, or why should one go on pilgrimages and seek God only in those specified places. When you have been able to imbibe the essence that is contained in the words, which describe Advaita and transform them into your experience, then you need not have to go to a specified place at all – you need not have to go anywhere at all. But, so long as you are content only with using words and just talking about Advaita and you have no experience at all, it is necessary that you should go to certain places. You have to make pilgrimages. Yes, for whatever you call Saguna, for whatever you call Sakara, you are seeking some Form. There is a place and time for that. But, once you have got over this feeling, if you are seeking the Nirguna, the ONE without attributes and the Nirakara, the One without Form, then there are no limitations of space or time.

Here is an example, which all the students know. Let us take the case of a cow. Inside the cow right through, there is the blood, which is flowing in its body. It is this blood, which is flowing in the body that gets converted into milk. We can infer that milk, in its essence, is present all through the body of the cow. But, if you get at the ear of the cow and twist it, are you going to get milk? Or if you get at the tail of the cow and twist it, are you going to get milk? If you want to get milk, you can do so, but there is chance of your getting milk only from a specified place. So also, while God is omnipresent and is everywhere, if you want to see Him, if you want to realise Him, then you have also to choose a place and a time.

But, in the teaching, which Uddalaka gave to his son in the beginning, sugar did appear as if it had a specific shape. It is only by taking the sugar, which had a shape and which had some attribute, and by putting it into water thereafter, it had lost its shape, it had lost its taste also to

Meditation

some extent, and Uddalaka could teach this shapeless, formless, attributeless thing by starting from sugar, which had a taste and which had a shape.

If you, as a young person, start your life by fixing a time and by fixing a form and begin your worship and gradually, by your practice, you reach a stage when out of that worship, you can just pick out a drop, a drop which has got a shape and taste and so on and put it into the large ocean, then the drop will mix with the large ocean and that will appear to you later on, as one infinite thing. For this, I will give you an example for what you initially experience as one, which has an attribute, which has a time, and which has specific shape, as against what you experience later on, as one which has no shape, which is present everywhere, and which is not bound by time. Let us take our own congregation at present, as the basis. I am now standing and talking and you are listening to what I am talking. But, I and all of you are all inside this Pandal. The talk, which I am now giving, you can listen to it for about one hour. The time is one hour. Look at this place, it is a small pandal and it is contained in a vast area and all of you are also grouped together as a body. In all of you, I am also one and am in everyone of you. After this, all of you, each one of you will go to your own place or your own village. When you have gone back to your village and at some moment, when you think of what happened now, you would say to yourselves that on such and such an evening, Swami was speaking to us, we were all sitting there, and He was saying the following things and so on. At that instant, when you recollect it, then all of us, including Myself, will all have gone into you. Thus, this picture, which has gone into your mind now, will stand as a picture, which is known to you all through your life. But this particular discourse, with a shape and with an attribute, has given you some experience and pleasure only for one hour. Because of the experience and the pleasure, which you have derived in one hour, looking with your eyes at the shape and hearing the discourse, this experience is going to remain in your heart and in your mind for all your life. But, if this did not happen for this one hour, if you had not witnessed all this, this will never have got imprinted in your memory. So, you should not speak lightly of and should not neglect the Saguna and the Sakara aspect. You have to accept and take it and with the help of that, reach the goal of Nirguna or Nirakara.

This process is called Meditation or is referred to as 'DHYANA'. However, today, in the world, many people are teaching in many different ways the meaning of the word Dhyana. What is the meaning of Dhyana? What is it that we are going to meditate about and who is going to do it? For what purpose are we going to meditate? If we make a proper enquiry in this manner, unless there is an object on which you could meditate, it is not possible to meditate. Such an object, on which you meditate or do Dhyana, is referred to as 'Dhyeya'. Without the object of concentration, you cannot concentrate. There is an object of meditation, but who is meditating? Therefore, there must be a third thing – 'Dhyata', which is you. You, who would be called Dhyata, through the path of meditation or Dhyana, you have to reach and experience the object of meditation or Dhyeya. These three are being referred to as three factors, one who receives the obeisance, one who gives the obeisance, and the process of giving obeisance. When the man, who meditates, takes to the object of meditation and goes through the process of meditation, then all these three, one who meditates, the one which is the object of meditation, and the process of meditation – unite and coalesce into one and only then, you achieve oneness. The one who loves, the one who is being loved, and the process of love are three factors. In prema – one who gives prema, one who receives prema, and the process of prema – we should regard all these three as one, through which the 'prematatwa' or the aspect of love is flowing. Even if any one of these three is missing, it is not possible to realise the completeness. If two, the one who loves and the process of love are there and there is no one to love, then it becomes useless. If the other two, the one who loves and the one who can be loved are there, but if there is no love between the two, then that becomes useless. On the other hand, there may be the process of love and there may be one who will be loved, but if there is nobody to love, then also it becomes useless. So, it is the oneness of all these three – one who will love, one who will be loved, and the process of loving – which will be referred to as Dhyana or meditation. In all these three, prema is present to the same extent. This is referred to by saying, "Love is God – Live in Love."

There is a need for us to make a proper enquiry into this path of meditation. This is a very good path to reach the Infinite. Although all these days, you have been listening to what is contained in many of our scriptures, like the Upanishads, like the Vedas, like the Darshanas and shastras, and so on, if you have not understood what is meant by Dhyana, the path by which to reach the destination, then all these may remain as book-knowledge and may create an allergy in you. For Dhyana, the time is important. This time, which is important, is referred to as 'Brahma Muhurta'. You will have to choose whatever form you like for the purpose of meditation, and during the time interval called the 'Brahma Muhurta', which is from 3 a.m. to 6 a.m., you will have to meditate on that at the same time, every day. There are also some methods and disciplines for this. You should not neglect and feel that there is no need for such specific methods.

There is a small example for this. We have put up a small fruit tree. When it is a small plant, we want to protect it by giving it fences. When it is a young plant, why do we put a fence around it and why do we try to protect it? It is because we feel that goat, sheep, and such other animals will come and probably eat it up and destroy the plant. We want it to grow well and we keep a fence around it. But, when that plant has grown and become a big tree, then we remove all that fencing. Why are we removing all the fence and protection at that time? The meaning of removing this fence is that the very same animals like goat, sheep, and cattle, which would have eaten up and destroyed the plant when it was tender, will then come and will seek shelter and shade, which the big tree now provides. The practice, which ultimately gives you moksha or liberation, should in the initial stages be regarded as a plant. For this practice, the fence, which we shall call discipline, is absolutely necessary. The reason for this is that bad company, bad ideas, bad association, and such other things may come and may destroy this young plant of practice. In order that they may not come and may not destroy, we will have to accept and observe discipline as the fence, which will protect us. When this young plant, which is seeking moksha by Dhyana, when it grows and becomes a big tree, then even though such bad ideas, bad company, and bad thoughts come close to the person, the big tree is such that all these visitors will only get pleasure and happiness out of that tree.

They cannot do any harm to that tree. That is why when we commence Dhyana and when we want to be in meditation, we should try and put ourselves in what is called a 'Padmasana'. For today's Padmasana, although there are not bad qualities and bad thoughts but the type of trousers, the drain-pipe pants which you are wearing are coming as an obstacle for you sitting in Padmasana. Maybe tomorrow, the person, who is giving you instruction in Asanas, will tell you what Padmasana is. You will have to abandon the pant, you will have to wear a dhoti, and you will have to sit in a Padmasana as has been shown by the teacher, who gives you the Asana lessons. Not only that, you should not sit on bare ground. You should sit on either a wooden plank or on a mat, or something like that. Not only that, you should not sit on a bare wooden plank. You should spread a piece of cloth over it. In the beginning, you should attempt to make a start with a wooden plank, which is above the ground by at least half an inch. There are some reasons for taking a wooden plank. The reasons are that the earth has got the power of conduction and diffusion. When we are sitting in meditation, because through you is passing the current of divine strength on account of your Dhyana, on account of the attraction which the earth has, you should not get disturbed. Therefore, you have got to have a plank. When we lay on electric wire inside a house, we also have a specially constructed wire, which is called the earth wire and which is put into the earth. So, we should regard our body as our house. While thus in the house of our body, we are in the process of giving rise to and establishing the divine current, then we should take all precautions that are necessary by isolating ourselves from the earth and by preventing the power or the strength in you from flowing away or dissipating into the earth. That is why our ancients have taught us that we should sit on a plank.

Not only this, that you are having the practice of getting up at 4:30 a.m. at the Brahma Muhurta, is also a very good habit. You are young and if while you are young, while your mind and body are still very sound and sturdy, if you do not start such good practices and get used to them at this age, when you grow a little older, when your body becomes a little more infirm and stiff, it will not be possible for you then to do so. It will be very difficult for you to acquire this practice at a late age. Truly, this age of yours is such that it is quite possible to understand many sacred things. It is quite possible to understand the Divine spirit. It is only in this context that we say, "Start early, drive slowly, reach safely." It is at this early age that you should begin early enough and reach safely. But, if you grow a little older and start practices late, you may not be able to get the happiness and benefit out of the practices. There are many people, who think that they will do all this after they retire. Before they retire, they always say duty is God, work is worship, and they go on doing all kinds of work, taking all kinds of jobs either under the Government, or under some private agency. But, this is not right. It is much better that you should do these things then and there and not go on postponing. This has been told to us in the Bhagavata. When the servants or the attendants of Yama come and pull you with a rope and ask you to move on, when they drag you with their rope and ask you to be quick and go along as your time is over, your own relations will say, "Now, there is no hope, put this body outside the house," and your wife and children will simply cry and say, "Now, it is all finished. There is no more hope." Under such conditions, is it possible for you to utter the name of the Lord and offer your devotion to God? So, at this young age, I am very hopeful that you will understand the significance of Dhyana and start Dhyana and become an ideal example for the rest of the country.

As I told you a little while ago, before you take your Padmasana and before you sit on the wooden plank, have a small jyoti – a candle light – in front of you. You look at that Jyoti, the light, well with open eyes. After one minute, close your eyes. After you have closed the eyes, feel that the light that you had seen before closing your eyes, is in your heart. You get the feeling and you have the feeling that inside the lotus of your heart, right at the centre is this particular Jyoti. If you are not able to picture the Jyoti in the lotus of your heart and get that feeling, then open your eyes, look at the light again, close your eyes, and try to picture it inside your heart once again. After that, you think of it and you picture to yourself, fix it in your mind, and feel that that particular Jyoti is put in the centre of this lotus. After that, you take this Jyoti from the centre of the heart and move it to each part of your body; bring it to your neck; from the neck, bring it to your mouth; from the mouth, bring it to your hand; from the hand, take it to your leg; from the leg, take it to your ear; take it to your eyes; take it to your head; from the head, bring it all around you; when you have brought it out of your head, you imagine that you have taken this Jyoti and give it to those, who are related to you; those, who are affectionate to you and your friends. Not only that, spread the light even amongst your enemies. After that, you picture to yourself that you have taken this Jyoti and given it to all the birds, the beasts, and everything around you.

Where this Jyoti or light has moved, there will be no darkness. It is in this context that all our Upanishads have said, "Tamasoma Jyotirgamaya." Since this Jyoti has reached your eyes, you will no longer have any bad vision or bad sight. Because this Jyoti has gone to your ears, you will not hear evil. Because this Jyoti has reached your tongue, out of your tongue will no longer come any bad words. Since this Jyoti has reached your head, evil thoughts should no longer go into your heart, nor will they arise in you. Since the same Jyoti has gone into your

Meditation

heart, bad ideas should no longer enter your heart. Since the same Jyoti has also touched your feet, your feet should no longer walk into bad places. Because to your hands, the same Jyoti has reached, your hands will no longer engage themselves in bad acts. The word bad is synonymous with darkness. In truth, if you have allowed this Jyoti to spread everywhere, there is no room anywhere for this darkness or bad to persist. If, while engaged in such Dhyana or meditation, you are still doing something bad, it simply means that this Jyoti has not reached that particular organ, which is doing bad.

By this meditation, not only bad traits, which are in you, will have been removed, but in their place, noble and sacred ideas and sacred actions would have entered; not only that, you would be able to get the glorious Darshan of Ishwara or you would experience Advaita, the experience of oneness, because the light that is in you is present in all human beings, because the light that is present in you is present in all the birds and animals, the light is everywhere. By realising this, you will also have established the truth of the saying, "Geetavakyam Idam Dharmam." Some of you may get a doubt and say to yourselves, "Well, we like Rama, He is our God; we like Krishna, He is our God; we like Swami, He is our God. Why should we not take and meditate on one of these Forms? Why should we have a light in front of us for meditation?" But, a shape or a particular form is not a permanent thing. That is a changing thing; that is also a fleeting thing. It is not right that you should put your concentration on something, which will change, which is not permanent. You must have something, which does not change. That is why you have to take the Jyoti. Having the Jyoti, which does not change, in your meditation, you can certainly put into it the 'Roopa' or form, which you want and which you want to pray to. There is nothing wrong in doing that. In this form of Roopa, there is always a growth and decline. This is also referred to as a change, as a transformation. Here is a small example for this. We fill up a tank completely with water. If each one takes a tumbler of water from that tank, to some extent the water level will come down in that tank. On one side, if we get some sand and put it up as a mound, and out of that sand, if each one takes a small quantity, then in time, the volume of that sand will also diminish. So it is that this body is something, which has been made up of the combination of elements, such as water, sand, and so on. That is the reason why this body is being referred to as something, which is made up of earth. On the contrary, if we have a Jyoti – or a light in one place, it does not matter how many people may come and light up their lamps from this one Jyoti, this Jyoti which is the source, is not going to diminish or lose anything. This first Jyoti, the source, is called the Akhanda Jyoti. Those, who come and light up their lamps, are called Jeevan Jyoties. So many Jeevan Jyoties, all of them have started from one single Akhanda Jyoti only. By putting this Jyoti in our heart, in each individual Jeeva's heart, then the result of the meditation will be that this single Jeevan Jyoti will go and merge itself in the Akhanda Jyoti and will teach you the nature of Advaita or the oneness of this world and the entire creation.

Meditation

For this, a time, a process, and a place are very essential. The place may change. Today, you may be in Brindavan, tomorrow you may be in Bangalore, the day after that, you may be in another place like Madras. For this body, which is travelling from place to place, it is not possible always to have a fixed place for the purpose of meditation. Even if there is a change with regard to the place where you meditate, you must take great care to see that the time, at which you meditate, does not change. In Brindavan, you can start your prayers at 4:30 a.m. Tomorrow, at 4:30 a.m., you may be travelling in a train. At that particular time, whether you are in Brindavan or whether you are in the train, you must take to meditation. Thus, at 4:30 tomorrow, in the train, if in your mind you recollect the place in Brindavan, where you sat the previous day, and start your meditation, then your mind will leave the train and will certainly come back to the place, where you started your meditation in Brindavan. It does not matter whether you are sitting in a train, or whether you are sitting in a plane, or anywhere else, if in your mind you recollect the original place where you started this meditation and stick to the time, then the time, the procedure for meditation, and also the place, which has gone into your mind, will all coalesce together and they will certainly give you peace and equanimity. Because the time is also as responsible as a servant, you should not change this time. Even a dog, which is like a servant, if you start giving it food say at 12'o'clock today and do it for four or five days like that, does not have to be called at 12'o'clock. The dog will come at 12'o'clock and will ask for food. So also, at the time that has been fixed for your Dhyana, if you, out of your heart, are willing to offer prema through your meditation, then surely at the appropriate time, God will come and will receive your prema and will give you all happiness. What you have to give God is prema. It must be prema coming from within your heart. It must be at the appropriate time. So, if you give heartfelt prema at the appropriate time, then God will certainly receive it and God will shower on you all happiness.

You must also have heard that God is SAT CHIT ANANDA (Satchidananda). I have now to tell you the meaning of BABA. BABA is B.A.B.A. The first B stands for Being; A stands for Awareness; the third letter B stands for Bliss; the fourth letter A is for Atman. The first B – BEING is SAT; the next letter A – AWARENESS is CHIT; third letter B is BLISS or ANANDA. The last letter, the fourth letter is ATMA, that means SATCHIDANANDA is ATMA. You also know the meaning of SATHYA; SATHYA is TRUTH. It is something, which is unchanging during all the times. The word SAI has three sounds in it – SA, AA, YE. SA stands for the sacred and Divine; AAYE means mother. In different languages, we have for the mother, Aayee, Mayee, and Tayee. Like that Aayee means mother, baba means father. SAI BABA is the Divine Mother and Father; SAAAYEE BABA – Divine Mother and Father. In the same way we use the letter SA for Divine, for mother we can use the word AMBA, for father we can use the word SIVA, SA AMBA SIVA (SAMBASIVA). Sambasiva or SAI BABA are exactly the same, there is no difference between the two.

Therefore, it becomes evident that this is 'Siva Shakti Atmaka Swaroopa'. So, if you want to taste and experience this Divinity, if you want to taste the nectar of bliss, then from tomorrow, you start on meditation and I am blessing you and I am hoping that you will be able to get the happiness and bliss of Divinity by such practices.

10.

Destiny And Divine Grace

The Mahabharata and Ramayana, which are the most precious jewels of India, are like vast oceans. If we look at these oceans from one side, we will have only a limited view, but if we climb up a hill and have a look at them, we get a fuller view and a better understanding of them. What we have to do is to delve into them and try to explore and understand the treasures contained in these big oceans. Ramayana and Mahabharata are very sacred books, which will directly tell us about many things, especially the ways in which we have to conduct ourselves. Ramayana and Mahabharata will help us in our daily life, like our two eyes. We are not able to know the true value of these jewels and we think that Mahabharata is merely a battle between the sons of two brothers, and that Ramayana is a story wherein a demon stole away the wife of Rama and Rama again won her back. It is not like that and these two epics are like the heart and the head of India, are as vital to India as the heart and the head are to a human body.

In the lecture delivered to you this morning, you have been told that, "Swadharmo Nidhanam Sreyaha, Paradharmo Bhayavaha." This means that in carrying out one's own dharma, even if one perishes, it is far better than taking to dharma not belonging to oneself. The latter path is beset with fear. We must try to first understand what dharma is. Then, we can try to know what is our own dharma or 'Swadharma'. In the word Swadharma, there are actually two words, 'Swa' and 'Dharma'. First comes the 'Swa', then comes 'Dharma'. These two are different words. They are not one word, but we use the words together. 'Swa' means 'I'; 'I' means 'Brahma Tatwa'. Therefore, by the word 'Swa', we have to mean 'Brahman' or 'Brahmatatwa'. 'Dharma' means Right Conduct. So, Swadharma means the path of the Brahman or the path of the Supreme Being. That thing that comes straight out of our heart must be considered as dharma. Between dharma and Sathya, there is yet another thing. The prompting that comes out of the heart or the feeling that emanates from the heart is called 'Ruta'. Ruta means the feelings and the ideas. They are of paramount importance. They set out all the guidelines for action and have a determining influence. So, the feeling that has been shaped in the heart, when it comes in the form of speech, is called 'Sathya' or Truth. If whatever is implied in these words, is put into practice, that is called 'Dharma'. We can say that Dharma is that, which is born from the heart, that which is then expressed in the shape of words and that which is then put into practice.

Dharma is not a thing that can be determined by each and every person, as per his whim. Some may say that the Dharma that comes out of one's heart is his Dharma; how can it become the Dharma of God? So, in your heart – not the physical heart, but the spiritual heart – you must try to locate and cognise the Atma Tatwa. The word 'I' belongs to Atma and never to the body. Thus, Dharma is that, which comes from our heart and which is to be put into practice by us. We try to put it into practice, according to the ideals of our culture and try to live up to that ideal. The 'Vyavaharika Dharma' or Dharma relating to the daily routine will be changing from day to day. Those things that will be changing from day to day are not real Dharma. Dharma is not changeable, it is eternal, it is immutable, it is truth. If it is changeable, why should we establish such a Dharma? Should we act according to it? Rama has been described in the Ramayana by the statement 'Ramo Vigrahavan Dharmaha', Rama is the Embodiment of Dharma. Even though Rama has a physical body, the Dharma, which He lived and set as an example and established in the world for eternity, is the eternal Dharma and unchanging truth.

All these things that begin with the word Swa have been born in the sanctity of our heart and they are not connected with the physical world. 'Swadharma', 'Swabhava', 'Swecha' are words, which begin with 'Swa'. When we think of these words, they will certainly tell us about our nature and about the Atma that is within ourselves. Swadharma is the Dharma of the Atma. Swabhava is the nature of the Atma. So also, Swecha means the freewill of the Atma. Swecha in the ordinary usage means freedom or liberty. We should not take it in the ordinary sense. Swecha means the will of the Atma. If we take it in the true sense and follow it up, we will be much benefitted by our action.

Brahman is described as having the nature of wisdom. That is why it has been said that the end of wisdom is freedom. So, freedom means Jnana Tatwa or the light of wisdom, but not the unrestrained way in which we try to live our lives in this world. There are many things, which we have to learn from our Puranas, from our Ithihasas, from our Vedas, and from the sayings of elders. For everything, speech is the authority. We are taking shabda or sound of the word as authority or proof. For all the words, Sathya or truth is the real basis.

You might have heard that of all the mandalas or the regions, the 'Dhruva Mandala' is the highest. We generally think that Dhruva Mandala is a place where Dhruva, the son of Uttanapada, lives, but it is a mistake. Dhruva means Truth. So, Dhruva Mandala means a region that is higher than all the other mandalas. That is why the saying has come that, "Truth is God." So, to attain the truth or the form of the truth, which is called the Parabrahman, we have to follow the truthful path, the path of truth. Whatever state we want to obtain, we have to follow the kind of path suited to it. So, if we want to reach the stage of Sathya, but follow the path of falsehood, we can never go to the sathya state. I shall give you a small example. When water is put in water, it will certainly get well mixed. There will be no difficulty. But, when oil is put in water,

Destiny And Divine Grace

they do not mix properly. Water will be separate and oil will be separate. Therefore, when sathya or truth is combined with sathya or truth, then there will be real sathya. But, if we mix untruth with truth, it will be just like trying to mix oil with water.

Many people have tried to comment upon our great Indian books and they have expressed many contradictory and conflicting views. I shall cite here an example. Dayananda Saraswati established what is called the Arya Samaj and gave certain ideas through that samaj. Though what Dayananda Saraswati gave us are really good ideas, in certain instances, they have some complex meanings also. On account of this, many people discussed what Dayananda Saraswati is alleged to have said and they never tried to understand him in the right spirit. From time immemorial, there has never been a dearth of critics in our country. Because there are no competent people in India, who can denounce the critics and their criticisms and oppose them, in some respects, India has come to the present stage. Indians are not people, who do not know the real situation. They know what there is in the Vedas, Puranas, Ithihasas, and other Texts. They were rather indifferent and felt that there was no need to challenge the ideas that have been expressed by people, who are not real scholars. But, we should not be indifferent like that. If we leave a small plant to take its own course, it will grow up into a big tree and sometimes, it spreads its thorns also around it.

Once, Dakshinamurti wanted to teach the people the real spirit of God and also, he wanted to enjoy himself.

He took a tree as his guru; he took a river as his guru; so also, he took a stone as his guru. He took nature as his preceptor and began to travel with joy. After some time, he reached the shore of an ocean. He sat on the shore of the ocean and was contemplating. At that time, a little dirt had fallen in the ocean. As soon as it fell in the ocean, the ocean became very furious and sent wave after wave and repelled that dirt to the shore. Dakshinamurti got angry with the sea. He said, "What is this? This dirt is a very small thing and the ocean is a very expansive one. Can it not contain this small piece of dirt in itself? How selfish is this ocean?" Generally, elders do not say or do anything without reason. So, he thought that because the ocean is very respectable, perhaps what it did was to give him some message; therefore, he felt he should not be angry with the ocean and prayerfully asked that he be given the reason for this and thus, make his heart and mind peaceful. Then, the ocean spoke thus, "I am very expansive and very large and in me are born many, many animals and creatures. Therefore, I always wish that my form should be very clean. If I give place to dirt, though it be very small, tomorrow it will make all my form unclean. Therefore, I did not want to give place to that little dirt and wanted to throw it back to the shore." This Dakshinamurti compared to Samsara or family. So, if in the family, we give place to a mean idea or a mean quality, it will certainly grow and will cover up and enmesh the whole family. Therefore, people leading a family life should try to see that not even a small, mean quality enters it. Samsara does not refer to family life alone. Our life itself is a Samsara. So, in this life, we should never give place to things that will mislead us or that will make us unclean.

Indians should never go against any religion or any idea or any one's feeling. Some people and some religions of other countries tell us that all of us are the children of God and so, we must live peacefully like brothers. India and our religions have taught us the saying, "Ishwara Sarvabhootanam," or the Lord is in all the living creatures. Our culture teaches us that not only human beings, but insects, animals, and all living things should be treated equally and all of them should try to live on a common basis. Indians worship the Bodhi tree. The meaning of this worship is that even trees have something good in them, that they have fragrance which indicates good. We are worshipping animals also; some people worship the Lion. It is called the vahana or the carriage of Devi or Lalitamba. We worship the cow. We worship all these, because we think that godliness is not only in human beings, but also in animals. So, among animals, we select the best of them, because we see God in them. Indians worship even snakes, which are considered to be very poisonous and harmful. To others, it may seem ridiculous that we worship the trees, the animals, and the poisonous snakes. However, it has a very significant meaning that in all these things, we see Godliness and treat all of them equally. So, our real religion points to unity and not to diversity. Indian scriptures and the Puranas teach us the highest truth.

Now, I shall try to answer the doubts that have arisen in the minds of some of the students, because these doubts if left unanswered, grow bigger and will go on pestering you, with bad results. Therefore, I want to clear all your doubts. One student mentioned about 'Prarabdha Karma and Sanchita Karma', the consequence of all our actions and asked whether with the grace of God, these can be overcome, especially the bad part of it. We should not try to worship God only for the sake of overcoming the consequence of all our actions. If you worship Him to get His grace, Prarabdha, Sanchita, and all other Karma will become ineffective by themselves. Before trying to rectify these things, first try to know what is Prarabdha, what is Sanchita, and what is Agami Karma. Prarabdha Karma is that, which we are presently undergoing and experiencing. Sanchita means all the past Karma. Agami refers to Karma that will follow in the future. Prarabdha is in between the Sanchita and Agami, and we are experiencing this Prarabdha on account of the previous Sanchita Karma. The result of what we do now will come in the future. I shall give you a small example from our daily life. We have got a store room in which we stock all our rice. We have already the old stock of rice in the store. So what we have stored in the room is called Sanchita. When we want to cook, we remove some rice from the store room and begin to cook it. What we bring from the store room for cooking today, is called Prarabdha. What we cook now and what we eat today will pass out of our body, tomorrow. Sometimes, what we eat may come out in the shape of a belch. Therefore, we cannot escape from Prarabdha, we must experience it in this life. In the store room, there is only rice. When we bring it, we will be able to convert it into many

Destiny And Divine Grace

preparations. In this way, we can make the rice into food, we can make it in the form of 'Pulihora'; we can cook it in the shape of 'Chakrapongal', it can be made into 'Daddhojana', we can make from it 'Idlies' and also 'Dosas' and so on, all of which are names for different preparations from rice. We never change the base, which is always rice. You have to start any preparation with rice only. Even though there is Sanchita, if you try to behave in a sathwic way, in a pious and good way, you will be able to change even Sanchita. You may say that in the rice store, there are big stones. They are the results of our bad actions. They are in the store mixed with the rice. Before we cook, do we not try to remove away the stones from the rice? So, it is quite necessary that when we experience Sanchita, we can overcome the bad effects to some extent or to a great extent and make them clean, just as we make the rice clean.

Here is another example. Prarabdha can be compared to the dust that follows in the wake of a bus. When the bus is going, the dust also will be following it. So, when the Karma, which can be compared to the bus, is running, the Prarabdha, which can be compared to the dust, will be pursuing it. When the bus stops and does not travel, then the dust comes and falls over it. But, when the bus does not stop and keeps on running, the dust will be only at a distance. So, when we are satisfactorily doing our daily duties without interruption, the dust or the prarabdha will be at a distance and behind us without affecting us. You may ask how long can we travel in a bus? We have to stop somewhere. It is not so. This road is of three kinds: work, worship, and wisdom. This work is related to Karma and dust will be only there. You may take this as a village road. But, if you pass some distance, then you will have a better road, a tar road. When the tar road comes, the dust will never fall on the bus. If you go still further, you shall reach the trunk road, the highway. So, the road of karma is called the village road. Bhakti or worship is the town road or the tar road. Wisdom is the highway, wherein there is no possibility of the dust coming. When we are following only the path of Karma, this Prarabdha will never come to an end. But, if we do the Karma in a way that we perform all actions for the pleasure and for the satisfaction of God, in worship and dedication to Him, no Prarabdha will trouble us.

From the examples of Dhruva and Markandeya, we know how Karma can be overcome. Markandeya's parents were to have a son, who would live only for 16 years. But, from the time of the birth of the child, not only the child, but the parents also were worshipping God in great devotion and the effect is that they could change even the sankalpa of God and as a result, Markandeya could live forever. There is this capacity of changing the sankalpa of even God by devotion. We need not be afraid of Prarabdha or Sanchita. If we think that the effect of the Prarabdha Karma is inescapable, then what is the use of worshipping God? Even though Prarabdha is there, the grace of God will certainly remove to a large extent the bad effects from the Prarabdha. Here is a small example for this. There is an injection bottle. It will be written on that, that the medicine inside can be used upto 1970. That bottle is there even in the year 1972 and the medicine is also there in the bottle, but the medicine will have no power. It cannot serve its purpose. So, in the same way, that in our destiny there may be the medicine of Prarabdha, but by the grace of God we can weaken its effect, blunt its effect. Even though it is there, it cannot trouble us. We can become beneficiaries of God's grace; we need not be afraid of either Prarabdha, or Sanchita, or Agami. If God is pleased with our worship, He will certainly annul the bad effects of Prarabdha and Sanchita. Therefore, the most important thing we have to try is to earn the grace of God by which we can overcome all these bad effects.

Another question is what we hear of the Kaliyuga. We must try to make the best of our present age only and try to do good things and live happily in this world. Past is past and it will never come again and we are not sure of the future. Present is not permanent. It will be always changing and moving. That is why we say, "Be good, do good, see good – that is the way to God." Try to be good, fill your heart with good, and lead a good life and the result also will be good. When one falls sick, it is not in any way useful to feel sorry over it. After falling sick, it is necessary that we should somehow try to take proper medicine and get over the sickness. Instead of weeping over the disease we have got, it is better to try and get it cured and help the body to get well. So also, instead of feeling sorry for the bad things that are happening in this Kaliyuga, we must try always to be good and remove the bad from this world. We are seeing many bad things and distractions among the students nowadays. You are all students and you have to try to remove all of those distractions and bad things. Try to be good so that you may reap happiness as a result. Truly speaking, these distractions are not created by students themselves. All the students are basically good. But, even in the hearts of the students, there are some possibilities for these bad qualities also to enter. Students should not give place to bad associations and bad ideas, and they should try to be good and also try to make others good. The right way of leading a good life in this world is the spiritual, moral, and ethical way. So, we must care for these three paths, the spiritual, the moral, and the dharmic. You always think that 'Pratyaksha', what we see directly, is the only proof and authority. But, Pratyaksha Pramana is not the only proof in this life. There are many things that are beyond the capacity of the human intellect and mind. We must first try to know what is not known to us. Then, it may lead to the welfare of the humanity. I shall give you an example about the 'Vikara' or the bad quality of our mind. A medicine as a finished product may cost only a little, but how much amount will have been spent for research on it and its discovery? As the science of medicine is progressing and advancing, the diseases also are growing faster and faster. If there is one doctor for each house, there are four patients in each house. If there is one lawyer for each house, there are many disputes and quarrels between the four brothers living in the same house. In this context, it is just madness to think that we are going forward in the field of medicine and also, in the field of law. It is not the law that we have to develop; it is love that we have to develop. Spirituality asserts that there is law in love. Where there is love, there is no possibility either for hatred, or for disease. When there is no love, there will be hatred towards others and that hatred will develop into a big disease. Jealousy, anger, and ego are the biggest diseases. If you want to keep yourself aloof from these three diseases, you must try to love everybody.

When one of the girl students spoke in the beginning, she addressed others as 'friends'. This friendship may develop into anything. Therefore, I asked her not to address others as friends. In the life of students today, this friendship is spreading along a blind path and without restraint. So, instead of considering others as friends, if you consider them as sisters and brothers, we know that towads a sister we shall never develop a bad feeling. Students must try to consider one another as brothers and sisters, and not mere friends, because even in friendship, sometimes there are bad meanings and bad interpretations. When Swami Vivekananda introduced a new form of address, instead of addressing them as 'Ladies and Gentlemen', he addressed them as 'Brothers and Sisters'. It was quite new to the foreigners and they were so much touched and moved by that gesture, that they applauded incessantly for 15 minutes. Of course, nowadays too, we are addressing the audience as sisters and brothers, but that feeling is not there in our heart even for the time we are on the platform. What we do not feel in our heart should not be expressed outwardly. We must give place to true feelings from our heart and we must try to practise good things in our life.

11.

Self-Control And Detachment

All religions teach us only good. We should try to understand this and follow them in practice. If we do like that, we will certainly be benefitted. Today, our programme began with Bharata Natya. We should know that our very life is a Bharata Natya. What is implied by this statement that our life is Bharata Natya and what is the platform? The world is the platform for the Bharata Natya of our life. Each individual is one of the many actors. Maya is the Tala. Maya will prompt this life to dance on the platform of the world. This NARTAKI, or the actress of Maya has got the capacity to attract certain scenes or 'Dhrisyas'. If Maya has not exercised her charm and spell on the minds of the people, man would not have come to such a condition. God is inside our heart, but Maya distracts our attention with her play and we miss the vision of God. To get over the spell cast on us by the actress Maya, we have to do certain practices and put in some effort. Just as if there are no accompaniments, no dance will have that appeal and beauty, so also when Maya is the actress, the song we have to sing as an accompaniment to her should be suitable to the actress. If both of them differ and do not match, there will be disharmony and the dance will not be attractive. This Maya can be given the name Nartaki, or actress. The word Nartaki contains three letters, NA-RTA-KI. If we read this word in the reverse manner – it becomes KI-RTA-NA, and so Kirtana will be able to control this actress or Maya. We have to ask what kind of Kirtana? Whose wealth is this Nartaki? She is the property of God. Because this Maya or Nartaki is the property of God, the Kirtana or the song about God will be very pleasant to her. Bhagawat Kirtana or the song about God will certainly give great pleasure to this Nartaki.

The hearing of God's name alone is 'Satkriti' or good tune and nothing else is Satkriti. So, our sages and seers based their life and activities on Satkriti and oriented it towards union with the Supreme Soul. The stage thus reached can be called 'Nivritti'. In order to reach that stage of Nivritti, we have to put in much effort. Water does not have any necessity for fish. But, fish cannot live without water. In the same way, there is no necessity of a disciple for a guru. But, if a disciple does not have an acharya or preceptor, he will find it very difficult. We are doing all these preparations of providing you with the right type of teachers to make you understand what the Upanishads have said, what the epics like Ramayana and Mahabharata have taught, so that you may be able to get to the state of Nivritti and also, obtain peace and tranquillity of mind and heart.

Self-Control And Detachment

You are having much of 'Sravana', hearing or listening to. You have to consider well and try to know what you have heard and how much of it you are going to put into practice. By merely hearing, your heart cannot attain a state of sanctity. You must think and contemplate over it. This is called 'Manana' and after Manana comes 'Nidhidhyasa'. Only after Nidhidyasa is completed will you be able to have the fruit and benefit of Sravana or listening. Today, 99 percent of the people think that they have done their business by hearing and they do not try to do Manana and Nidhidyasa. Sravana or listening can be compared with the cooking that is done in a kitchen. If we bring what is cooked to the dining room and eat it, that can be compared to manana or contemplation. After eating, if we try to digest what we have eaten, that can be compared to Nidhidyasa. Only when all these three actions are done will what we eat give strength and nourishment to our body. Nowadays, everything is ready in the kitchen, but we are not able to bring it to the dining room, eat it, and digest it. Without these, how can we get the strength that is required? Knowledge of every kind is ever available in the form of Vedas and Puranas. We are not trying to bring out what is said in those texts to our experience. The sole reason for this is that we do not have a sincere desire for doing so.

We must try to strengthen our mental capacity. The mind has immence potency and there is no other power that is equal to it. If we can only cultivate and improve this mental capacity, then we will gain an immense potential. The mind itself is the sole cause for everything, either for bondage, or for freedom, for happiness as well as for misery and for so many other things. A small example to illustrate this is in the story about Prahlada and Hiranyakasapa. Prahlada is the son and Hiranyakasapa is the father. We must try to know the distinction between the father and the son. Because Lord Narayana killed his brother, Hiranyakasapa was very angry with Him and he tried to search for Him and when he could not see Him anywhere, he told his son that Narayana or God is nowhere in this world. But, Prahlada argued with his father and asserted that God Narayana is everywhere. He said, "Do not doubt, God is not only here, but He is everywhere. Wherever you search for Him, He will be present there." Then, Hiranyakasapa told his son, "Mad boy, I have searched every place. There is no place which I have not searched. I have searched even the ocean, but I could not find Him." But, Prahlada had complete faith and confidence in God and he told his father, "It is only a defect of your vision and the malady of your mind, if you could not find Him. Search for Him sincerely and with faith. You will be able to find Him." Then, the father asked, "Is He present in this pillar?" "Yes, He is there without fail," said the son. Then, Hiranyakasapa broke the pillar. Instantaneously, God appeared in the form of 'NARAHARI', half-lion and half-man. God was not found by Hiranyakasapa, when he searched for Him everywhere, but He made Himself visible in the pillar, when Prahlada told his father that God is everywhere. The reason is this; Hiranyakasapa never believed in his heart that there is God, but Prahlada believed with great faith that God is there and that He is omnipresent.

Therefore, according to the idea Hiranyakasapa had, he could not find God, and according to the idea Prahlada had, he could find God everywhere.

If we try to make our mind pure, then we shall be able to discover anything and everything. In our Sadhana, the first thing we have to do is to deepen and steady our faith. God is all pervading and He is everywhere and so, the Atmatatwa that flows out of our mind will be very near God. Because God comes out of our heart in the form of speech, we must try to make our speech as pure and as clean as possible. God is also in the form of Truth. So, whatever we will be telling through our speech, God will be saying, "Let it be so!" There is a small story for this. A traveller was going on his way. After going some distance, he was tired on account of the summer heat. By the side of the path, there was a big tree and he went there to take rest under the shade of that tree. When he went into that cool shade, he was overjoyed. Then, he said to himself, "I am able to find a very cool place; how fortunate will I be if I will be able to get a glass of cool water also, here?" Instantaneously, a tumbler of water came down. After he drank that water, he thought, "Now I have quenched my thirst, but how happy will I be if there is a good bed here, because this floor is hard and rough." At once, a big, soft bed came down. He then thought, "Even in my house, I do not possess such a bed and such a pillow. If my wife comes here and sees, how happy will she feel?" Immediately, the wife also came. He saw her and thought, "Is she my wife or is she a demon? Will she eat me?" No sooner he said this, she ate him. The tree under the shade of which he sat is 'Kalpavriksha'. Kalpavriksha is a tree that fulfils all desires. When the traveller sat under the Kalpavriksha, whatever good things he thought of, he got them instantly. But, when he thought about bad things, bad things also came to him. This world is a part of Kalpavriksha. We are sitting under the shade of this Kalpavriksha. If we think badly, bad happens to us and if we think in a good manner, good happens to us. So, when our thoughts, when our contemplation and when our deeds are pure, Kalpavriksha of the world will be giving the good things desired by us. Both good and bad will come only from our heart. They never come from outside. That is why in the beginning, we have to make our heart as pure as possible.

All these sacred stories and texts will be preaching us an inner meaning. When we read the story of Prahlada, we will be thinking that Prahlada is good and that Hiranyakasapa is the atheist. But, we must also think about what happened to them. If we go deep into the story, it will teach us that when we think in a good way, good things will happen to us and if we think in a bad way, bad things will happen to us. So, in this way, for everything, the mind or our sankalpa, the desire is the cause.

In the morning, I told you about Gajendra Moksha and other stories. Who is this Gajendra or the Lord of Elephants? Our story tells us that Gajendra was a king in his previous birth and he took the form of an elephant on account of a curse given to him by a sage. While he was going with the female elephants in the forest, he saw a lake. He wanted to take water from it; he went into the

Self-Control And Detachment

lake and a crocodile caught his foot. This Gajendra in his previous birth was a great king. King signifies another form of Atma. Atma is the King and Paramatma is the kingmaker. So, the individual, who is one with the state of Atma, has become an animal on account of the curse given to him by a sage. When a king changed into an elephant, what does it mean? He let go his 'Atmadrishti' or oneness with the Atma and degraded himself into the form of an animal. Atmadrishti is just like the gait of a lion. When the lion is walking, it will be always going straight, but will never try to look back. And Jivadrishti is just like the gait of a sheep. The sheep will never go straight. It will be afraid and it will be always going with some fear in his mind. If we go with Atmadristhi, we shall be able to go straight and get happiness. But, if we fall from the Atmadrishti to Jivadrishti, sometimes we may become like animals. Like the king, who became an elephant, we may experience difficulties in life. In the daily life also, if we happen to do a thing that is very bad, the elders remark, "Why did you do this? Are you an animal?" It does not mean that we are real animals. But, our behaviour in doing such an action is just like that of an animal. This elephant has forgotten the Atmatatwa and was leading a life of attachment, of falsehood, conceit, and arrogance. It is in a state of intoxication and illusion. This elephant is entering the forest of life. When it is wandering in the forest of life, it becomes thirsty. What kind of thirst was it? It is related to the enjoyment of the senses. Immediately, it sees a lake. What is that lake? It is full of worldly desires and that is called the Samsara or family. He wanted to enjoy the pleasures of that Samsara and he went and got down into that lake. He is too much seized with desires, which never let one think over what he is doing. Therefore, he put both his legs in the lake. At once, a crocodile, which can be compared to 'Mamakara' or attachment or 'Ahamkara' or ego, caught hold of its leg. When it caught its leg, the elephant was not able to escape from it. He tried all means. The elephant found that its body has become very weak. Then, it wanted to depend upon its mental capacity. It found that even the mental strength was also insufficient and could not help. Then, it thought only of divine strength.

Nowadays, men are leading their lives just like that elephant. Man is depending entirely upon the strength of his body, upon the strength of his intellect, upon the strength of his relations, and upon the strength of his learning. He is not counting and depending upon the divine strength. When the elephant found that it lost all its strength, he thought that he should pray to God. Why did not the elephant pray to God for such a long time and why did it try to pray to God in the last moments only? We must try to find out the reason for both these. We are leading our lives entirely depending upon the strength of the body and the strength of the mind. If one depends entirely on these two strengths alone, he will not be able to get happiness. Even though he pretends to look happy outside, really speaking he has no laughter or happiness in his heart. The reason is that the strength of the body and the strength of the mind are not capable of giving any happiness or peace to man. When we dedicate these two strengths to God and if we think that everything

Self-Control And Detachment

depends upon the grace of God, then we may get peace and happiness with the grace and kindness of God.

We read in the Bhagavata story, that when the elephant prayed, God sent His Chakra, which is called 'Sudarshana Chakra'. We must try to know the inner meaning of this Sudarshana. Sudarshana is not merely a weapon, or an instrument. When the elephant tried to turn his looks to God, the looks of God also were turned towards the elephant. Su-Darshana means good look. When the elephant tried to look towards God, good looks of God also fell upon the elephant. That is why it is called Sudarshana. I used to say when I was in Shirdi, "You look to me and I shall certainly look to you." When your looks fall on me, my looks certainly will fall on you. When the good looks of the elephant were directed towards God, the kind looks of God were sent to save the elephant. When the kind look of God fell on the elephant, then it was able to get rid of the bondage.

We have to think about the crocodile also. If the crocodile is on the ground, it will not have any strength. When it is in the water, its natural habitation, it will be very strong. So also, Dharma will hold with all its strength, not in words but in practice. Dharma protects you, when you practise it. Bhagawan said in Gita, "Dharma-Samsthapanaya Sambhavami Yuge Yuge" – in every Yuga or Age, I am taking birth for the sake of establishing Dharma. In fact, Dharma is eternal and is present at all times, present, past, and the future. What then is the necessity for establishing it? It simply means that people are not practising it and Krishna wanted to restore or reestablish the practice of Dharma.

There are many things, which we do not know and about which we will be having doubts. With faith and confidence and thinking earnestly, we must try to clear those doubts and try to be happy. Our puranas teach nothing but truth and things are explained so clearly that no doubts need be left. These doubts come on account of the distorted meanings we give to the words or sayings of the Puranas. I shall give you a small example. We must try to have pure thoughts in our mind and put such thoughts in the form of pure speech. For instance, we must try to know the relationship of Jeeva with other things in the world. A prince, son of a king, once went to the forest in his princely attire. There was a sage in the hermitage. He saw this prince and asked him, "You appear to be a prince. Whose son are you?" The prince replied, "Our kingdom is Jitendriya Rajya and I am the son of King Jitendriya." The sage was astonished. He asked himself in disbelief, "Is there a kingdom like Jitendriya? Is there a king by name Jitendriya? Perhaps he is only using words like this. I don't think there is such a king living in this world." Then, the prince said, "Oh sage, it is true! Our kingdom is Jitendriya and all the people in our kingdom are Jitendriyas – they have full control and mastery over their indriyas. Not only the people, but every living being in the kingdom is a Jitendriya. The king is Jitendriya and the king's son, myself, am also a Jitendriya."

The sage was much astonished. He thought, "We, the sages, are going through severe austerities and efforts for controlling our senses and even then, we are not able to succeed; how can the king, the prince, and the people of this kingdom control their senses?" He wanted to test it. Then, he said, "Oh Prince, give me your princely dress and take my Sanyasi dress yourself." Because he was the prince of Jitendriya, he at once gave his dress to the sage. The sage then brought the blood of an animal, poured that blood on the dress given to him by the prince, and with that dress went to the kingdom of Jitendriya. He entered the kingdom, entered the main gate, told the gate-keepers, "Your prince came to our forest; he was hunting in the forest and was killed by a beast. Therefore, I have taken his dress and have come here to show it to you, as proof of the death of your prince." The gate-keepers laughed at him and said, "So, you have come for this purpose?" With cheer on their faces, they sent him in. He went to the king. As soon as he went to the king and showed these clothes to the king, he said, "Oh king! Your son was killed by a beast. I have brought his clothes." The king also merely smiled away and said, "Oh! He is not my son, nor am I his father. We are just like birds on a tree that will come and rest themselves on the tree, in the evening and will fly away as soon as it is morning, each in its own way. Like that, on the tree of this Samsara, all of us have come to stay here for some time and the bird of my son has flown away. That is all to it."

The sage thought that perhaps this king, for some reason, might not have sufficient love for the son and he wanted to show the clothes to the queen. He thought that, because she is the mother, she would certainly react with grief on seeing these clothes. He went to the queen and showed the clothes to her and told her, "Oh mother!

Your son has been killed and he will not be returning." Then, the queen also smiled away. She said, "All these jeevas or living beings are pilgrims in the Kshetra or Karma. We have come on a pilgrimage to this Karmakshetra and we are taking our rest in this choultry. After taking rest for some time, everybody will leave the choultry and go on his own way. In that way, we are all living in this choultry. There is, in fact, no relationship as father, mother, and son."

Then, the sage thought that if he went to the wife of that prince, she may certainly be stricken with grief, because it is her husband that has been dead. He took the clothes to the wife of that prince and wept, showing those clothes to her. She said, "Swami, you wear the dress of a sanyasi, but the way of your weeping and crying appears to be like that of an ordinary man. Will you please tell me the reason why you are weeping?" Then, he told her that her husband has been killed. She also smiled away and said, "There is a tree in a forest and one of its branches will be breaking and will fall in a stream. There is another tree in that forest and the branch of that tree also will be breaking and will fall in another stream. These two branches will go along these two streams and they will come together in a big stream, will move together for a while, and after some time, they will get separated and each will drift in its own way. In the same manner, I am the branch of a certain tree and my husband is the branch of another tree. We have, for some time, come together and now, we are separated. There is nothing to be astonished in this. For these branches, which are flowing in the stream of life, it is inevitable that

Self-Control And Detachment

they will have 'Samyoga', union and 'Viyoga', separation as well." Then, the sage thought that what the prince told him was entirely true and returned to his hermitage. He wanted still to test the mind of the prince and as soon as he went to him, began to weep very loudly. The prince told him, "Sage, your way of weeping atonishes me. Will you please tell me the reason for your weeping?" Then, the sage told him, "Prince, I went to your kingdom, your king was killed; your queen was killed, your wife was also killed. That is why I am weeping." Then, the prince taught a lesson to the sage by asking, "Who is the king? Who is the queen? Who is the princess? They are not related to me. The only king is Paramatma Himself. It is He that gave the kingdom to us and it is He that has taken it away from us. Therefore, I need not feel sorry for this. The only thing we should take care of is to do good deeds in this life and try to get salvation. Therefore, I do not weep or feel sorry on account of the news that is brought by you." Then, he taught him that there is no mother, there is no father, there is no brother, and there is no spouse. There is a verse to this effect and he taught that verse to that sage, "Mata Nasti, Pita Nasti, Nasti Bandhu Sahodaraha; Tubhyam Nasti, Griham Nasti, Tasmat Jagrata Jagrata."

This life is just like a water bubble and we should not consider that this jeeva has some relationship with other jeevas. This body is a leather bag having nine holes – it is not a gem that has got great effulgence. It will be giving out foul smell every moment – there is no good fragrance in it. So, we have to clean this body every day and also, decorate it. In this body, there is God. If God goes out of this body, there is no body at all. This body is such that it will make even sacred things impious.

I shall give you a small example. Once, Narada went to God Narayana. Narayana asked Narada, "You will be always wandering in all the three worlds. Did you see any strange thing in this creation of mine? Please tell Me if you have seen such a thing at any time." Then, Narada said, "Lord, you think that there is no mean thing or an impious thing in this world, but I have seen many impious things and also many mean things in this world. There is no place at all in this world, where they are not seen." Then, Narayana asked, "Is there something unholy and mean in the creation that was done by Me?" Narada replied, "Every day, every preson as soon as he wakes up, will be excreting 'mala' or reject matter. Is there anything more unsacred than this?" Then, Narayana said, "Oh! Narada, are you considering that as unsacred? No, it is not unsacred, it is good." Then, Narada said, "If I say that excreta is sacred and also good, people will certainly admit me in a mental hospital." Then, Narayana asked him, "You go and ask the excreta itself." He had no other work and he was always wandering in the world and so, uttering the name of Lord Narayana, he went to ask this question of that 'mala' itself. When he was going near it, the excreta told him, "Oh! Narada, don't come near me." Then, Narada thought that he should have asked that foul matter to be at a distance, but instead the foul matter itself is asking him to keep away. He felt that he was the son of Brahma and was such a great sage and that the foul matter should treat him like that is strange.

From a distance, he addressed the excreta and said, "You are very dirty. What is the meaning in asking me to get away from you?" Then, he got the reply, "Last night, I was in the shape of an apple, I was in the shape of a sweet, I was in the shape of good rice, and I was in the shape of so many good things, but as soon as I entered the body of man, I got such a mean state. When I entered man's body only once, my state has become like this; if I have some relationship with man again, how meaner will be my state?"

The nature of this human body is like that; it will make impure anything, however good it is. We known even a flour mill behaves better. If we put rice on the top of that, then rice flour will come. If we put wheat on the top, wheat flour will come. If we pour any other kind of grain, the flour of that grain will come. But, in the mill of our body, if we put fruits, mala will be coming. If we put pickles in a jar, it will be preserved for at least one year, but if we put anything in this body, it will become dirty in less than twelve hours. Even in so dirty a body, there is a possibility of seeing pure Atma. If we try sincerely, we shall be able to see in this impure body, the pure Atma or the Supreme Being. If we want to keep our jewels safely, we put them in an iron safe. The jewels that are put inside are very valuable, but the box is not as valuable as they are. If we put valuable jewels in a valuable box, thieves will take away the valuable box and the jewels also along with it. So, it is natural and also safe that valuable jewels should be put in a box that is not very valuable. The Atma is pure and very valuable. We are putting such a jewel in this box of body, which is not very valuable. We must never forget that we have taken this box for the sake of protecting the jewel. We must always remember the main and only reason, for which we have been give by God this body. If there are no good ideas in the body, what is the use of this body? Even the thieves will throw off the box, after taking the jewels. We must always remember that this box, the body, is for the sake of the jewels, namely God and all the good qualities, divine virtues, associated with Him.

12.

Sankara Jayanti

In the word Gita, there are two parts 'GI' and 'TA'. 'GI' indicates sacrifice and 'TA' indicates spirituality. Therefore, this book Gita teaches us both sacrifice and the real nature of the Soul. If we understand the spirit of Gita, we will know that it has taught us that the most important feature of a human being should be sacrifice. Gita has also taught us what kind of sacrifice it is. That should be 'Karma Phala Tyaga' or sacrifice of the fruits of the deeds we do. Gita never taught us that we should give up action. It has taught us to do everything, undertake every action for the pleasure of God, and never desire for the fruits thereof.

India has been the seat of such great sacrifices. Not only that, India is also a Yoga Bhoomi, the land of Yoga. On the east, there is Bay of Bengal and on the west, there is the Arabian Sea. The union or confluence of these two seas is 'The Hindu Maha Samudram' or the Indian Ocean.

The confluence symbolises the real meaning of that word HINDU and teaches us the Unity between the Jiva and the Brahman. Such people, who lived in India, leading an ideal life, must be considered as ideal 'Jyotis' or lights to all of us. While history is very important and not useless, we should realise that real history is not that which teaches us about the kings and about the periods when they ruled, but is that which teaches us about the real spirit of India.

'Adhyatmika Jivitha' or spiritual life does not mean leaving the home and living in a solitary place. Spiritual life really means that everybody should think that all people are ONE and he himself is one with all. True spiritual life is that, which teaches us Unity or oneness and makes us lead a life of selflessness and love. Instead of filling our mind with theories and subtleties of Shastras and our head with books and scriptures, it is always better to fill our heart with love and spiritual aspirations. When we are able to fill our hearts with real love, then it will be possible for us to obtain tranquillity of thought and peace of mind.

Today, in the world, we see many associations, institutions, and organisations. We must try to understand what an association really means. Only a group of people does not connote a 'Samaja' or association. The real meaning of Samaja is equanimity and peace due to a feeling of oneness. We must try to improve the society by equanimity and by spreading the thinking that all are equal. The real meaning of Samaja is to lead our life on one word and along one path. It is not possible for us to visually see the Samaja or the association. Samaja is not a special form of the basic elements. The individuals that form the society have got a form, but not the society or the association. We can see the individuals that compose an association, but we cannot see the association. If there is no individual, there is no association. In the same way, we are able to see the world but we are not able to see the Lord of the world – 'Jagadishwara'. If there is no Lord of the world, there will have been no world at all. As the individual is an important part and a limb of the society, so also God is an important and essential aspect of the world. He is the real basis of the Universe.

In the present context, people must first try to improve themselves and then the society and then their country. If the individual does not improve himself, but tries to improve the society, it is no use and the attempt will be a failure. We must first try to set right our home. Then, we must try to improve the village; afterwards our district; next our province and next the whole country. We must go step by step like this. But, without knowing ourselves first, it will be meaningless attempting to improve the society and the whole country. If we want to experience the 'Satchitananda', we will be able to do so only in the society. It is madness to go to the forest and try to experience Satchitananda instead of improving our home and the society in which we are living. God is all-pervading; He is found in the hearts of all living beings. How can a heart, which cannot love the living fellow beings, love God? People will be, on the one hand, praying to God and on the other, they will be harming other people. This is not proper. We shall be able to love God only when we are able to love the people, our fellow-beings. If we are not able to love the people, we will never be successful in this world.

In India, many great people were born to teach us the spirit of this love and also to teach us the oneness of all the beings in this world. Among the people who propagated such lofty ideals, Sankaracharya is one. We will not be showing real gratitude to Sankaracharya, if we merely treat this day as a festive day without trying to understand what he said and what he taught. When we are able to function with the fullness of heart according to his teachings, then only will we be celebrating his Jayanti properly. If we do not try to know what he taught and if we do not try to lead a pattern of life according to his teachings, but instead if we just satisfy ourselves with sweets and feasting today, the day of Sankara Jayanti, that is not a proper celebration. All the festive days of India are not meant for just 'Ahara' and 'Vihara' – food and enjoyment, but they are oriented towards efforts at gaining knowledge of the Supreme Being. They have all a spiritual basis. On these festival days, we must try to know the full meaning of at least one saying said by such great men, and try to put it into practice. All the holidays that are generally given on such occasions, Jayantis and Sacred days, should not merely be considered as holidays, but as 'HOLYDAYS'. We must spend the time usefully and make our life meaningful. We must try to imbibe the spirit of the country, in which we are born. Is there a man, who does not say, "This is my motherland! This is my mother tongue!" It is a great pity that sometimes, the Indians themselves do not have much faith in their precious culture! The country of India is like a beautiful garden. Just as the garden looks beautiful on account of many colourful flowers, so also India is beautiful in being full of great many religions. We see all the religions co-existing only in India. There is also a variety of races in India. Inspite of all the variation in races, the people of India lead their lives with an underlying unity, considering one another as brothers and sisters. Therefore, it will not be possible for us to see such a unique country elsewhere. We must try to make our country prosperous. Prosperity does not come from the sky. It does not come from anywhere else. It comes only from our endeavour.

The age, in which you are now, is very propitious. At this propitious age of yours, you must endeavour and must try to have a determination for its fulfilment. You must have one aim, choose a destination or goal, and try for the attainment of that goal or destination. Man has been born in this world to achieve something sacred, but not to spend his time in 'Ahara', 'Nidra', and 'Bhaya', or eating, sleeping, and worrying with fear.

Sankara demonstrated the real nature and value of our Indian culture through his own life. Sankara tried hard to earn the grace of God as it is said, "Brahmavid Brahmaiva Bhavati" – one, who understands the supreme being will himself become the supreme being. Sankaracharya was one like that. Among all the animals, the life of a human being is the greatest and it is also not easily obtainable. When Sankara was a little boy, his father had to go to a neighbouring village on some important errand. In the house of Sankara, there used to be daily worship and daily offering to God. His father used to worship like that and he also used to offer 'Naivedya' to God and later, distribute the prasad to all the people, who came there. On one day, as the father went to the neighbouring village and as the mother was out of the house, the responsibility of worshipping God and offering naivedya fell on Sankara's shoulders. Sankara knows the real meaning of the vedic words, "Matru Devo Bhava, Pitru Devo Bhava." When his father left the house, he told his son, "My dear son, I am daily worshipping God and distributing naivedya to all the people. So also, in my absence and in the absence of your mother, you will please try to do like that." Sankara promised to do so without fail. He poured some milk in a cup, put it before the Idol of the Goddess and prayed to Her, "Mother! Take this milk, which I am offering." Though he prayed for a long time, the Mother did not take the milk, nor did She appear. He was very much disappointed. He said again, "Mother! Mother! You are daily taking the offerings that are given to you by my father. What sin these hands of mine have committed that You are not accepting the offering, which I am giving to You?" He prayed to Her earnestly from the innermost depths of his heart. He was prepared to sacrifice even his life and told himself, "My father asked me to offer this milk to the Goddess, but I am not able to do so, because the Goddess is not receiving the offering which I made. It is better that I die." He went out and brought a big stone to kill himself. The Mother of the Universe is very compassionate and She was very much moved and touched by Sankara's sincerity and She at once appeared before him and drank the milk that he offered. She drank the whole milk and placed the empty cup before him.

The boy was very glad that the Mother of the Universe came and drank the milk, but there was nothing in the cup to distribute to others. He thought that his father will certainly ask for the naivedya of the God after his return. He feared that the father may think that he drank away all the milk and he may be angry with him. Therefore, he prayed to the Goddesss, "Goddess, give me at least a drop of milk, so that I may be able to give it to my father." But, the Goddess did not come. He again sincerely continued to pray; the Goddess was moved and She again appeared. Because She was not able to give the milk that She drank, She gave Her own milk and filled the cup. There is a belief that because Sankara tasted that Divine milk, he was able to attain the highest learning, knowledge, and wisdom that is ever possible. So, the essence of the Grace of the Goddess became the essence of the learning of Sankara. In order to please his father, he tried hard and was able to get the Goddess of the Universe to manifest Herself before him. From this story, we must learn to revere and obey the orders of our fathers implicitly and sincerely.

Let us also remember his great love for his mother. He knew that if he does not please his mother, he will not be successful in his Sadhana. So, even though he desired to take Sanyasa, he was not prepared to take it without the prior permission of his mother. Because he was the only son, the mother also was not willing to permit him to take Sanyasa. But, the Sanyasa taken on by Sankara is not like the monkship of today. By merely wearing a saffron coloured robe, devotion and detachment do not descend on a person. You know the crocodile incident and how Sankara got his mother's permission for taking Sanyasa. After Sankara came to the shore of the river, he told his mother, "Mother, it is not a real crocodile that caught me in the waters, but it is the crocodile of Samsara or family that has caught me." Sankara used his skill and his intelligence, but never did he do a thing without the permission of his parents. We do some actions now and then, but they are not sometimes appropriate to the time and situation. When the iron is red hot, if you beat it with a hammer, you can mould it as you want and it will yield to you. But, when it becomes black and also cold, even though a very strong man comes and beats it, it will not yield. Thus, our actions should be appropriate to the time and situation and always be for the right purpose and in the right direction. Now, your age is the right age for doing anything. You must know that you are being trained to become the future citizens of India and also the future soldiers in the moral and spiritual army of India. These summer classes have been started to protect India from all dangers and in all ways. We must try to establish and nurture and maintain our own culture. If we forsake our culture, our life in this world will be futile.

Now, I shall describe to you a beautiful incident from the life of Sankaracharya. One day, when he was in Benares, he was returning from the river through a narrow lane and a person, who was considered to be an untouchable, was coming opposite him. Then, Sankara asked him to move out and keep away at a distance so that himself, a brahmin, could move on unpolluted. Then, that untouchable asked Sankara, "Are you asking the body to keep at a distance? If that is so, one body, which is 'Jada' or inert, is asking another inert body and it has no authority to do so. If you are asking the soul to keep away and at a distance, the Soul that is in me is the same as the Soul or Atma that is in you. Therefore, the same Atma cannot ask itself to move away from itself and be aloof." Then, Sankara thought, "This so-called untouchable is one, who knows what is real Atma and what is real Anatma, what is Kshetra and what is Kshetrajna and I must respect him." So saying, he prostrated before the 'untouchable'. The untouchable was none other than Lord Viswanata Himself. He then appeared in His true Form to Sankara. Let him be a brahmin or let him belong to any caste, if he knows well the Advaita Tatwa, then he has the true spiritual enlightenment.

Different religions may look different and their paths may look different, but the goal is only one. The clothes, which different people wear, may be different, but the material with which the clothes are made is one. The ornaments may be different, but the gold with which they are made is one. The colours of different cows may be different, but the milk that they all give is only one. The darshanas or philosophies may be different, but the God, about Whom they speak, is only One. The flowers may be different, but the offering will be the same. People delude themselves into ignorance of this basic truth. They create for themselves an illusion of plurality, build up walls of difference among themselves, and plunge into suffering and grief. One must try to get at the source of knowledge and realise the basic unity of all creation. That will make our life sacred and meaningful. Here is a small example for this. There is a tree. There will be cool shade under it. Many living beings come, sit under the shade and enjoy. But, the tree never feels the ego or vanity that all these animals are sitting under its cool shade and are enjoying. But, man is selfish and egoistic and consequently, suffers false vanity. He suffers because of his own hallucinations and illusions.

We have a mistaken notion that some people belong to us and they are ours and others are not. When you think about yourself and you, then you will be able to know your people in the true perspective. You first try to know yourself. The attempt to know yourself is called 'Sankhyajnana'. And 'Tarkajnana' is that, by which to know what the 'I' is and wherefrom this 'I' has come. Living steadily in the state of 'I', if a person tries to know the truth, that state is called 'Amanaska'. So, every individual should try to know and attain the state of complete 'Amanaska'.

Today, we are celebrating the Jayanti of Sankaracharya, the Jayanti of Ramanujacharya, the Jayanti of Madhvacharya, and the Jayanti of several other great men as well. We are thinking that all these names are different. Today is not only Sankara's Jayanti, but it is the Jayanti of Ramanuja also. Instead of knowing the oneness and unity in all such philosophies, we think that they are different and thereby, promote hatred. There is really no room to have any differences on the subject of God.

If the Vaishnavites and Saivites do not like each other, it is only because of their ignorance of the underlying inner truth. The youth of today should try to know that Unity. They should not give room for differences or distinctions. They should try to be amicable and happy. I shall give you an example for this oneness or unity. We think that God Siva has got the 'Damaruka' or the drum in one hand and 'Trisula' in the other hand and we visualise His Form in that way. So also, in one hand of Vishnu, there is the 'Chakra' and in the other hand, there is the 'Sankha' or the Conch. Sankha means sound. Chakra means time. So, it is that God Vishnu has taken the aspects of sound and time in both His hands. And in the case of Siva, Damaruka or the drum represents sound and Trisula is 'Tri-Kala', the symbol of time past, present, and future. What Vishnu has in His hands is sound and time. Similarly, what Siva has in His hands is also sound and time. Where then, is the difference between them? The difference is in Form and Name only, but the Energy or the Power is the same. Even in Quoran and in the Bible, just as in the Vedas, the principle of Advaita only has been taught. In our Upanishads, it has been stated that Ishwara is everywhere and that the world is pervaded by God in every place and in every atom. You read something similar in the Bible, wherein it has been stated that, "All world is one, my dear son, be good to everyone." It is only on account of our pride and ego, we create such differences among ourselves and we make our lives miserable and unhappy.

On the sacred day, on which this Sankara Jayanti is celebrated, we must know what Sankara taught us and try to put what all he said into practice. Even though some things appear to be lifeless, when they come and combine with ourselves in life, they will also become the most important significant. For instance, we cook the vegetables and eat them. So also, we boil the rice and eat it. By cooking, the life principle is removed from the vegetables and rice. When they are cooked, we must think that they have become 'jadas' or lifeless, but when they go into our body, they will turn into 'chaitanya' and give us vitality and strength.

Today, you have been told that there are three truths: 'Pratibhasika Satya', 'Vyavaharika Satya', and 'Paramarthika Satya'. Truth is only one and it is never threefold. We only think that it is of three kinds. It is never of three kinds. I shall give you examples for these three kinds to make it clear that this classification is superficial. Pratibhasika Satya has neither basis, nor an existence. It is our illusion. When there is twilight, a little light, and a little darkness, we come by a rope and mistake it to be a snake. Really speaking, there is no snake there. The snake is only in our mind and the thing that is really there is only the rope. This is Pratibhasika Satya. If we stand before a mirror, we see our reflection in it. When we move away, the reflection vanishes. Therefore, the reflection is not true. When the original object is there, then only we will see the reflection. Here, there is one basis, namely the original thing. Without the original, there is no reflection. This is an illustration of Vyavaharika Satya. On the other hand, Paramartika Satya is an Entity, which is present everywhere and at all times. This is the true and eternal Reality. Here is an example. There is a silver cup in our hand. We give this to a goldsmith and ask him to prepare a plate. After some time, we give this plate to the goldsmith and ask him to prepare a box. First, it is in the shape of a cup, then it is in the shape of a plate, then it is in the shape of a box. Here, the form and the name have changed, but silver never changes. We are giving value to silver and not to the form and the name. We are giving only wages for preparing the objects. This is an illustration of the Paramartika Satya. All these multiple forms we notice in the world are just like various cups, plates, and tumblers. The Atma of Silver, the core in all the forms, is only one. It does not change. There are many bulbs with many different voltages and different colours. But, in all these bulbs with different voltages and different colours, there is only one current. Even though we see many forms, many names, various things in this world, many races, many creeds, and many castes in this world, we must know that the God that is present in all of them, the inner Being, is in reality only One. Our students should try to get such 'Samadrishti' and 'Sama bhava'.

The youth of today, whether they are at home, or in the college or in the society, should not give room to bad ideas in their heart. They must try to lead a moral, spiritual, peaceful, and happy life. We must try to get away from seeing evil and listening to evil.

Students go to the college on some vehicle, either on a bicycle or on a car, these days. The parents will be very anxious until their children, who go to college, come back home safely. What is the reason? Is it due to the busy traffic? No. Because there is a tendency to see evil, there is a possibility of many accidents. When you are going on a bicycle, you must try to see the road, you should not see this side or that side, look for cinema posters or something else. If you do that, accidents do happen. So, when you are doing a certain thing, you should observe the discipline related to that. But, you should never turn your eyes to other things. Because you are very young, there are many things, which you have to practice in your daily life. If you treat others unfairly or ridicule them, they will feel greatly pained. You must know that if others treat you in the same way, you will feel greatly pained. If you look at a sister of somebody else with a bad idea, the brother of that sister will certainly be pained in his heart. So, if somebody looks at your sister with a bad idea, you also feel very badly in your heart. If you think of these two things, then you must come to know how you should behave towards others.

We do not see these days 'papabheeti' or 'daivapreeti' – fear of sin and love of God anywhere. With fear of sin and love of God, we must try to lead our lives in a disciplined way. This will give us all happiness. We must try to respect our parents first. If you respect your parents now, your children will know and will certainly respect their parents, you and your wife. "Matru Devo Bhava, Pitru Devo Bhava, Acharya Devo Bhava, Atithi Devo Bhava" are injunctions given to us in our traditions. After the worship of these four; mother, father, teacher, and guest, come to the worship of God. You

Sankara Jayanti

may ask Me, "Why did they put God in the last place? Why did they not put Him in the first place?" God is the same to all and every one has got the same claim towards God, but to an individual, his parents are the real authority. God is the Creator of all and for an individual, his parents are the creators. For our life, the real creators are our parents and we must treat them as God, as His visible manifestations. Though God is the Creator of all, for this body, the creators are our parents. We must have such an idea. God is the Mother and Father of the world. Our parents are the mother and father of this body. When we can show gratitude to our parents, who gave this body, then we will be able to show gratitude to God, Who has given this world to us.

Lord Ishwara and Goddess Parvati are the Creators of this world. Here is a beautiful story acclaiming the supremacy of mother and father over all else. The first son of Ishwara and Parvati is Ganapati or Vighneshwara. The second son is Subhramanyeshwara. They told them, "Sons, you must go round the world and whoever comes first will receive a special prize." As soon as Subhramanyeshwara heard this, he got up on his vahana, the Peacock. Peacock is a big bird and it can fly in the air also. Subhramanyeshwara is a small child and so, he could go round the world on his peacock very easily. Vighneshwara is very big and huge in size and his vahana, the rat, is very small. It is very difficult for a body of such a big size to fit on such a small carrier, the rat, and go round the world. So, he was not prepared for this journey. He sat near his parents. The mother used to ask him why he was not going round the world? He used to say, "I shall go, I shall go." Subhramanya went round the world and was returning. Ganapati saw him at a distance and immediately went round his parents and said that he went round the world. Then, the father said, "Subhramanyeshwara has gone round the world. You have gone only round us. Therefore, I think that Subhramanyeshwara is greater than you." Then, Vighneshwara said, "When I round the parents, I have gone round the world, because it is the parents, who have given me this body. On account of this body, I have been able to see this world. Therefore, the parents are the world for me and when I have gone round the parents, it means that I have gone round the world." Then, the Lord was much pleased and gave him the name Ganesa – the Lord of Ganas. If children try to please their parents, then they will be pleasing God as well.

13.

Customs And Character

By holding a sword, does a man become a great warrior? By holding a Veena, will he become a great musician? By holding a pen, will he become a great writer? By holding a bow and arrow, will he become a great archer? Even though the ladle is in the sweet, it cannot experience its flavour. Can frogs that move around the lotuses in the water enjoy the honey in the lotuses? Can a stone, on which sandalwood paste is made, experience the fragrance of the sandalwood pieces? Can a blind man see his beauty in a mirror? These are situations, over which we should ponder.

The mighty Himalayas are in the north of India. Indians should compare these mountains to Sathya, Dharma, and Ahimsa. We must consider Sathya, Dharma, and Ahimsa as manifesting themselves to us in the form of silvery mountains. The great Ganges is considered to be sacred and pious and has been born on this mountain.

The culture of India is just like the stream of the Ganges. If we consider the culture of India, like the Ganges, as having been born on the Himalayas, then we know that there is no impurity in Indian culture. The Himalayas are clean, sacred, pious, and clear. Clarity is peace. We see now that even Indians are trying to exterminate Indian culture. This is not possible. These ignorant people, who want to do such a thing, can be compared to those, who want to make the Ganges run dry. Just as the Ganges can never become dry, so also Indian culture can never be rooted out.

While Indian culture can be compared to the Ganges, the deeds we do can be compared to the sacred Yamuna. Saraswati, the third river, is the spiritual stream, which flows in our lives like blood flows in our bodies. We see that the blood of the Indians is the Saraswati river, the performance of deeds of Indians is just like the Yamuna, and their cultural life is like the Ganga. The combination of these three rivers is the country of India. We cannot say that an Indian is a combination of just flesh and blood or a combination of earth and water. We should regard an Indian as the combination of the three rivers Ganges, Yamuna, and Saraswati. Many Indians are trying to go in an improper way, because they are not aware of the sacred stream flowing in them internally. This stream is full of knowledge. Saraswati does not mean only literature, but also is the Goddess, Who gives us perfect bliss or ananda. She will root out the impurity of man and make him sacred and pious. This Saraswati will establish the atma tatwa and is the stream connecting man with God. We must consider her as the stream flowing internally and never as the stream flowing externally. Education is more in the shape of enlightenment than pure knowledge.

Man today lives a life, from which sacredness, modesty, and all other good qualities have disappeared. Though he has some good qualities, he does not make any use of them. There are good books in India, the Ramayana and the Mahabharata, which teach us our culture. Ramayana is a version of our daily life and it gives us extreme bliss. It proclaims in truth, how members in a family should behave to one another and towards society. Ramayana has three alternative names and these are 'The killing of Ravana', 'The Story of Sita', and 'Srimad Ramayana'. We must know why these names have been given to Ramayana and the meaning in each case. It is called Srimad Ramayana, because it describes the qualities of Sri Rama. Sita is an ideal woman, possessing all the qualities that an Indian woman should possess, such as chastity, purity, and so on. Because Ramayana describes all these qualities perfectly, it is called 'The story of Sita'. We must concentrate deeply and understand why Ramayana is so called. When Rama was going into the forest to make the words of his father truthful, Sita wanted to follow him. He tried to dissuade her by advising her. Sita is the embodiment of all the dharmas that are found in the world. She is called Bhoojata, daughter of the Goddess of Earth and she has the qualities of her Mother. The main characteristics of Sita are chastity, tranqullity, and good character. But, when necessity arises, she is also able to teach Rama the path of dharma. As an illustration of this, we may consider the situation, when Rama said to Sita, "You are very delicate and cannot experience the conditions in the forest. I shall return soon and I request you to stay in Ayodhya and take care of your mother-in-law and father-in-law." Prior to that, Rama went to His mother and told her that He was going into the forest for 14 years to make the words of His father come true and asked her to give Him her blessings. The mother then said that she could not leave Him for a moment and she, too, would follow Him into the forest. Rama taught some principles of dharma even to his mother, saying, "Mother, father is old. Stay and serve him. I am going into the forest for his sake and will be back after 14 years. Serve father, who is like God to us. To you, your husband is greater than everyone else and must be looked after. While I am away, look after his health." Recalling this, Sita said, "You have taught some principles and dharma to your mother and you have asked her to stay and look after her husband. Does the same not apply to me, Your wife? Should I not follow You and serve my Husband? Looking after one's husband is as important to Kausalya as it is to me. Husband is God to a wife. I consider You as God and I must follow You to the forest." Rama tried then to pacify her in another way. He said, "You may be able to bear all the conditions of the forest, but if you come with us, you will be a great responsibility on our shoulders, because the forest is full of wild animals and we will have to protect you as well as ourselves. Stay at home and do not cause us trouble." Sita replied, "You say that there are many cruel animals in the forest and the most cruel animal amongst them is the lion, the king of beasts. When the lion of my Husband is with me, how can other animals harm me?" He said, "Even if there are no animals that may harm you, I will have to leave you at times to go and get something to eat. If at that time, some harm comes to you, it will be very difficult for me or my brother to protect you." At once, Sita replied, "Rama, You are a great warrior, a great Hero, and a very capable Person. This fact was proved, when you broke the bow of God Shiva. I know Your abilities fully. The words You spoke to me just now are not befitting of Your dignity. If Rama is not able to protect one person, how will He protect the whole world? Even to protect You from such infamy, I should follow You into the forest."

Rama could not say much more. He quietly said to her, "My mother will be stricken with grief at My going away. It would be better, if you stay behind and console her." Sita then said, "You are Rama and I am Sita. You are the moon and I am the moonlight. If the moon is in the forest, how can moonlight be in Ayodhya? Where there is moon, moonlight will always be there." Rama could not reply. Rama tried to tell her to stay in Ayodhya, but Sita did not listen to those words. She said pitiably, "Rama, I am very young. You will be away for 14 years, while your brothers enjoy the company of their wives and the maids of the palace enjoy the company of their husbands. Seeing this, I will get jealous and bad ideas will form in my mind. To rid me of such thoughts, take me with you." There is no possibility of bad thoughts ever entering Sita's mind. Rama said, "Your heart is pure, your character is perfect and I know that such bad ideas will never enter your heart." She then fell at His feet and said, "You are going into the forest, where there will be many thorns on the way. Because my Mother is the Goddess of the Earth, She will be very kind to me. I can request Her to let You go happily on Your way. At least for this, take me with You." I have narrated this sequence of incidents, leading to Sita falling at the feet of Rama, because Rama's heart melted only when she fell at His feet.

A similar situation also comes in the Mahabharata. Arjuna argued with Krishna and put many logical ideas before Him. During that time, Krishna did not teach him the sacred Gita. Only after he surrendered completely did He teach Arjuna the Gita. As long as you control your body and mind, God may try to be independent in His own way and protect you, but God becomes more independent when you surrender and dedicate everything of yours to Him. Here is a small example. In order to make some jewellery, you give some gold to the goldsmith. He melts it, beats and hammers it, and does many other things. Then, the jewel is prepared. If you want to make some jewellery and do not give the goldsmith any gold, then he will not be able to make anything. If you give him the gold and tell him not to melt, beat, and hammer it, he will still not be able to make anything out of the gold. If we offer the gold of our mind to God and tell Him not to interfere with it, how can God prepare the jewel of peace? If you allow Him to do whatever He wants, then He will prepare the ornament of peace for you.

If you, in any seriousness, ask what is yours here, you will get the answer that nothing really belongs to you.

You are under the mistaken idea that one thing or another is yours, but this is incorrect. If this body is yours and some limb is ill, why can you not rectify the sickness? When you are not able to rectify a small defect in your body, is it yours? If the mind is yours and if you can put it under control, why does it act like a monkey? Why do you think that this world is yours? If it is yours, how does it move without your permission? Life is not yours.

Those, who catch monkeys, prepare a pot with a small opening in it and fill it with some sweet. The monkey, who desires the food, will put his hand inside the pot and take a big handful of the food. Thus, the monkey becomes unable to draw his hand out through the opening. Only on releasing the grip will the monkey be able to take his hand out. It is his desire for the food that has bound his hands. Because it took with his hand some food to fulfil its desire, it was bound there. This wide world is like that pot and our 'samsaras' or the families are like the narrow top. Our desires are the sweets in the pot. The world being the pot, containing the desires as sweets, man puts his hand in the pot. When he sheds his desires, he will be able to live in the world freely. To get freedom, the first thing to do is to sacrifice. In philosophical terms, this is called renunciation.

If any man possesses dharma along with wealth, power, and riches, there is none greater than him. Even now, if a poor but pure man goes to the court and follows dharma, the court will do justice to the poor man and punish the rich. Dharma displays morality. However learned we may be, if we have no morality, we shall become the brothers of Ravana. Because he left the path of dharma, he had to fight the monkeys, who in the end killed him. When he has about to die, his wife Mandodari came to him and said to Rama, "I am not sorry that Ravana has died and been separated from me, but I wonder at the fact that such a great man, possessing such great strength, had been killed by the monkeys. This must be because my husband gave himself upto bad desires and he had to fall."

We come to the same conclusion in the story of the Kauravas. They had greater wealth and a larger army compared to the Pandavas. Because they did not follow the path of dharma, they waged war on the Pandavas, who had many good qualities. Whatever kinds of strength we have, if we do not have the strength of dharma, all is futile. Real strength is 'Daivabala and dharmabala', the strengths that come from God and from dharma.

The customs and manners that go with Indian culture make us very respectable and there is no need to abandon them. Young people, with their peculiar dress imitating the westerners, appear just like clowns. In olden days, people wearing old pants looked just like elephant trainers. These people think that tight pants make them look beautiful. How can pants, large on the top and narrow as they come down, fit every one? Those, who have a big belly, will look very awkward in them. Those big bellied people with tight pants look like question marks. It is not right on our part to bring disrespect to India with such peculiar dresses. There is nothing wrong in wearing rich and beautiful clothing, but they should be fitting to our

Indian culture and be such as will create some respect for our country. There are some bush shirts, which are made of cloth used for furniture, bedsheets, and so on. When men walk with such bush shirts, even animals will be afraid. If little boys wear such clothes, there is some meaning. Indians must be very careful about the way of dressing and the fashions they adopt. Indians traditionally look at the forehead of the baby, when it is born and if it is very broad, they presume the child is very fortunate. They think that God writes the future on the forehead. But, people now try to cover their forehead with their hair. This is not beautiful either. Some people close one eye with their hair. This is not proper either. We must be able to look well and see things in a proper way. Our sight is 'srishti' and srishti or creation is our 'drishti'. Drishti is also called knowledge. We are ruining our knowledge with the mistaken idea that what we do makes us very beautiful. Among the students here, there are no such people, but I should ask that when you go out of here, you should never do such things. Protect your respect and honour.

Wherever you walk, never walk in the middle of the road. Nowadays, young people hold hands on the road, thus blocking the road and obstructing the vehicles. Follow the rules of the traffic and behave in such a way that you do not disturb others. Students are prone to go on a strike meaninglessly. Students going from out of here must never partake in strikes. For what purpose do you admit yourselves into a college? Follow that purpose first. If you partake in strikes, the teaching course, which is generally two years, stretches over to five, thus wasting the money your parents send you. In the name of strikes, people throw stones on buses and hit non-offenders too. This is not right. We have established this summer course to put an end to such agitations, so far as you are concerned. You should behave properly in the future. The Guru is Brahma, the guru is Vishnu, the guru is Ishwara, and if you go a step further, the guru is Parabrahma. We must go to the preceptors, who educate us in a humble manner.

14.

The Perishable And The Imperishable

It is difficult to properly and fully understand the multifaceted Indian culture, which indeed is in some ways the source of all religions of the world. Many people have tried to explain the speciality of Indian culture, but they were able to explain or express only what little they could comprehend with their limited knowledge. They were not able to portray satisfactorily and fully the spirit of Indian culture. Indian culture is born of the heart and of intuitive wisdom. It is not connected with odd and futile things such as the objects of the material world. Indian culture can be compared with '*Kalpavriksha*', the tree that gives all one wants. Approach with reverence and in a spirit of earnest enquiry alone will enable you to comprehend it. If you approach it in a superficial way, it will ever remain elusive.

It is ridiculous if we, having been born as Indians, calling ourselves Indians and esteemed by others as sons of India, are not able to understand the inner meaning and the real significance of Indian culture. Just as the elephant does not know its own strength, so we the Indians today have become unaware of our own strength. The elephant is very strong, but when the trainer asks it to sit, it sits. When he asks it to bend its head, it bends its head. In spite of its immense strength, the elephant can be controlled by the trainer. Likewise, Indians have become weak by imitation and by running after wrong traditions. They are not able to follow and tread the true path. When we have gold in our Indian scriptures, why hanker after other base material and superficial values? Even though there is ample scope for us for understanding our culture, we never make an earnest and whole-hearted effort. What is found in *Mahabharata* may be found in all other religions and scriptures, but what is not found in *Mahabharata* cannot be found anywhere else. But, we generally find the cheap preparations of our neighbours much more tasteful than the rich delicacies made in our own homes. This trend is more prevalent among the modern students. We must try to revitalise and resuscitate Indian culture, Indian dharma, and Indian religion. Present day students must come forward to follow the sacred path. The present educational system is not at all giving the right and proper direction. This is the main reason for the decadence among students. Actually, the fault is not of the students, but is of the educational system. Students should not be satisfied by reading only their text books. They should also read books written by great men of wisdom. Reading such scriptures whenever they get time is also a kind of Sadhana. It is the real study and education.

The Perishable And The Imperishable

This is wanting among the students, primarily because of lack of acquaintance with our sacred scriptures, like *Ramayana*, *Mahabharata*, and *Bhagavata*.

There was a good Queen by name Meenavati. She had a son by name Gopichand. When Gopichand was a boy of ten years, the maids were giving him an oil bath scented with perfumes, making him sit on a stool, and telling him various worldly things. Meenavati saw this through the doors of her apartments. Seeing them whiling away time in futile talk and pleasantries, she felt sorry. She came to the place where Gopichand was being bathed and stood there with tears flowing from her eyes. The son asked, "Mother, why are you crying?" She was silent. The son again asked for the reason. The mother said, "The only thing left of your grandfather, forefathers, and your father who enjoyed all these physical pleasures, is one handful of ash; we do not see them any more; at least you should be wise and try to enjoy the eternal bliss of the Jiva instead of enjoying these worldly pleasures connected with the body. The great Harishchandra, who always spoke the truth – did he not die and leave this world? Could Nala, who ruled the entire Earth, take a portion of the Earth with him? Did Mandhata, who was a gem among kings, take away treasures with him? Does Rama, Who built the 'Sethu' or bridge across the ocean – remain on the earth now? No one has taken these earthly treasures or achievements with him. Do you hope to take this kingdom and pleasures with you? We must experience only the eternal bliss with the Jiva and not the worldly things. We must perform good actions with the body and must have good promptings by the mind. It is only such things that please God and draw forth His Grace."

Whatever things we do with this body, we are leading to a rebirth of this body. Any actions, good or bad, can be compared to seeds. In order not to sow such seeds, we should do all actions without desire. All actions should be done in and only for the pleasure of God. If you sweep a place, think that you are doing that for cleaning the heart, the shrine of God. When you help or harm others, think that you are doing it for yourselves. Then, you will never let yourself harm anyone else.

Students must forget two things. Firstly, you must forget whatever help you have done to others. Secondly, you must forget whatever harm others have done to you. Because, when you remember the harm done by others to you, you always plan to take revenge. When you do not remember this, you will not do any harm. If you remember the help rendered by you to someone, you will be looking forward for the reward. On the contrary, there are two things that you must always remember. One is that God is One and the other, that death is One. In whatever manner you may look at them, these two are the eternal truths. If you do not want to go to a marriage, you can cancel the engagement. Similarly, if you do not want to go for a cinema, you can postpone it for the next day. But the last journey, the journey to your death, can neither be cancelled, nor postponed. We make preparations when we want to go for a marriage or a cinema. What preparations are we making for the final journey?

The Perishable And The Imperishable

There are three friends for us in this world. You may yourself determine who is important of the three. Kauravas thought they had the support of great warriors, like Karna and great teachers, like Drona. They never depended on themselves. Depending on the strength of these people, they harassed the Pandavas. In the same way, thinking that we have these three friends with us, we behave in a reckless manner. On account of this recklessness, we are doing many improper and wrong things. When we are doing something we are not supposed to do, we are liable to punishment. Sometimes, we are dragged to the court to receive the punishment. Generally, we go to the first friend to win the court case. We go to him and ask him to be a witness. He says, "I will sit at home and give evidence, but I will not come to the Court." Thinking that this friend is not the right one, we go to the second friend and ask him to be a witness and help. This friend says, "I will come up to the Court, but not inside." Then, we go to the third friend and that friend says, "I will come wherever you want me to come. Even if you go to the jail, I will come along with you." Of these three, the true friend of course is only the third one. We have kept two friends for this life. The first one is wealth and the second one is the relative. Meritorious deeds, which we perform, constitute the third friend. When we die and ask our friends to accompany us, the first friend, namely wealth, will say, "No, I will stay at home, I am not going to come with you." When the dead body is taken to the burial ground, the wealth stocked does not follow the body. The second friend, the relative says, "I will come only up to the court - only up to the burial ground. From there, you should go on your own." But, the good deeds that you do go with you. They go with you inside the court to bear witness. They accompany you beyond the cremation ground. Therefore, the good deeds alone that you do with a pure heart will be your true escort, but not your wealth and your relatives. The reason why great men preach that we perform good deeds and lead a pure life is only because the good deeds alone will be our ultimate succour. They are the only things that protect us, even as the eyelids protect the eyes.

King Harishchandra, who gave his life for truth, became a guard at the burial ground. He saw the body of a wealthy man being brought in a big, decorated carriage, to the cremation ground. They brought him there, kept him on the pyre, lit the fire, and went away. The only person that was left was Harishchandra. He watched it for a while. While the body was burning and when the fire touched the "Sushumna Nadi", the body started rising up. To prevent this happening, usually a heavy wooden piece is put on the stomach. When life in the "Sushumna Nadi" evaporates and leaves the body, the body again falls back. Harishchandra began musing on the rising and sinking back of the body. He wondered whether the corpse rose up to see if any of his beloved relatives are around, but seeing that no one is there, slept again.

Imagining that this world, which is full of Maya, is paramount and permanent, we develop attachments to the wife and the son. But finally, neither the wife, nor the son will follow us. As long as there is life in the body, we feel everyone and everything is ours. When life has ebbed out of the body, we cast it into the fire without any consideration whatsoever. What sort of relationship it is that we have with this body is to be thought over and enquired into; wealth is so dear to us and we worry lest we lose it or part from it. After putting the body in fire, the relatives think only of the insurance policies he had and whether he had left enough property for them or not. Therefore, there is no relationship between this body of yours and anyone else. Whatever deeds you do with the body relate to the body only and not to the Jiva.

Here is a small example to illustrate the relationship between the body and the Jiva. When we go on a good tar road, our shadow falls on dirt that is in the side drain. Even if you go on a beautiful road, the shadow may fall on dirty things. But, the dirt does not cling to the shadow. You must try to tread on the right path, but do not fall in the dirt along with the shadow. What you must learn is to do good things with the body; you should contemplate about good things with your mind. Cultivate good thoughts and perform good deeds. Sometimes, people ask – Yes, we should learn to love everyone, but what should be done if the other party hates us in spite of our loving them so much? Why should you be bothered whether others reciprocate your love or not? Your duty is to see that you are not swerving from the right path. Since someone is doing harm, if you also hate, how can you claim that you are still good? Therefore, you must never swerve from doing good. You must also endeavour to see that others act in the same manner. If you want to delve deep and experience true love, you leave all bodily considerations, cultivate the Atma-drishti. Then, you will have the right vision. The same Atma exists in all. You should see everyone with Atma-drishti, but not differentiate them by looking at attributes, such as height, weight, and status.

I will give the example with Myself as the basis; I love everyone – I love even those, who do not love Me. I do not ask whether they are loving Me or not. We must see whether our love is pure or not. Hatred has no place at all in Me. People, who do not want Me, also come to Me, when need arises and bend before Me.

15.

Worship Your Parents

The honour of a nation depends upon the morality of that nation. A nation without morality will be doomed. For the last several days, many experienced and learned scholars were giving you discourses on Vedas, Shastras, and Puranas and expounding the greatness of Indian culture. Mere listening to and knowing about the nature of Indian culture will not be rewarding. It has to be reflected in one's conduct. The prestige of an individual depends upon the purity of the individual. When the individual reforms himself and undergoes the process of samskara or purification, then only will he be able to truly recognise the greatness of our culture. Individuals make the society. A village depends upon the condition of the society and the state depends upon several such villages. The country or a nation is an assembly of such states. The welfare of the nation thus depends ultimately upon the quality and nature of the individual. Therefore, reforming the individual is of primary importance. Reforming the individual has two aspects: first weeding out the evil thoughts and bad habits within him and second, cultivating of good habits. Students must put into practice these two things: doing away with evil habits and cultivating good habits in their place.

The future of the country depends upon the condition and quality of the students. Students may be described as the very roots of the nation. Therefore, we must pour the water of 'Divyashakti' or the divine force into the very roots. Students may also be compared to the creepers bearing flowers. If we allow these creepers to grow as they please, they grow in a wild and disorderly manner without beauty and symmetry. Therefore, we must prune each creeper so that its shape may be beautiful and it may grow in a wild fashion without any beauty. The beauty of life depends upon our good habits. The period of student-days is so sacred and most important in life. So, the students must be disciplined in their minds and habits and must fill their minds with pure thoughts and try to enforce and put into practice all those good thoughts in day-to-day life and in their day-to-day activities. Only then can they attain the right stage of development. The intention of organising this summer course is not simply to transmit information, which is given by these scholars who are delivering the lectures. More important than giving information is the transformation that we wish to bring about and that is the purpose of this summer course. Instead of jotting down things in the note book, it is more essential that every one of you should jot down the ideas on the tablet of your mind. It is desirable for every one of you to think over and ponder over every day, questioning within yourselves, "How far have I changed in my conduct? How far have I been transformed by listening to these lectures?" This is very essential. If you are not transformed, all this will be just a waste of time and energy and nothing but trouble to elders. The stage, through which you are now passing, is really a sacred one. By cultivating a spiritual outlook right from this stage, it will be possible, when you grow old, that you will be able to spend your time and your life in a very calm, quiet, peaceful, and happy manner. During the monsoon season and when the rains are abundant, it is desirable and necessary to fill all the tanks, because if the rivers and tanks are dry, it will not be possible to save anything or preserve anything for the summer days. This is the right period when you should fill your mind with thoughts about your own future, about the future of the country, and about the future of the race and that of the nation, and with things of such profound importance. If you do not attempt to move in the right direction now, even as your body is strong and when your faculties and powers are good, it will not at all be possible for you to do so at a later stage, when your body grows old and fatigued, when the mind has lost its alterness and all your powers have dried up and withered away.

These scholars and pandits, who are delivering these lectures, may be learned, very experienced, very old, but they can only point the direction; they cannot do the walking for you. The walking must be done by you. You must proceed along the path that is indicated. These elders may be compared to guide posts. They can simply point out that if you go along a particular way, you will reach this destination and that if you go along another way, you will reach another destination and so on, but they cannot tread the path for you. Your effort is essential in this regard. If you look at the conditions of today, the Government is not in a position to introduce reform in the lives of the people, because the kind of reform needed is not there in the rulers themselves and the people are not in a position to infuse that kind of enthusiasm in the rulers. I shall clarify to you this connection or the relationship, which obtains between the people and the Government with the help of a little analogy. A small snake has caught a big frog. The snake is trying its best to devour the frog and the frog is trying its best to escape from the snake. The frog cannot emancipate itself from the snake and the snake is not in a position to devour the frog. As a result of this struggle, the reward or the final achievement is only exhaustion for both. Either the Government must have the capacity to educate and reform the people, or the people must have the capacity to educate the Government. Unfortunately, both the Government as well as the people are lacking this power very badly. Both are getting exhausted. Therefore, you, who are the future hope of this country, should give the needed leadership both for the people as well as the Government.

The dignitaries, high officials, and great scholars, who have delivered these lectures, you must remember, were also students like you at one time. Those, who were students a few years ago, have today become teachers and guides and you, who are the students of today, also would become teachers and guides of tomorrow. Some of you, who are students of today, may in future become even leaders and preachers. The greatness of any individual depends upon the reform of his character. It does not depend upon his power, money, or position. Thus, you must try to first increase the good qualities or virtues in you. You have joined the colleges not simply to score marks and secure a pass. It is more important that you should not receive bad remarks; that is more important than securing marks. It is necessary today for every one of you to examine why you are getting educated. Is it for the sake of understanding the truth of life or is it simply to get some job and a salary? Is it for knowledge or for a salary? You should not join colleges just for a salary or to get the capacity to earn a salary. You should get educated for the sake of gaining knowledge of life, or 'Vignana'. True education is that, which enables you to stand on your feet. Therefore, try to develop self-confidence and try to improve your character through the processes of samskara or purification. You must develop culture, which is moral, spiritual, and ethical. You must cultivate an independent approach.

You must develop the habit of taking pains and undergoing any amount of trouble in order to discharge your duties satisfactorily and correctly. You must be ready to lay down your life to sacrifice yourselves for the welfare of the country and for the welfare of the nation. Today, we find many individuals, who exploit others for their own happiness. We rarely come across an individual, who sacrifices himself for the sake of others' welfare. Therefore, one man must suffer in order that ten people may be happy. We should not cultivate the habit of subjecting ten people to unhappiness, just for one's own sake, just for the benefit of a single individual.

We must consider here quantity versus quality. If the action is bad, you are not justified in suffering for the happiness of ten people. If ten people are working for something noble, then there is every justification for you to sacrifice your own happiness and to support them with your endeavour. At times, it becomes necessary to analyse the matters deeper. Though there may be thousands of bad people, one good man would be able to control those thousands of bad people and this control is possible only through the power of love. We must try to understand the policy adopted by the country, the method followed by the country, and the method followed by the society. We should never join the mob in a blind manner, without discrimination and reason. There is such a tendency among the students. If they feel that one student is insulted, then they all support him in a blind way. They must consider whether that student really deserves support and whether he was right or wrong. If we are able to set right that one student, when he is in the wrong, the institution would be benefited. On the other hand, if you blindly support the one student, who is definitely in the wrong, then the prestige of the institution will be damaged.

We must help a good cause and we must never support a bad cause. When we are able to show discrimination and do not err into wrong judgement, then our educational institutions will be greatly benefited. Sometimes, we may want something good and reasonable. Then, you may represent it to the officer in charge and you have the right to represent it. When you approach a higher authority, you must always adopt an attitude of humility. When you make a proper representation, in the right spirit and with proper humility, the officer also will be pleased to grant it. On the other hand, if you commit a blunder and show an attitude of defiance, naturally, the man in power would be antagonistic towards you.

Therefore, every student must be a 'Vidyarthi' in the full sense; namely one, who seeks education and not one, who seeks fulfilling his desires. Vidya is enriched by Vinaya or humility. True education is judged from the cultivation of good character and good conduct, and not merely from the attainment of degrees. Education does not mean ignoring the sacrifices made by your poor parents at home. It does not mean at all that you should move about luxuriously dressed, displeasing your elders, disregarding all those, who are more knowledgeable than you. That is no education at all. Your parents will always feel happy when they find you endowed with good character.

There are several parents, who undergo many privations and sacrifices for the sake of the future of their children. There are several fathers and mothers, who even starve themselves in order to provide education for their children. So, education, which does not teach the right attitude which a student should adopt towards his parents, who undergo so much suffering, is not education at all. One should even call it bad education. The words of Indian Wisdom – "Sathyam Vada, Dharmam Chara" – Speak the truth, do the right thing – and the injunctions of our culture – "Matru Devo Bhava, Pitru Devo Bhava" – worship your mother as God, worship your father as God – deserve to be preserved in the caskets of our hearts like precious gems.

North Indians and people from Maharashtra are very familiar with the story of Pundarik. Pundarik was an ideal son, who spent all his time in the service of his venerable parents. When the parents had fever or other discomfort, Pundarik used to serve them, attend on them, touch their feet, and do all sorts of service for them. Today, when the mother is laid up with high fever, the son, not caring for the condition of the mother, runs to the film show. Mother is the Goddess, who has given us this blood, this body, and this individuality and therefore, she deserves all consideration and worship. By disregarding the mother, we shall never be able to prosper in life and we shall never be able to become good in life.

When Pundarik was serving his mother, Panduranga came there. Pundarik was pressing the feet of his mother and he did not care to look at Panduranga. In the meantime, Tukaram, his guru, also came there. Tukaram asked, "My dear Pundarik, do you know Who has come? It is God Panduranga! You are not caring for Him. How is it?" Then, Pundarik replied, "The culture of Two Gods is not important for me, but the culture of EK HARA or One God is important for me." Tukaram said, "He is God." Then, Pundarik said, "Yes, He is God; this is also God. The real God for me is my parent and not

Panduranga. From the moment of my birth, I have been seeing this form and this form of my mother was responsible for the birth, growth, for the nourishment and sustenance of my body. Therefore, I worship her. The Goddess, who has been right in front of me for the last 18 years, is more important than the God, Who appears for a few moments and vanishes. If Panduranga cares to grant me darshan, let Him wait until I complete the service of my mother." So saying, he threw a brick as a sort of Asana or seat for Panduranga to sit and wait. Even God Panduranga waited, until Pundarik completed the service of his mother and then, granted darshan to him. Even God would wait for you. Do not think that He would go away, but you must discharge your duty to the best of your ability and to your utmost satisfaction. That must be your pledge.

Krishna is described as having tilak – 'Kasturi Tilak' on His forehead, 'Kaustubha' on His chest, 'Navamouktika' on the tip of His nose, and 'Kankana' on His hand. Kasturi Tilak is not the ordinary tilak. It is the Gnana or wisdom itself. So, He has the symbol of Jnana or wisdom on His forehead. Kaustubha is not an external ornament, but it is the emotion on tenderness and love within the heart. There is yet another significance why a pearl should be worn under the tip of the nose. The Navamouktika or the pearl is the indication that we should always focus our attention on the tip of our nose, in order that we may have real wisdom. You may question why our vision should be focussed on the tip of our nose? When we sit down to worship God and keep our eyes wide open, then there is very possibility that our attention gets diverted and scattered. If we keep our eyes completely closed, then we may be induced to sleep. Therefore, we must keep our eyes half closed and we must concentrate our vision on the tip of our nose, so that we do not sleep and also, our attention does not get diverted. The poets have described this pearl at the tip of the nose in order to drive home the truth that our attention must always be concentrated on the tip of the nose. Now, coming to Kankana or the bracelet on the hand, Indians use the bracelet on two occasions. Once, at the time of the marriage and a second time when they perform a Yagna or Yaga. The meaning of the Kankana is that we have decided and determined to undertake some noble action. Then, you may ask the question why Krishna should have Kankana on His hand? Is He going to get married every day or is He going to perform a sacrifice every day? No, He has taken some pledges and therefore, He is wearing the Kankana. The first pledge is to protect the right and the good and to protect Dharma when Dharma is in danger. The second pledge is to look after the welfare of those, who devote themselves with single mindedness to God, who think only of Him and no one else. He said, "When you have abjured all Dharma and have taken shelter at My feet, I shall liberate you from all the sins that you have committed." Krishna has put on this Kankana in order to carry out this pledge. Because we are not endeavouring to gain the grace of Krishna, the Kankana is still there and continues to be there. We are not able to derive the benefit of the Kankana, because we do not practise thinking of Him only and of none else. He said, "If you do think of Me only and of none else and if you worship – if you do all these three, I shall take care of your welfare." We do not undertake to do any of these three duties and yet, we ask the question, "Why is it Krishna is not taking care of me?"

Leadership requires that you should lead the others in the right direction. What you want others to do, you must be the first to practise. Today, leaders are experts in saying things, issuing orders, and giving advice to others, but they do not follow. In every walk of life, whether it is political, economic, social, cultural, or religious, they pose as great people and speak as if they are all great 'Heroes'. When we look at their actions, they are only big 'Zeroes'. Therefore, the students of today must make it a point to endorse in their daily action what they listen to from others. They must lead other people in the right direction. Today, you criticise your leaders that they have gone wrong here and they have gone wrong there. Tomorrow, when you become leaders, you must take care to see that you do not commit the same blunders and you should not let yourselves become the objects of the same criticism.

There are five fingers to the palm. We point out, when we come across a bad man, with the pointing finger. When you point at others, only one finger points out at them and three fingers point back at you. So, when you point out one fault in others, you must be able to examine three times whether there is a fault in you. There is a device for this. When you come across a big fault in others, you just consider it to be a very trivial one or a very unimportant one. Then, you will not be unhappy.

Suppose there is a small fault in you. Then, you try to magnify it and you feel you should never let in a similar fault again. By looking at it in that way, you will not have occasion to be guilty of the same fault again. On the other hand, if you conceal your fault and try to point out the fault of others, it will not be safe either for you, or for the others. Do not always go forward in pointing out the faults of others. On the other hand, if any one points out any fault in you, you must prostrate before him, because you, by yourself, will not be able to find out where you are in the wrong. Because your eyes are directed outward, you will be able to find the fault in others only, but you will not be able to find the fault in your own nature.

Here is a small story. During the summer season, in places round about Nagpur, water will be very scarce. Things might have improved now, but in old days, things were very bad. An orthodox old Brahmin lady set out on pilgrimage. She was so orthodox that she did not touch anything or anyone and she did not permit anyone to touch her. She started on a pilgrimage with such an orthodox mentality. By the time she reached Nagpur, she felt that the climate was very hot. She turned on the water taps, but not a drop of water came out of them. Her thirst increased. The Government made some arrangement in that station for supply of water. The skin of an animal was used to make a bag. They filled water in such bags and supplied that water to the thirsty people. When several people were drinking the water that was served from that bag of leather, this lady, though she was thirsty, was hestitating in her mind whether the man, who was serving the water, may belong to a low caste, the bag may not be pure and may not have been cleaned well and so on. She was hesitating to take that water. After much hesitation, the lady, who could not suppress her thirst, went forward. She questioned the man, who was serving the water, "My dear sir, is this bag pure? Is it clean?" The man, who was serving the water, was clever. He said, "The bag of leather, from which water is being served, is cleaner than the bag into which that water will be poured after service, namely your body. This bag is cleaner than your interior."

Today, we are cultivating this undesirable tendency of looking at the impurity of the bag, but not caring to remove the impurity from within our own body. First of all, we must try to purify what is within us and then only can we rectify what is external to us. This is essential for the students to know. Because, tomorrow, you may become high officers though you are students today. Therefore, if you fill your mind with good thoughts now, then when you grow in life and occupy high positions, you will be able to serve the country properly.

Though many students have been attending this course for over 20 days, listening to several discourses on very important topics, there are still some students, who are not able to avoid their previous bad habits. It is a very pitiable situation. It will be good augury for the future, if you are able to shed the bad habits that you had before coming here. In their place, cultivate good habits. Here, in the morning and in the evening, the Name of the Lord is dancing on your lips. You are feeding your tongue with the sweetness of the Lord's name. If the same tongue that is made sweet by the name of the Lord in the morning and in the evening, is filled with the fire of the cigarette in the evening, then all the good effects are counteracted and wholly nullified. So, you must get rid of the bad habit of smoking. The smoking habit does not give you any happiness. On the other hand, it spoils your health, damages your lungs, and doctors say that sometimes even cancer may be the result of smoking. The lips of the students will get charred and become black by smoking. Why should you continue this habit, which damages your beauty and also your health?

If you return home in the same bad condition, in which you have come here, then your stay here will not be fruitful at all. On the other hand, when you return home, if your friends, your relations, and your parents feel that you have returned from the workshop almost as a new personality and in a perfect condition, then we also feel happy that all our endeavour has not gone waste and has been rewarded.

16.

Anger - The Greatest Enemy

He, who is able to fully control his senses, will be in a position to attain liberation or moksha. Vemana, the well known philosopher-poet, has written a verse, which says that one, who has eaten the dog, is considered a great yogi; one, who has eaten a pig, is considered a greater yogi; one, who has eaten an elephant, is considered as the wisest among the yogis. We must go deep into the meaning of these three statements. The word 'dog' stands for anger and the word 'pig' stands for ego and the word 'elephant' stands for attachments. One, who is able to control and overcome his anger, ego, and attachments, becomes a great yogi.

Not only in India, but in several parts of the world, people are getting interested in the knowledge and practice of yoga. Though there are many schools of yoga, the most significant is the Patanjali yoga. Patanjali defines yoga as the regulation and control of the tendencies of the mind. Without controlling the senses, we cannot attain happiness in any walk of life or in any endeavour. If we just let go of our senses in a wild fashion, the result will be sorrow and not joy. But today, Indians are not paying proper attention to the nature of their senses. Some people are under the misapprehension that they miss the very essence of life, if they control their senses and deny themselves the pleasure of the senses. This is a mistaken idea. We should not think that we are controlling or restraining the senses. The real meaning and significance of this process is not that we are restraining the senses from performing their functions, but that we are directing and regulating them along the proper channels. Thus, we shall be able to enjoy the real delight of the mind and the real pleasure of the spirit.

Anger, pride, and other passions reduce man to the level of a lunatic and sometimes, degrade him to the level of an animal. Therefore, it is very necessary that we should recognise vignana, pragnana, and sugnana, which are latent in man and direct them along the proper channel and thus, achieve the highest state of supreme bliss. The cause for all the troubles, confusion, and turmoil is the fact that we have lost mastery over our senses. We let them go in a wild fashion. By leaving the senses unfettered and unregulated, we will not be able to discriminate properly, think coolly, calmly, and rationally. Thus, many times, we are misled into wrong actions. Anger is like an intoxicant. Internally, it induces us to do wrong things. This is the source of all the sins. It is a great demon. Anger leads us to commit all other sins. In the case of

Anger - The Greatest Enemy

Viswamitra, we know that all the good he acquired by 'tapas' was nullified by this one evil, anger. The merit he had accumulated through tapas undertaken for thousands of years was all lost in a moment of anger.

We need not go as far as Viswamitra. In our daily lives, we know that when we become angry, our nerves become weak and feeble and we lose grip over ourselves. Even a moment of anger takes away our strength, which we gather by eating good food for three months. Anger not only debilitates us and takes away the merit of our good deeds, but also enfeebles our condition. If we are able to control this anger, we shall be in a position to attain merit through the utterance of the Lord's name.

Vasishta attained the title of 'Brahmarshi' and Viswamitra also wanted to attain the title of 'Brahmarshi'. But even after years of tapas, he could not attain the same. Viswamitra became furious, because even when the world honoured him with the appellation of Brahmarshi, Vasishta did not agree to call him so. This indignation led to many other evil qualities. Anger induced the thought in Viswamitra that if he eliminated Vasishta from the world, then everyone else would honour him with the name of Brahmarshi. Once, on a moonlit night, Vasishta was describing to his pupil the qualities of Viswamitra. Viswamitra, who was hiding behind a bush with a sword in his hand to stab Vasishta, happened to hear the glorifying tributes Vasishta was paying Viswamitra. Vasishta was not aware that Viswamitra was hiding behind the bush and in his normal manner was describing the good qualities of Viswamitra's tapas, which he compared to the moonlight. This brought about a sudden transformation in Viswamitra. He began to repent in his mind his decision to kill Vasishta, who was such a great man and who was so kind towards him, talking about his fine qualities. He thought how bad he was when he entertained the thought of killing him. He felt that he must make amends and fell at the feet of Vasishta, expressing his repentance. He did so and Vasishta with a beautiful smile said, "Great Brahmarshi, wherefrom have you come?" When Vasishta addressed him thus, Viswamitra was surprised and felt quite repentant. Vasishta said, "Today, you really deserve the appellation of Brahmarshi, because you have eliminated all your anger and ego and you fell at my feet in a mood of utter repentance."

We must recognise the truth. So long as there is the feeling of anger and ego in our hearts, we will not be able to feel well in our life and will feel sick in our mind. One's anger is one's greatest enemy and one's calmness is one's own protection. One's joy is one's heaven and one's sorrow is one's hell. He, who is possessed by anger, will be hated by people, because he will commit a number of bad deeds. Anger leads to many great sins. First, we must endeavour to control this emotion of anger. Sometimes, ego also enters the feeling of anger. One's wealth leads to one's humilitation. The presitge of an individual is sometimes undermined by one's own wealth and one's pride in wealth. One's wealth brings a kind of distance between him and his kith and kin. People lose everything and are exposed to bad suffering, because of their anger.

If we aim at transcendental reality and Divinity, we must decide to bring this great emotion of anger under control. Anger is caused by weakness. It is not the weakness of the body, but of the mind. To give strength to our mind and remove the weaknesses from our mind, it is necessary to fill it with good thoughts, good feelings, and good ideas. While the funeral pyre consumes the dead, 'chinta' or an agitated mind reduces to ashes the living body. It is a living death, if one is obsessed by pride, ego, and anger. A state of mind, in which one overcomes these things, is described as 'sthitapragna'. A sthitapragna is one, who neither elated by joy, nor depressed by sorrow. He can take joy and sorrow in his stride with the same equanimity of mind.

Perhaps, you think it is not easy to control our senses. Even if it is not easy to control them, it is very easy to divert all of them in the direction of God and give them a new orientation. The Gopikas give classic examples of such supreme self control. By directing the powers of your senses towards God, all the impurities of the senses are eliminated in the process. The first step is cultivation of love towards all living creatures. This helps you to control your senses and direct them towards God.

There are three fish in a pond. One fish said to the other two, "The water in this pond will run dry after day. A time will come, when the pond may become completely dry and before the fisherman comes to catch us, it is necessary that we go and stay in some place where there is perennial supply of water." The second fish said, "You are imagining. Your mind is full of needless fears. The pond will not run dry. The fisherman will not come to bother us. Enjoy your present state." The third fish said the same thing. The first fish was discouraged when the other two did not accept its advice and so, it had to share their fate. As anticipated, the fisherman came and trapped them, cooked them and ate them. Our life may be compared to a pond and the length of our life to the water. The three fish are the three gunas, "Tama, raja, and satwa." The sathwic tendency always decides to follow the path of good and fixes its attention on things, which are permanent. It decides that before the level of water runs down, it should save itself and it always thinks of noble things. Water has been compared to the length of life and day by day, it recedes and at any time, death may overcome it. The fisherman is the emblem of death. Tama and raja are antagonistic to satwa and therefore, even the merit of satwa is counteracted by the other two. These two gunas, tama and raja, mislead our senses and send them along the wrong path. We should first try to control tama and raja and thereby, attain mastery over our senses. If we follow good methods, even raja and tama may be conquered by close association with satwa. We should believe that holy, sacred, and perennial love can be found in every human heart, where God resides. We should believe that God is the Indweller of the heart and must follow the teaching that comes from the heart and adopt good methods to follow such a teaching.

Our ancients have given us sacred paths of yoga and dhyana to overcome evils and gain control over our senses. To control anger and hatred, ancient sages have left their villages and gone into the forest. Today, it is not necessary to retire to the forest to get rid of anger and hatred. Virtue cannot be practised in a vacuum. If you live in an atmosphere of anger and are able to control it, then it is a meritorious achievement. But, if you live in a forest, where there is no room for anger, and say that you have controlled your anger, it is not meaningful. You must therefore remain in the worldly surroundings, where there is ample scope for the rising up of emotions of anger and hatred and then, learn to control them. That will be a meritorious achievement.

The sages used to perform 'yagnas' and 'yagas' for gaining mastery over their senses. The real nature and meaning of a 'yagna' is the overcoming of all our evil tendencies, throwing them into the fire of sacrifice. This is described as 'bhootabali'. The word bhootabali has been misinterpreted and some people think it means 'animal sacrifice' and this has given rise to evil practices. This is not the right way. 'Bali' means tax. Today, we are paying taxes on our property, on our houses, and on our income. But, the intention of levying taxes in the olden times was different from the intention of taxing today. Today, taxes are often collected, but misappropriated by the people in power. Taxes of olden days were used to further improve and increase the welfare of the people. Where there was not water supply, they used to provide water; where there were no roads, they used to build roads. By sacrificing all our evil tendencies to Gods, we are blessed with what is beyond man and what man badly needs in this world.

We offer to God so many things, because offering gives us pleasure. We offer flowers to God not because God does not have flowers, but because it makes us happy to offer flowers to Him. Many students say, "If we pass with a first class, I will break five coconuts at Your feet." Is it that God does not have coconuts at His disposal? All the objects we offer, like leaf, flowers, water, and all others have an allegorical significance. The word leaf does not refer to 'tulsi' or any other leaf. Our body is a leaf. Our body is offered as a sacred leaf to God. Because this body is full of the three gunas, we consider it as a leaf and make an offering of it to God. The word 'pushpa' stands for the flower of the heart. The flowers we talk of in the context of God do not refer to the earthly flowers, which fade away. Similarly, the word fruit is the fruit of the mind. It means that we must do our deeds without expecting any reward and if action is done in that spirit, it becomes a holy sacrifice. Water does not mean that, which is drawn from the taps. It refers to the tears of joy that spring from the depths of your heart. You should not offer leaves gathered from trees, which are external, or flowers from plants in the garden, or water drawn from the well, or fruit got somewhere else, but you must offer all these from the tree of your body, which is sacred, to God. Whatever offering you make, when you offer those things born out of the tree of your own body, then the full merit will be bestowed on you.

The word 'narikela' stands for a coconut. Every Indian must grasp the hidden significance or the inner meaning of offering a coconut to God. We never offer the coconut as it is. We remove the fibre that covers it and offer the fruit that is free from all the external fibre. Only then is it possible to break the coconut. By breaking the coconut, the water in it flows out. The heart is the coconut and it is covered by the fibre of desire. The water that flows out is the 'samskara' or purification. The fibres on the surface are the desires. We must strip the heart of all desires and offer the core without the fibre. It then becomes an offering to God. If we aim at a state of no birth and want liberation from the cycle of birth and death, the core acquires a different significance. If we plant a coconut as it is, in course of time and by watering it, another plant will grow out of it. At the time of germination, there is water in it. At that time, the kernel will be clinging to the sides of the fruit. The water, in due time, gets dried up and the kernel shrivels and begins to drift away from the external surface of the coconut. If we try to get the kernel out, plant it, and water it, nothing will happen. Our body may be compared to the shell and our life to the kernel. Our samskaras are the waters inside the coconut. As long as there are samskaras within us, the heart will always cling to the body consciousness, just as the kernel clings to the fruit.

Control over the senses is the golden way to get rid of evil tendencies clinging to the body consciousness. Control of the senses helps us to get rid of all evil tendencies. When your mind is troubled by bad thoughts, try to sit in a place and think of God, then you will be happy. Several great saints have taught the path of acquiring control over your senses. They used to offer to God all the tendencies that arise from the senses. They used to dedicate all their actions to God. Because they could divert their senses in the right channel, their senses were not touched by the temptations of the sins. When you do any action just to please God, there will be no evil result, which flows out and it does not cause you any suffering. What is offered to God is totally free from all defects and imperfections.

Gowranga was the original name of Chaitanya. As he grew up, he directed all thoughts towards God. He used to wander along the streets, singing kirtan and beating cymbals in his hands. In those days, there were enemies of such 'nagar sankirtan' or singing on the streets and they used to take away the instruments from the hands of those, who used to go along the streets chanting the name of God. Even at such moments, Chaitanya never exhibited any trace of anger. When any one took away the 'tala' from his hands, he used to think that the will of God was that He wanted him to chant His name without any accessories. The harm done to him was interpreted by him as a great benefit done to him. If anyone abused him beyond endurance, he used to utter the name of Krishna and thus, tune his mind to the mood of Krishna. When he uttered the name of Krishna, Chaitanya lost consciousness of his body. Because he lost his consciousness whenever the name of Krishna was uttered, he was known by the name of Krishna Chaitanya. Such titles won in those days were because of deserving merit and not like the titles conferred today on good, bad, worthy, and unworthy people, all alike. In those days, people never cared for worldly titles. Every person considered himself as the child of immortality. The removal of immortality is the way to attain immortality. Injustice, impropriety, and inequity are weaknesses, which must be got rid of. With a pure heart filled with the spirit of love, we must get ready to serve our country. In any field of life, you will be able to do well and shine well, if you are filled with love in your heart, if you have kindness, and if you have the right spirit of sacrifice and service in every action that you take up. You must visualise the Deity you worship as manifesting Himself or Herself in all human beings. With this kind of universal love, you must try to gain mastery over your senses. Though you may not read Vedas and Shastras, though you may not perform yagnas and yagas, it is possible to gain the grace of God by the cultivation of love.

Satwic food, which is congenial for the mind, is necessary to develop these qualities of love. Today, many people think that satwic diet consists of milk, curd, and so many other things. This is not correct and you must try to understand the real nature of satwic diet. You take the satwic diet through your mouth. The mouth is only one of the five sense organs. Satwic diet does not mean simply the food we take through our mouth, but also means the pure air we breathe through our nose, the pure vision we see through our eyes, the pure sounds we listen through our ears, and the pure objects we touch through our feet. All that we take in through the doors of the five sense organs may be described as the satwic diet. Listening to bad sounds, looking at bad sights, touching bad things do not constitute satwic diet. If we simply live on curd or milk, it does not mean that we are nourished by satwic diet. It may be that through the mouth, we are taking sathwic diet and through the other four sense organs, we are filling ourselves with many kinds of impurities. Satwic diet means the synthesis of sathwic food, breathing pure air, listening to good sounds, looking at good sights, and touching pure objects. Only then, we may be said to be satwic in our habits.

We must believe that it is the duty of Indians to control and develop the senses along proper channels. Today, India is considered a weak nation, because the people have not exercised such control as our ancestors used to, over their senses. We must also try to bring about unity in diversity. One piece of straw cannot bind even a tiny ant. But, if we weave a rope out of a thousand pieces of straw, we can bind even a wild elephant. Therefore, it is possible for us to achieve great things through unity. Indians must all be united and through unity, try to safeguard the higher values of Indian culture. India has been a leader and a sacred country, which has given spiritual leadership to the entire world for centuries. All the great cultures, which have been accepted in other countries, originated at some time or other and in some form or other in this sacred land.

17.

The Path Of Devotion

You all rejoice when you look at the pictures on the screen and mistake them for reality. What you should really do is to keep your attention rivetted upon what lies behind the screen, and if you are able to understand what is real and what is not real, all your doubts will be set at rest.

The foolish crow will live upon rotten flesh and other putrefied objects. On the other hand, parrots and cuckoos drink the honey that is hidden in the flowers and thereby, they feel thrilled with delight. In the same manner, foolish people run after temporal objects and worldly things and waste their time and energy. On the other hand, those, who have pure minds, drink the nectar of God-realisation and the nectar of Godly love and experience supreme happiness.

'No pains, no gains' is a common principle and we derive the fruit only if we are prepared to undertake the work. This truth is seen in all walks of life. We cannot achieve any fruit without paying the price for it. It is not proper to follow our mind and live according to the dictates of its whims. Life, which is lived according to the shastras, is the real life. Shastras alone contain an authoritative declaration of the real goal of life. It is even not necessary for us to read the different shastras in order to realise the nature, the significance, and the purpose of life. If you follow the truth, which flows from your heart, you will be led the perfect way.

Today, we do not believe that what the shastras have laid down is really the expression of truth or of the 'Sathya Swarupa'. The purport of shastras is known by different names and this variety of names sometimes leads to confusion. When we listen to discourses delivered by experienced and wise elders, we land ourselves in doubt whether to adopt this one or the other, and we do not know which is the right path and which is not. The sentences of the shastras may sometimes be interpreted differently and sometimes, we land ourselves into trouble by trying to follow the different interpretations that are put upon the sentences of the shastras.

Today, with the help of an analogy, we will be able to realise whether God is serving man or man is serving God. We imagine that man, Manava, is offering everything that he has for the sake of the realisation of God, Madhava. It is not very difficult for the man to follow the path and try to realise Madhava. Every discipline and every action, which leads man to God, is not difficult to be implemented. For instance, Vedic Brahmin takes the holy water of the

The Path Of Devotion

Ganges in the palm of his hand and offers the same water back to the sacred river. The truth is that he is not offering his property or his father's property or his grandfather's property, but he is offering the holy water that he has drawn from the sacred river back to the river. Similarly, when we look at the objects offered by man to God, they are all created, preserved, and bestowed upon man by God Himself. Man is not offering anything of his own, except when he is offering his devotion arising from his heart. God takes care of that devotee, who completely surrenders himself with single minded devotion at the Lotus Feet of the Lord. If one is intoxicated with the Divine Love and forgets all worldly responsibilities, God Himself will take upon all the responsibilities of that devotee.

Our shastras teach us many good things through the examples of the lives of great saints and great teachers. One devotee addressed God thus, "I am not Sakkubai to let you get bound to the pillar and beaten up in my place. I am not Ramdas to demand the return of the money that I have spent for you. I am not Jayadeva to demand that the ruined house should once more be repaired and that the roof should be put over it and covered with hay." We find several such devotees in our history, who have thus served God and made God serve them. All our shastras unanimously declare that love alone is the criterion and the one essential requisite for developing unswerving devotion. Realisation, which is not possible through logic, which is not possible through offering sacrifices, and which is not possible through discussion and other disciplines, can be achieved only through love. Therefore, we should examine why we should cultivate and cherish this love.

The nature of the body, the nature of the mind and of the desires and senses are not conducive to the realisation of God. We all hear about the Lord, Who sleeps on 'Ksheerasagara', the ocean of milk. Our 'Antahkarana' or the inner subtle body is the 'Ksheerasagara' or the ocean of milk. And that which remains after dhyana – the sesha or the remnant – is the 'Adisesha' or the great serpent. The consciousness that lies in between the two is Lord Vishnu Himself. And the one, who worships, or the worshipper is Goddess Lakshmi. Several great men have taught us how to make God sleep on the ocean of milk – in our own 'antahkarana' or in our own heart.

There is a hidden meaning as to why we think of the 'sadhaka' as Lakshmi. Unless the inert nature is completely shaken off, the Jeevi cannot be called Purusha. It is possible to attain that principle of Purusha through the feminine nature or 'Stree-tatwa'. We must examine what this 'Jadatwa' or inertness is. There are five phases or aspects of this inertness. The first one is called 'Ghatakasha' – the sky within the pot. The second is 'Jalakasha', the sky reflected in the water. The third is the 'Daharakasha', the sky that is reflected in the heart. The fourth one is 'Chidakasha' and the fifth one is 'Mahadakasha' or the grand sky. So, when we look at these five kinds of 'akashas', they are all inert or 'Jada'.

Each one of you has got a name. The name refers to the body, but not the 'Atma' or the soul in you. The name would have been given by the parents to the body, which is inert, and it refers only to the body, but not to the 'Atma'. 'Ghatakasha' is that state, which says, "This is I. This is I." Man uses the word 'I', referring to the body, though there is deeply lodged within him the higher principle of 'Atma' or the soul. Even when we are lost in the knowledge of the body, thinking only of the body, still there is that feel for the Atma within us.

Then, coming to 'Jalakasha', it is that state which is full of 'sankalpa' or intention and may be described as the sky reflected in the water. If in a little pond of water, the blue sky is reflected and the sky may also have the shining moon, we have the illusion that the sky and the moon reflected in the water seem to be mobile or moving. The sky and the moon do not move, but only the water moves when the breeze blows over it. The 'sankalpa' and the 'vikalpas' in us are the water. 'Daharakasha' is the state, when one looks at 'sankalpas' and 'vikalpas', but one is aware that he is looking at them.

Let us take an example. We pour water into a tub and we look at it. We see our own face reflected in it and we say that it is a reflection. Even though that image reflected in the water is beaten, not even a single stroke is felt by the object, namely the body. So, if the object and the image were one, any injury done to the image must be felt by the object also. Though your face is reflected in the water, the goodness or the badness of the image does not affect you, the object. You may then question, "Is it not my reflection?" Yes, it is yours. When the image is hurt and that injury is not registered by you, it is 'not you'. But, when you are abused, you and the image become one. When the image is hurt physically by anybody, that injury is not felt by the object, but when the image is insulted and abused by anybody, then the object, whose reflection is found in the water, also feels the insult. You feel angry, because you are there in the image also. In 'shabda' or sound, there is unity, but in action or 'kriya', there is no unity. And the nature of 'Shabda-brahma-tatwa' is hidden there. Thus, in 'Jalakasha', we also find the nature of 'Daharakasha'.

Now, coming to 'Chidakasha', this refers to man remaining a mere spectator. 'Chidakasha' is the state when man, without being upset, without being in any way influenced by emotion, just observes and remains like an observer or a spectator. Whatever may happen to the body – it may be insulted and injured – the person is not affected by them; he is always engrossed in the higher consciousness and that is the state of 'Chidakasha'. The pot may be broken, the pond may run dry, the canvas may be torn to shreds, but that 'akasha' stands there. The sky reflected in the pot, the sky painted on the canvas, only refer to the media, but not to the great sky itself. Though this is reflected in our body, mind, and senses, this 'tatwa' is something, which transcends all of them.

Only when the senses are brought under control and when there is a state of 'Nirvikalpa', we reach the highest state of realisation. It is possible for us to realise the nature of the 'Mahadakasha' or the great sky in the state known as 'Nirvikalpa'. 'Nirvikalpa' means arresting the activity of all the senses and assuming supreme control over them. Then, the consciousness is not lost in the body or in any part of the body, but it is entirely devoted to that higher or the transcendental state. And the 'Mahadakasha' is called 'akasha', because it has an element of 'Jada' or inertness in it.

We sometimes call a conglomeration of clouds by the name of sky. The sky has no separate entity or existence. It is not a shape, which is concrete and made up of the five elements. It has only one quality, namely 'shabda' or sound. And this sound is all-pervading. It is wrong to identify 'shabda' only with the sky. The sky is known by several names, such as 'akasha', 'gagana', 'shunya', or nothingness and so on. There is nothing there in the sky. The state of nothingness is called by the name of the sky. When we sometimes refer to our heart and say, this is 'hridayakasha', it is because there is no shape for the 'hridaya' or heart in a spiritual sense. The 'akasha' has to be cleared of all baser intentions and instincts, all 'sankalpas' and 'vikalpas'. The sky reflected in the water, the sky painted on the canvas, are only steps and have no special existence or validity.

If a boy is admitted to a school, he gradually progresses from the nursery to the first standard, from the first to the second, third, and so on. He does not suddenly jump from the nursery to the highest class in the school. When we take the nature of the school, we cannot but say that this boy is progressing from one class to another, year after year. The same boy, if he remains at home and undergoes private studies and takes the help of tutors, it is possible for him to go straight to the 6th standard. When we gain God's grace and love, it is possible for us straight to go to the highest state of 'Mahadakasha', without passing through all the various stages of 'Ghatakasha', 'Jalakasha', and so on. It is necessary for us to search for the path that easily takes us to the feet of the Lord and realise Him.

Though we know that the world is false, it is desirable that we recognise the truth even in this falsehood. Let us examine carefully whatever truth there is in it. Even in boyhood, we have all the qualities of the old age latent and hidden. We do not find any basic changes though we may pass on from the state of adolescence to youth, to middle age, and to old age. And the same body is present through all these stages of change, from boyhood to old age. Nobody can identify exactly the point of transition, when boyhood comes to an end and youth begins, when youth comes to an end and old age comes. The body does not undergo any death. The body remains and within the same body, these changes come about. When we contemplate upon this, we verifly find truth in falsehood, falsehood in truth, truth in truth, and falsehood in falsehood.

In this world, which is false, we are leading a life which is false. Therefore, it is not a life of truth when we question what kind of life we are leading. If this world was real, why do we, after our dinner and retiring to sleep, forget all the lectures that we have listened to during the day and all the experiences of the day? Nothing remains in our mind. It is not forgetting, but we simply become unaware of all the experiences, through which we have gone during the day. Though your body may be resting in the shed at Brindavan, your mind may be dreaming at night, wandering in the streets of Delhi. In the dream, you think that you are moving in Delhi in body. The truth is that though your body is here and you are dreaming that the body has gone to Delhi and has gone shopping, your body has not gone there at all and you are remaining here. When you are sleeping, you feel that you have gone to Delhi. You have not gone and your body is here itself. What is true in the waking state is false in the dream state and what is true in the dream state becomes false in the waking state. Therefore, this is falsehood in falsehood.

The sun shines brilliantly when there is no obstruction, but when we build a house and fit it with doors and windows and close all of them, there is only darkness but no light inside that house. When we want the sun's light to penetrate into the house, either of two things must be done by us. We must remove the top or we must get rid of 'deha bhranti'. We demolish the top, which is made of 'ahamkara' or ego and 'Mamakara' or attachment. Alternatively, we can fit a mirror and see that the sun is reflected into the house. Then, the mirror also will be able to radiate the effulgence of the sun. It is possible by moving the mirror to spread the light in the dark interior of the house. But, does the light come from the sun or does it come from the mirror? The mirror is inert and it is not luminous by nature. The moon also is like the mirror and the moon has no brightness of its own. The light of the sun is reflected on the surface of the moon and therefore, the light of the moon is so cool and so pleasant.

Our Vedas teach that the moon is like the mind, which reflects the glory of the soul. If the light of the 'Atma' is reflected in the mirror of the 'buddhi' or intelligence, then the entire dark mind may be seen shining with light. Mind is responsible for our being able to derive 'prajnana', even though we are in the state of 'ajnana'. If we make our mind radiant and illumined, then there is no room for darkness of 'ajnana' or ignorance. When we turn our 'buddhi' towards 'Atma', we shall be able to dispel all the darkness from our mind. Mind is the master of the senses and intelligence is the master of the mind. 'Atma' is the master of intelligence. And what is grasped in intelligence is beyond the senses. It transcends the senses. The attempt to gain liberation ultimately by passing through all these intermediate stages is known by the name of 'Moksha Marga' or the path for liberation.

Some days back, I said that I would deal with the subject of the different 'padas' in the different Yugas and explain how dharma has lost its 'padas', in spite of the appearance of the great Avatars. I shall elucidate it now. Dharma used to live and move about in Krita Yuga on four feet. The four feet are 'Yajna', 'Yaga', 'Yoga', and 'Tapa'. I told you that expression of sound or 'shabda' that emanates from the heart is called 'Rita'. Further expression of this 'Rita' through word of mouth is called 'Truth'. Thus, 'Rita' means the 'Sathya Sankalpa' in the heart itself. Truth is the expression of that thought through word. Implementing truth into action is dharma. There is a saying that there is no dharma higher than truth. Truth is the basis of all dharma and truth depends upon the 'Rita'

The Path Of Devotion

or the 'sankalpa'. So, these three – Rita, Sathya, and Dharma are inseparably and inextricably connected. Rishis in Krita Yuga followed these four-fold paths, described in the foregoing as the four feet, in order to gain harmony between thought, word, and deed.

The loss of one 'pada' in Treta Yuga really means the loss of one 'sadhana', namely Tapas. The word of the 'pada' is to help man walk. Tapas also is the process of enforcement in action. It was possible in Treta Yuga to attain dharma without Tapas, by following the other three, namely yajna, yaga, and yoga. In the Dwapara Yuga, with the help of only two, Yaga and Yoga, it was possible to attain liberation. Yajna has been eliminated. In Kali Yuga, dharma has only one 'Pada', namely Yoga. Yaga is gone and Yoga alone remains. "What kind of Yoga?" you may ask the question. That Yoga, which is relevant is Bhakti Yoga, the yoga of devotion. There is no other way to attain liberation in this Kali Yuga, except through the path of devotion. In Treta Yuga, people were able to enjoy the proximity to Divinity through the three methods, Yajna, Yaga, and Yoga. In Dwapara Yuga, the same could be achieved with the help of only two 'padas', Yaga and Yoga. It is possible to attain this in Kali Yuga through Yoga alone. Thus, the inner meaning is that they have facilitated the process, eliminated the difficult ones and the one that is easily accessible to all, the path of devotion is what remains in the Kali Yuga.

It used to take two months for people to reach Banares, some 50 years ago. Ten years ago, it used to take 3 days for going by train. Today, it is possible for us to reach Banares by plane within 3 hours. Kashi or Banares has not undergone any change. The City of Bangalore has not undergone any change. The four feet we used in the early journeys have finally dwindled into one foot at the present time. Our methods have only been facilitated. Let us take our life itself as an example. Until you are one year old, you use all the four limbs to move. After a few months, you walk on two feet taking the help of the wall with your hands. Sometimes, you may take the help of the mother's hand. In that stage, you use three limbs. After some time, you do not depend upon either the mother, or the wall. You can just walk on your two feet. Later, when you want to be very swift in your movement, you use only one foot. When you run, the two feet do not touch the ground at the same time. Only one foot touches the ground at a time. Because you set only one foot on the ground, you are able to reach the destination very quickly. Dharma has not changed. Only the means of attainment have been facilitated. Dharma remains the same. When Krishna said that dharma is endangered, He meant that some danger has overtaken Dharma. Dharma is not destroyed at all. Dharma is imperishable and indestructible. That is the reason why Rama is described as the very embodiment of dharma, dharma which is imperishable.

18.

Dvaita, Advaita, and Vishishtadvaita

In the Atma tatwa, all are eternal. In the world-sense, all are ephemeral. Though we know that this body and the sense of the work-a-day world are purely ephemeral, we make the mistake of treating them as permanent. Atma tatwa, which is Jnana, is permanent. Though we do not accept it, it still exists. It is above all experiences of losses and difficulties and nothing can shake it. This Atma tatwa is the embodiment of truth. It is also the embodiment of delight or the 'Ananda Swarupa'.

There are several instances in the Gita, where the eternal existence of soul has been referred to. 'Na twevaham Jatu nasam' is the first such reference. That is, 'I, who am the Divine Swarupa, always remain.' The second such reference is 'Na twam', that is, 'you, who are the Jiva Swarupa, are also there. There was never a time when you were not there. All the others, Bhishma, Drona, and others also have been ever there. The world is also there always. I, who am the Ishwara, you, who are the Jiva and this world, which is Jagat – all the three have always been existing.' These three, Jiva, Ishwara, and Prakriti have been in existence at all times – they were there even before the creation and they will continue to be there. Though the physical bodies may be undergoing transformation, this Atma tatwa remains eternal and changeless.

There are three approaches or three philosophies, which have been propounded to enable us to know this tatwa. These three are Dvaita, Advaita, and Vishishtadvaita. Let us first try to understand what is Dvaita or duality. Dvaita propounds that Jiva and Prakriti always exist, are always there, and they will never become one. The permanence of these two entities, though they are different, is accepted.

If we take into consideration the Vishishtadvaita, it postulates 'Chit' and 'Achit' in the phenomenal world and accepts the phenomena of appearance and illusion. It states that both are true and valid. Vishishtadvaita has also established the oneness of Jagat, which is 'Jada' or inert and of Jiva, which is full of consciousness. Vishishtadvaita also says that Jada and Chaitanya, i.e. inertness and consciousness, are the manifestations of the same principle of Divinity and therefore, are considered equally valid. Because these two entities cannot merge with each other, they have been postulated as different aspects of the same form and as part and parcel of the same principle.

Jagat, the world, Jiva, the consciousness, and Purusha, the Supreme are not three separate entities, but are one and the same from the ultimate point of view. The greatness of Vishishtadvaita lies in proclaiming their unity. Though the appearances may be different and there may be varieties of experiences, it is asserted that in all these, there is one thing present, namely the unifying spirit. Followers of Vishishtadvaita use the analogy of gold. Though the ornaments may be of different shape, the gold is the same. They go even a step further. If God has not these subtle and gross bodies, the very nature of God will be incomplete. I will give an example. Let us take the king, the kingdom, and his people. Without the king, there cannot be the kingdom; without the kingdom, there cannot be the people; without the people, there can be no kingdom, and without the kingdom there can be no king. They are all interdependent. Because all these three are in a way inextricably interconnected with one another, Vishishtadvaita has propounded the unity of the three entities. When we take into consideration the nature of the king and the people, then we shall be able to grasp that there is also the principle of non-duality or Advaita here. The king also is one among the people and he is also a man. The king is the law-giver and the people are those, who are regulated and bound by the law. Though the ruler and the ruled may appear to be separate, as human beings, they are one and the same.

Just as we are told about the oneness of Jada and the Chaitanya, we find Chaitanya or consciousness in inertness and we find the features of inertness in consciousness as well. Therefore, in a way, they are inseparable. The inertness cannot exist without consciousness. Consciousness cannot exist without inertness. In the work-a-day world, we may mistake and think that conscious force cannot enter into inert matter and vice-versa. But, that is a mistaken idea. We all believe that this whole world is permeated by shabda or sound. But, where there is a movement or motion, there alone does shabda originate. We close our eyes many a time every minute. As our eyelids move, they do make a little noise, but the noise is so inaudible that we are unaware of it. Because it is inaudible, we cannot deny the presence of sound. Just as we are not able to recognise the sound, which is inaudible, in the same way, we are not able to recognise the consciousness in Jada and we are not able to recognise the element of Jada in consciousness.

There are two aspects present in this illusion. One is 'Parinama' or evolution. The other is 'Vivarta'. Vivarta is the property, which makes us think that there is change though the substance remains the same. It is made to appear to have a different shape and form. When we are walking alone, we may come across a rope, but get deluded to imagine it as a serpent. The rope does not go and the serpent does not come. It is all an illusion. Vivarta is the quality, which makes us forget the real thing and makes us impose upon that, some other thing which is not there. It is the effect of Maya. Parinama is the property of evolution or change like milk turning into curd. If there is no milk, we cannot change it into curd. Parinama is that, which changes what is there. Maya is present both in Parinama and Vivarta.

Today, we live under the influence of Vivarta. Though we are Atma Swarupa, we forget the Supreme Reality and we live with that Dehabhranti or the bodily illusion. We mistake our ephemeral existence to be the real existence. We are not afraid of the rope, but we are terribly afraid of the serpent. We are not afraid of the Atma, but we are afraid of life. Though we are Atma Swarupas and should be free from fear, unfortunately, we are lost in the fear and illusion.

'Upadhis' or containers apart, there is only one Reality, just as there is only one sun shining in the sky. But, when we fill a thousand pots with water, the same one sun is reflected in these thousand pots. Because the thousand pots are there and they are filled with water, which has the quality of reflection, the one sun seems to be split up into a thousand suns. This is only a feeling and is not true. The truth is that there is only one sun shining in the sky. Likewise, this body may be compared with the pot, which is filled with water and one and the same Atma is reflected in each pot, and appears to be separate.

Several persons put the question, "Swami, please tell us where the Atma goes after the death of the body." When the pot breaks and the water spills on the ground, where does the sun, who has hitherto been reflected in the water, go? The sun has not come and has not gone. But, he has appeared as a reflection, because there is the pot and there is water in the pot. And when the pot is broken and the water has run out, the reflection has disappeared.

There is another question. If the same sun is reflected in all pots, would not all the reflections have the same value? The reflection has the same value, but the pots are of different value. One pot may be an earthen pot, another may be one of copper, another of brass, another of silver, and another of gold. Therefore, the value of the pot varies according to the material, with which it is made, but the reflection has the same value. This body has the value, which varies according to one's wealth, one's position, one's education, but the Atma Swarupa has the same value. So, all these differences are illusory. They are created by things relating to the body. The Atma Tatwa is one and indivisible.

On the bank of a river, once, a group fo children were tending their cows. It was the monsoon and all of a sudden, a furious current of water developed. Because it was a fast current, one bear, which slipped into the water, was drawn into the midstream and was being carried away. One of the boys looked at the floating mass and from a distance, it appeared to him to be a bundle of blankets floating in the water. He said to his companions, "I shall jump into the water and get the bundle of blankets out," and so, he jumped into the water. With the mistaken idea that it is a bundle of blankets, the boy embraced with his hands the bear. Then, the bear also embraced him with its own hands. However much the boy tried to extricate himself, the bear did not leave him. It held him fast. The boys on the shore shouted, "Oh, my dear companion, leave that bundle and you come away." The boy in the water, struggling to escape, cried out, "Though I want to escape from it, it does not allow me to escape." So, in this river of life, maya plays like the bear and we mistake it to be a bundle of blankets. Hoping that it would offer us solace, comfort, and happiness, we jump into the river and try to catch it. At a later stage, when we want to extricate ourselves from it, we find it impossible to do so. This illusion is created by maya, but the Divine principle is always one. Visishtadvaita has been teaching from time immemorial that though the forms are different, there is only one Purusha, which is the Unity in the diversity and multiplicity of forms.

Coming to Advaita, we have to understand the word to mean non-duality. What is not two is Advaita. What is that is not two? Brahman alone is not two. In the Gita, Lord Krishna taught this principle to Arjuna at several places. He says for instance,

"Vrishninam Vasudevosmi; Pandavanam Dhananjaya."

"Among the Vrishnees, I am Vasudeva. Because I am the son of Vasudeva, I am Vasudeva. Among the Pandavas, I am Arjuna." Though He is One, here He represents Himself as two. He further says, "I am Ishwara, you are the Jiva, and the heroes, who are ranged against you, constitute the Jagat, the world. This jagat is all reflected as in a mirror. You are considering that you are separate and all these people are separate from you. You are thinking that you and they are different. Jiva, Ishwara, and Prakriti as three entities have been there from time immemorial." Then, Arjuna questioned, "If these entities, Jiva, Ishwara, and Prakriti have been ever in existence and Jiva and Ishwara are one, how do You know about Jagat and why do I not know anything about it? When You and I are one, how is it that You know and I do not know? Please tell me the secret of this." Krishna said, "Arjuna! You also can know, but you do not focus your mind upon the goal. Therefore, you do not know. But, My mind is always steadily rivetted on that Reality. Therefore, I know it. And that is the essential difference between us two." Arjuna could not grasp this. He said, "You are trying to hoodwink me, oh Krishna!" To this, Krishna said, "Arjuna! I shall never utter false or deceitful words. I am Satya Swarupa. Truth is My breath. The world is brought about by My Sankalpa. Therefore, there is no place for falsehood or deceit in My words. It is because of the effect of Maya that you have become subjected to illusion and you are attributing falsehood even to Me!"

Then, He wanted to teach Arjuna by an example. He asked Arjuna, "How old are you?" Arjuna said, "I am eighty years old." Krishna asked, "Tell Me, three years ago, on such and such a day, where were you?" Arjuna could not recollect and said, "Lord! I do not remember where I was on that day, three years ago." Krishna said, "Then you do not remember where you were. You accept you were in a particular place three years ago. If you were not there three years ago, how could you be here today? You admit today that you do not know where you were three years ago." Krishna patted Arjuna on his back and continued, "Do not feel embarrassed. I shall put to you another question. Please tell Me how old you were when King Drupada was bound and brought by you to your kingdom." Arjuna replied, "I was at that time 16 years old, oh Lord!" Krishna then asked, "Do you remember when you got married to Subhadra?" Arjuna said immediately, "I certainly remember, I was married in my twenty-second year." Then, Krishna questioned, "An event such as the marriage, which took place fifty years ago and the incident of bringing King Drupada bound to your capital, which happened long, long ago, are remembered by you, but you do not remember what happened just three years ago. Why is it? The secret is this. The nature of maya is that it makes you attach importance to some events, such as birthdays and wedding days, but not to others."

To experience joy and sorrow alike is the secret of Samadhi. Only Rama has been able to demonstrate this Samadhi quality, i.e. one, who is not elated by joy and one, who is not downcast or depressed by sorrow, however enormous it may be. Not only Rama, but all Avatars have demonstrated this state of Samadhi. Rama, Who got ready for the coronation ceremony at 7'o'clock, at the same time and in the same stride, took the decision and went away to the forest. So, He was not elated at the prospect of becoming the future king and He did not get depressed or frustrated when He was asked to go to the forest. Krishna always used to be smiling whether it is Rudrabhumi, the sacrificial field, or Yuddhabhumi, the battlefield. Wherever He used to be, He remained an embodiment of ananda. That was why His words, which were uttered on the battlefield, have acquired the name of Gita. Gita means song. We sing when we are happy. Does one sing, when one is unhappy or sorry? When Krishna could sing even in the midst of a battle, it means that He can always remain cheerful and happy.

And the real nature of Avataras is that they are always overflowing with the spirit of delight and joy. Just as the ocean rises and surges up when there is full moon in the sky, in the same way, when I look at the devotees, My Heart overflows with limitless, boundless love for them. Everything is Rasa swarupa. There can be no change in the attitude, in the affection, and in the thoughts of God, but the ignorant attribute the changes they imagine or differences they see to God out of their petty-mindedness.

When Divine power fulfils some of our desires, we praise God, but when the same power does not satisfy our desires, we straightaway condemn Him. Man commits sins and he has to undergo the punishment for the sin. But, then he says, "Oh God! You have no mercy, You are subjecting me to this punishment." People cannot stand test and trial. They speak sweet words in My presence. They are mostly pretensions and they are not true. Our nature is Ananda. 'Swa' is Brahma tatwa. 'Bhava' is Swabhava. 'Swa' does not refer to the individual. 'Swa' refers to Brahma. 'Swecha' means the Will of the Lord and 'Swabhava' means the Bhava of the Lord.

People remember those days, to which they attach some special significance and they do not forget them.

Because they do not attach importance to other days, they do not find a place in their memory. And there lies the difference between Jiva and Deva. Jiva imagines some as necessary and others as unnecessary and dwells on differences. As far as Deva is concerned, there is nothing which is necessary for Him and which is not necessary for Him. He remains a spectator of all. For a spectator, the past, the present, and the future are all the same. He can visualise all the three periods of time. He remains as Atma Swarupa during all the three periods of time.

Though God is one, as a result of our love for him, we establish different kinds of relationship with God. Some may address Him as Father, others as Mother, others as Christ, others as Siva, others as Hari, and so on. It is only the difference, which is born out of illusion, but there is only one God behind all these relationships.

I will give you another example, which is within the range of the experience of all. Everyday, we take and enjoy ghee, butter, buttermilk, curd, etc. All these are ultimately derived from milk. Milk is Advaita. Butter is Vishishtadvaita. Buttermilk is Dvaita. Both the Dvaita and Vishishtadvaita are derived from Advaita. Therefore, it is said that wisdom is advaita darshanam. Wisdom reveals to us the Brahma Tatwa. It is described as 'Sathyam Jnanam Anantam Brahma'. Brahma is that which is truth, that which is endless, and that which is all knowing. The word Brahma is derived from the root: 'Bruhi'. Bruhi means that, which does not change. It is called Brahma tatwa, because it does not change and because it remains eternal. We must adopt the theory of 'Raso Vai Saha' in order to attain this Brahma tatwa. The entire world or universe is born out of Rasa, God Himself, Who is Rasa Swarupa. That, which is born out of Rasa, cannot be 'Nirasa' or devoid of rasa.

Pandits classify Rasa into nine categories. They are called Navarasas. According to My view, there are no Navarasas or nine rasas. There are only two rasas. One is Karuna rasa and the other is Sringara rasa. The emotions of Daya, Prema, and Anugraha merge in Karuna rasa. The emotions of Kama, Krodha, and Lobha merge in Sringara rasa. Sringara rasa misleads us, whereas Karuna rasa leads us. Therefore, to recognise our duty, we must take recourse to Karuna rasa. Only through Karuna rasa can we enjoy the proximity of the Lord. That is the real ecstasy or bliss. Karuna rasa offers us pure selfless love. Selfish love leads to an aspect of Sringara rasa and that is Moha. Moha rasa may be compared to the water that is stagnating in the pond. Karuna rasa may be compared to the water that flows through a river. Moving water ever remains pure. Still water gets contaminated and becomes stagnant. Stagnant water sometimes becomes poisonous, because worms breed in it. Flowing water always remains pure and surely and finally reaches the ocean of Anugraha or God's grace. Moha expresses itself in desiring things. Desires go on multiplying. Moha may be compared to the water that is bound in a lake.

I will give now an example. There is a girl in one house. There is a young man in another house. Their houses are almost side by side. But, the girl does not know anything about the young man and the young man does not know anything about the girl living in the neighbouring house. One day, the girl fell seriously ill. That day, all the people in the house were hectic and they were all anxious and several doctors were called in. When the boy in the neighbouring house heard the noise, he thought it was a disturbance for his studies and, therefore, he closed his window and started reading. But, in course of time, as a result of destiny, this boy, who was living in that house, got married to that girl in the neighbouring house. The marriage took place in the morning. In the afternoon, the girl developed a stomach ache and this bridegroom felt very anxious for the girl and her stomach ache. Where and when has he developed this attachment to the girl? Because he got married to her, even a little stomach ache upsets him now. Though the same girl fell dangerously ill some time ago, he did not feel even the slightest anxiety for her, because at that time, there was no attachment or relationship with that girl. So, abhimana and mamakara, affection and attachment are responsible for all joys and sorrows. This is all the result of illusion, but we are all intrinsically embodiments of happiness. We must also try to attain that serene state of mind, the equanimity which enables you not to be elated by joy or depressed by sorrow. When you are able to attain that equanimity of mind, which is above the experience of joy and sorrow, then you can also attain the Samadhi.

The word Samadhi has been variously interpreted by our scholars. When someone falls unconscious during Sankirtan or when someone becomes stiff during yoga, they think it is a state of Samadhi. But, this is not real Samadhi. The very meaning of the word is conveyed by the two syllables that makes the word 'Sama' and 'Dhi' – Sama means equal, Dhi means buddhi. So, to be untouched by joy and sorrow, to take them in the same stride is Samadhi. In Dvaita, duality always remains. Visishtadvaita teaches us that there may be differences of Rupa and Nama, form and name, but the Purusha behind them is the same. They also accept the permanence of both Jada and Chaitanya, the inert and the conscious. They hold that Jada is as true as Chaitanya and Chaitanya is as true as Jada. Because we have one-sided look, we are not able to look at the other side of the picture. When we are able to recognise both, then only we will be able to realise the unity. We must attempt to reach unity through duality. If we want to attain Advaita state, we must first pass through the process of Dvaita state. Therefore, it is not possible to live without Dvaita.

Earlier, I was dealing wth the four Purusharthas, namely Dharma, Artha, Kama, and Moksha. These are comparable to the steps of the ladder. Dharma is firmly planted on the ground and if we ascend the ladder step by step, we reach the highest rung, the goal of Moksha. So, we deem Prakriti as Dharma. And our destination is Moksha or Purusha. Artha and Kama are the intermediary stages between Purusha on the one hand and Prakriti on the other. Without the basis of Dharma and without the goal of Moksha, Artha and Kama in the middle are of no significance. So, we shall be able to find the oneness of all the four Purusharthas, when we are able to understand the nature of each. Dharma and Artha may be grouped together. Moksha and Kama may be grouped together. Adopt Artha for Dharma and develop Kama for Moksha. Our Kama or desire should be oriented towards Moksha and the Artha that we amass must be for establishing Dharma. When we give predominance to these two things, Dharma and Moksha, then Artha and Kama also become sanctified.

There is no use of listening to discourses on Advaita. It is something that must be realised through action. It must be manifested in your conduct. You must make it a point not to hurt or offend anybody, give pain to anybody, and must realise the philosophy of Advaita in action. Today, there is an eruption, almost like an earthquake, among the youth in the country. It is not proper on the part of the students to embark upon violent agitations in a mood of irrational and blind passion. From today, the students must get ready to open the eyes of the leaders of this unrest and drive home even into their hearts the philosophy of Advaita and spiritual message. You may derive some emotional satisfaction when you indulge in some violent acts, but in the long run, that action will only do you harm. Whatever be the action, which you take up, if you do it in a spirit of purity, harmony, and unity, you shall be able to derive the fruits thereof, which are pure and immaculate.

19.

God's Love Is Like Sun-shine

There is nothing greater than Karma or duty and that duty must be done in a disinterested manner without having any attachment to the fruit of the action. After the action is performed in a spirit of detachment, it will lead us to greater happiness in this world.

You should clearly understand the meaning of Karma, bhakti, or jnana. Yoga must be considered to be the common factor in all these. Patanjali has described yoga as the control of the faculties of the mind and only after that can we undertake anyone of these paths, namely that of Karma, bhakti, or jnana. It is not possible for anyone to abstain from action. Action is the basis for our existence. This body has been given to us for the sake of action. It is the need of man's life that he must sanctify it through action and purify his time by right action. This stream of action flows through jnana also and ultimately leads us to the highest stages of realisation.

We think that karma, bhakti, and jnana are separate, but according to our philosophy, they are indivisible and not separate. Even if they appear to be separate, they are same in form, time, name, and nature. Here is an illustration. At first, we find on a tree a small bud. By preserving this bud, it develops into an unripe fruit. This unripe fruit develops into the ripe and mellow fruit. When the fruit becomes mellow, it becomes sweet. The bud, the unripe fruit, and the ripe fruit are the three manifestations of the same reality. The path of karma may be compared to a path, which is wrought with certain difficulties. When we think of the path of bhakti, it seems to be less difficult and more delightful. To attain the ability to go along the path of jnana or superior wisdom, action or the path of karma is inevitable. To give you another analogy, the path of karma may be described as a train journey. During the journey by a train, we get down at one station and get into another train and thus, travel by different trains. The path of bhakti may, on the other hand, be described as a journey in a through carriage. The path of jnana is like travelling in a through train.

Though the path of karma is difficult, it gives us varied experiences. There are three kinds of karma, namely, karma, vikarma, and akarma. According to the Gita, these are three ramifications. Karma may be described as the ordained duty. Vikarma deals with certain actions, which are prohibited. But, such prohibited actions, if and when they are undertaken for God realisation, become sanctified. Akarma is described as pure laziness or idleness. The karmas are clarified by the Gita and must be enforced in action and not merely talked about. Karma is our responsibility since our birth. The Gita refers to man as karmaja. Man is born through and for karma. Moksha or liberation and janma or birth are all derived from karma. It is not possible for us to spend one minute without karma. Though it takes a gross physical form, action helps us to spend our time usefully. As long as we have five senses of our body properly functioning, we cannot but undertake some type of action or other. Action will always lead to a reward or a fruit. The fruit of action is a reaction, a reflection, and a resound of the action itself. But, the Gita teaches us that the actions we undertake for God realisation must be free from any consideration for a reward or a fruit. All those, who propagate the message of Gita, say that man has only the right to act and has not the right to claim the fruit of that action. But, the Gita has not said that man has no authority to enjoy the fruit of the action. Gita has said that man should voluntarily give up the right to enjoy the fruit of the action. It has not said 'Na Phaleshu' or there is no fruit. It has said 'Ma Phaleshu' or though there is the fruit, the injunction is that you must give up the desire for the fruit of the action. It is also described in our sacred Vedas that man achieves real happiness by voluntarily giving up the desire for the fruit.

One ponders over how man can enjoy through sacrifice. Without thyaga or sacrifice, we cannot have either 'bhoga' or yoga, but have only 'roga' or disease. Take the example of our inhaling. After we inhale, if we do not exhale the air that we have inhaled, the lungs will be damaged. Similarly, our stomach will be upset, if we do not excrete the food we have taken. If the blood that flows through the arteries does not flow through a particular point of the body, it will be stagnant there and then, we will get a boil. Therefore, all our welfare is inextricably tied up with tyaga or sacrifice. If the child does not register natural growth, the mother gets very anxious about it. We are giving up the body that we inherit at the time of birth and by growing, we sacrifice the original state and attain the new one. Whether we do it knowingly or unknowingly, tyaga leads us to happiness. Sacrifice gives us supreme satisfaction. Knowingly, we may not be able to do any sacrifice, but doing it consciously leads to great happiness. We must give up this body and enjoyment of the senses. For this kind of sacrifice, there must be a higher basis.

We do not know when this body, made up of the five sense organs, will drop off. Though they say that hundred years is the limit, do not believe it. We may die in childhood, in youth, in middle age, or in old age. This we do not know. Whether we will die in our own village or in the wilderness, we do not know. Death is the ultimate certainty. The wise man must realise the truth about death, during his lifetime. If you give up this 'deha bhranti', the body illusion during your lifetime, you will be able to develop the higher notion, the 'tyaga bhranti'. There must be a limit up to which you may nourish this body, which can be compared to a boat. Your life is the river. One side of the river is this world and on the other side is the other world. You have undertaken a voyage from this world to the other world, using the body as the boat and you must take care of this body, until you reach the other shore. This body must be looked upon as a boat; as a means to an end, but not as an end in itself.

We must take the Bhagavad Gita as the basis of knowing what pefect bliss is. God, Who is Mahakarma Swarupa, has assumed the Karma roopa and appears as Krishna. When Krishna in a Karma roopa is delivering a message, Arjuna takes the stula roopa. As long as Arjuna listened to the Gita in the gross form, he was not able to comprehend its significance. Arjuna prayed to the Lord to remove that great veil, which is born in the stula roopa and only when it was removed could he assimilate the Gita. All that Arjuna experienced is the result of that stula roopa. Arjuna became subject to that great agony in his mind because he was thinking of the people in front of him to be important as his kith and kin and as his forefathers, as his fathers, as his brothers and others of the same family. Later, Arjuna was able to absorb the spirit of the message of Gita and he was able to have a glimpse of the Viswa Roopa. Dhritarashtra also listened to the same Gita. He could not find any wisdom, because he simply listened to it in his stula roopa. When we listen to anything, we must listen to it in our awakened consciousness. What we gather through our ears is not enough, but we should try to meditate upon it and then assimilate it into our own system. Only then, it gives us real nourishment, enlightenment, and enjoyment. All our enjoyment may be classified into three parts, 'priya', 'pramoda', and 'moda'. When we look at an object, which is after our own liking and feel happy about it, it is priya. Moda is the joy we feel, when we acquire the object we like. Pramoda is the higher joy, the joy we feel at what we have really acquired. Today, we use the word priya in a meaningless manner. Priya means only looking at the object and not getting it or enjoying it. We must develop that attitude of pramoda and through pramoda, develop priya towards the object. We cannot enjoy real happiness through priya and moda. You want to have the darshan of the form of God. If you only look at it, it is priya and it does not give you much satisfaction. If you try to gain and master it, it gives greater happiness. When you are able to enjoy it completely, you become a part of it and vice versa. You do not get your stomach filled, when you look at a sweet in the shop. But, when you have the sweet in your hand, you have the guarantee that you can eat it any time. But, it is only half the achievement. When you have the sweet in your hand and whilst talking to some friend, a monkey may come and snatch it away. You cannot be absolutely sure of enjoying it. You get full satisfaction only after eating it and after it becomes a part of the digestive system.

The sadhana involved here is that it is no use looking at a sweet, but you should buy it, eat it, assimilate it, and make it a part of your own system. That gives you full happiness. You must always conduct your enquiry in such a way that the object you see becomes a part of your body by proper enjoyment and assimilation. This is described as step wise discipline. Following the right discipline leads to duty. If you look at a sweet and snatch it, it may amount to theft and acquisition in an improper manner. If you have the money, you pay the price and purchase the sweet. If the desire to eat is strong and you do not have the money, you may request the shopkeeper to give you one. He will give you one. Similarly, when you want to taste the moksha and feel you do not have sufficient strength, you may pray to God and God in His great mercy will give you the needed faculty. That, which you can procure in this manner, is truth.

Truth is God. Truth can be easily gained. Unfortunately, today, owing to your ignorance, you undertake many enterprises for the sake of falsehood. You should never give up the habit of discipline. When you reach the state of perfection only, you do not have to think of regulations or discipline. You must carry on your duties and responsibilities as long as you remain in these ashramas, beginning with brahmacharya and ending with sanyasa. If you want to build a house in the village, you certainly require the permission of the department, which controls it. If you want to roam in the forest, you may not require any permission from any office. On the other hand, as long as you are living in a society, you must necessarily discharge all your responsibilities and duties that are built around the society. Even the sanyasi and the brahmachari have their own duties set aside for each of them. Today, we find great agitations for rights, but very few people discharge their duties and realise their responsibilities. Remember that only when you are able to discharge your duties properly, you get the authority. You should not hanker after power, without doing your duty.

We must undertake sadhana and behave in a way that is like the Divine. This is the chief doctrine preached to Arjuna. Arjuna asked, "After having killed my kith and kin, what can I do with this kingdom? Instead, I shall become a beggar and go about begging." Then, Krishna asked, "Do you want to act according to your liking or according to My liking? If you want to follow your desire, then go as you please, but if you want to abide by My desire, then you must abide by what I say." It is for the Divine to discriminate in this matter and decide what is right and what is wrong. In Arjuna's thinking, greater importance had been given to the physical relationship of the body to body than the Divine relationship between man and man. Any love that is related to the body has an element of selfishness in it and this can be compared to the electric bulb we have in a room. The light of the bulb is limited by the walls of the room and this is like selfish love. Love, if it is on a higher plane, can be compared to moonlight. There is, in that case, light within and without. This light, too, is hazy and not clear. Pure love, which is entirely selfless, is like sun-shine. Sun-light gives us a clear view of all objects. God's love is like sun-shine. Human love is like the moonlight. Individual love is like the bulb in the room. You rise from the individual love and get into the state of mutual love.

One question is being often asked. Krishna is the Lord of the universe. He was all pervading and yet, the same Krishna was responsible for the destruction of forty lakhs of men on the battlefield. Is it violence or non-violence? This is My answer to this question. An individual, let us say, has developed cancer on his back. There are millions of germs in that cancerous boil. Does the doctor pause and ask, "Should I kill so many millions of germs?" Is it not the duty of the doctor to save the life of the patient? Which is of greater importance? Should he protect the life of the patient or should he have consideration for the germs? The doctor comes to the conclusion that these germs are dangerous and kills them and saves the patient's life. In this process, the doctor has taken into consideration quality and not quantity. In the same manner, the world at that time had developed a cancer in the shape of Kauravas. When Krishna found that these Kauravas were like cancer, He became a surgeon, took Arjuna as His assistant, and performed the great operation. In that operation, forty lakhs of germs were killed. So, we must always take into consideration the greater need for protection of dharma. The protection of dharma is more important than anything else.

Our life becomes one of fulfilment, when we lead it as one of morality. The greatness of life is not in amassing wealth. Remember that money comes and goes, but morality comes and grows. This view of morality has been safeguarding India from time immemorial. We do not now find morality in our society, our economics, our politics, our spirituality, and other walks of life. Today, I hope and wish that the students will always bear in mind that through morality, they will make their lives pure and can thus uphold the great culture of India. A bright future awaits them, if they follow the path of dharma.

20.

Pleasure And Pain

You cannot kill a snake by just beating on your ankle with a stick. Without conquering your body, you cannot know the truth; in this way, without conquering hunger and thirst, you cannot know the supreme reality; and if you do not have knowledge of the self, you cannot be called human.

Young students! For the last one month, you have been listening to very inspiring discourses and sacred talks and this one month must be a golden epoch and a memorable period in your lives. It is not enough, if you think that by listening to all these discourses, you have God's grace in full measure and that it will enable you to attain spirituality. You must preserve all the gems of truth in the casket of your hearts, you must cherish them and safeguard them forever. It is not enough if you simply think that you had the good luck to be admitted to this course. Though all the birds may be green, can all of them twitter like parrots? There may be many worms crawling on flowers, but can you call all of them bees? If an ass covers itself with the skin of a tiger, can that ass become a yogi? Alas, it cannot become even a tiger.

There is nothing in the world of today, which one cannot fathom or comprehend and which one cannot understand. One can purify his life, his body, and his time through the teachings that you had the good fortune to hear. But, if man does not realise his real nature, if he is simply engrossed in his worldly activities, which make him forget his real identity, he will not be able to gain anything at all. Man must first try to know who he is. Only then can he easily acquire the fruits of his endeavours. Man is classed as one among animals and to acquire the birth of man is really very difficult, because man occupies a supreme place among the animals. Everyone knows how the animals are all the time worried about getting food and filling their bellies. That seems to be the only engrossing activity of animals.

You may have seen cows in your house. As soon as the rope is loosened, the cow immediately goes to the place where there is green grass and tries to fill its belly with the grass. During the time of feeding, the animal brooks no delay at all and it eats up quickly all that is available. It does not mean that the food is digested simultaneously. Only when it returns to the cattle-shed, it tries to ruminate the food it ate before. Only after it ruminates the food, that food becomes part of its strength, because it gets assimilated into the system. The cow first eats as much as it can and later, digests the

Pleasure And Pain

food. In the same manner, all those, who had the privilege of benefiting from the Summer Course from morning to night, have been taking in eagerly all that they can lay their hands on, like the greedy animal, whose hunger is not easily satisfied. During the last month, you have been eating and eating. But, it is not the ordinary food, which one can eat at any eating place. For the past month, you have been supplied with this wonderful diet called the Sathwic diet in the shape of several discourses form learned elders. When you go back to your own places, you must try to ruminate over this sacred spiritual diet, which you have been eating during your stay here. This process of rumination may be described as 'manana', that is, thinking of it over and over again. Even in the case of an animal, if it does not ruminate, it is considered to be struck with some disease. You must enjoy all that you have amassed in this one month and make it your own through the process of manana and then, your stay here will be regarded as having been fulfilled. On the other hand, if you leave what you have heard here itself and return to your homes and relapse to the old ways of your life, then your lives will be disgusting and unattractive. But, the youth of today are in such a state that they do not know the difference between good and evil, between pure and impure, between truth and untruth. Not only young men, but also all human beings born in this kali yuga are becoming confused, because they do not know how to differentiate between good and evil, between sin and virtue, and between joy and sorrow. The sense of discrimination is being put to a severe test in us, because what seems to be good at one time seems to be bad at another time; what seems to be desirable at one time seems undesirable at another, what seems to be conducive to our health at one time seems to be dangerous to our health at another and so on.

We consume pure food and water, but in a very short time, it gets converted into impure matter worthy of only excretion. It is not easy to distinguish between what is pure food and pure water and what is not. We should not leave it at that, considering it to be prakriti dharma or a natural phenomenon. In nature, there will be impurities at first and we have to transform them by suitable processes. Scientists, specially those belonging to the geological department, know this very well. When they prospect for gold, they find out the spot where gold is, then dig deep into the earth and find impure lumps of raw gold mixed with other elements. In this natural state, gold is found to be in the company of other impurities. At a later stage, they purify the impure mass and get pure gold from it. All natural laws will be like this. It is a natural law to answer calls of nature, to sleep, to feed, and so on. But, by just following these laws of nature, we will not be able to go anywhere or reach any higher destinations. From the same heart, we find two emotions, one anger and the other mercy. Thus, we find it difficult to understand this nature, by which two contradicting emotions emanate from the same heart. Because the heart is the source of both good and evil, it is the bounden duty of students to understand how our ancestors were able to constantly focus their attention on good alone. Some people argue that man is born just for the

Pleasure And Pain

gratification of his senses. Some people think that they should amass food and wealth for the sake of joy and happiness only. If man simply consumes food like the other animals, how does man differ from them? Is it necessary to be born as a man to amass food? The bird, which is hungry and has not stored food, just goes straight to the food to satisfy its hunger. On the other hand, man stores food for the sake of future gratification. Man is not born to go in quest of food. He is born to go in quest of the atma.

We should develop our intelligence, because our intelligence enables us to know good from bad through the process of constant thought and discrimination. We should not stuff our heads with all worldly matters. We must implement the good principles, which we have stored in our minds. The discourses of elders and the messages of great books point out to the great principles of finding unity in diversity. But, this principle remains only theoretical, if it is not implemented in our daily lives. Several holy texts are exhorting us to find unity in diversity and recognise diversity in unity. This is being preached, but we cannot find one person, who by his actions is able to drive home the truth into our hearts. If we want to recognise unity in diversity, we must first know the meaning of these words. We may easily say that the elimination of sorrow and acquisition of joy is the simple path, which leads to spiritual illumination. Even in this regard, we must know the nature of sorrow. Only then, can we destroy or eliminate it. Sometimes, when we consider one experience to be sorrowful, after sometime, it may turn out to be a pleasurable one. And when we consider an experience to be a case of joy, it may turn out to be one of sorrow or anguish in due course.

I shall illustrate this in a small example. A mother longed for the birth of a son and her wish was granted. She gave birth to a son, but unfortunately, the next day, he developed a high temperature and died. Is this a matter of joy or sorrow? That birth, which was considered the source of joy, turned out to be a case for her anguish. Before the birth, she had undergone the pangs of birth. The same mother, when she looked at the face of her baby, forgot all her pain and was happy. What she considered to be a source of joy turned out to be one of sorrow and what she considered to be sorrow turned out to be delight.

We read in the papers about several incidents that happen in the world. A young couple, who are enjoying the thrill of their first day of wedded life, are travelling on a bus with some friends and relatives. Unfortunately, the bus meets with an accident and their joy is turned into sorrow. We exult in winning a lottery and feel very happy about the one lakh of rupees we have won. But, the same night, it may be pilfered by a robber. Sometimes, we are perturbed, not knowing how to spend the money. There is joy on one hand in having the money, but also anxiety on the other hand.

Several businessmen rejoice over the profits they have made, but are agonised on the heavy income tax that will be levied. Therefore, life is a symphony of joy

Pleasure And Pain

and sorrow, a mixture of pleasure and pain. Man cannot decide for himself the difference between joy and sorrow. It is not possible for us to have joy without sorrow or sorrow without joy. We must develop the attitude that all sorrow leads to happiness and that all happiness leads to sorrow, because man cannot choose for himself only joy or only sorrow. He must cultivate the attitude of synthesis of joy and sorrow and develop equanimity. He should not be exhilarated by pleasure and he should not be depressed by pain. Pleasure and pain always follow each other and no one can separate one from the other. A synthesis of these two can be obtained only through spiritual paths and not through any other path.

It is possible for us to develop this knowledge of oneness and thereby, develop the right attitude towards joy and sorrow. Though you have come from several parts of the country, you are able to mingle together like brothers and sisters, because there is that undercurrent of unity that you are all Sai devotees. Here, Sai is one, but the individuals are many. It helps us to recognise unity in diversity among the people here. In this baffling multiplicity is the shining unity of Sai. This garland in My hand may be regarded as one of the flowers, consisting of various colours and perfumes. The flowers are many, but the thread that binds the flowers together is one. Sai is the thread. You are all the flowers of various colours. We must take into consideration another aspect. Some flowers may be buds today. Tomorrow, they will blossom and the day after, they will be full blown. You are young today and after 10 years, you may become householders and after 50 years, you will become old. This process of evolution is inevitable. The flowers undergo change, but the thread remains the same. This thread is the eternal unchanging thread, called the Brahmasutra. That principle, which is changeless, is Brahmatatwa.

Human life is made up of several stages. Birth, growth, ageing, getting debilitated, and death are the various stages of the changing body. In this field, which is full of change, the principle which remains unchanged is the Divinity. The body is full of 'Vikaras', but the atma is the 'Nirvikara'. These are referred to in the Gita as 'Kshetra' and 'Kshetragna'. 'Kshetra' is the body, which is the field and the 'kshetragna' is Paramatma. We question ourselves as to why we visit the field. It is not to see the field, but to see the master of the field. When we go on a pilgrimage to Kashi, it is not to see Kashi, but to have the darshan of Lord Viswanath of Kashi. Because Viswanath lives in Kashi, it becomes a place of pilgrimage. Why do we nourish and protect the body, which is the Kshetra? It is only for the Kshetragna residing in this body. Those, who lose sight of Kshetragna, and those, who are engrossed only in the Kshetra, should be termed businessmen. Several businessmen go to Banaras to buy saris and never visit the temple of Viswanath. But, he, who goes to Banaras for darshan, goes to the shrine of the Lord and then visits the market. Therefore, every individual must clearly bear in mind that the ultimate aim of the Kshetra is to enable the darshan of the Kshetragna residing in him.

In the Gita, Lord Krishna says He is both the Kshetra and the Kshetragna. The Kshetra is not purposeful without the Kshetragna and vice versa. Both are interdependent. Because of this, Lord Krishna said that He is both the Kshetra and Kshetragna. He said that He is all pervading through both, but there is a little distinction between these two. It is clear that by taking into consideration the letters of kshetra, which are two syllables, we can see that it is different from kshetragna, which has three syllables. The vital difference is in the syllable 'gna', which means 'Gnana Swarupa'! Kshetragna is that, which is Gnana Swarupa and without that, it is merely kshetra. We will never enter into bad ways and have evil thoughts, when we bear this in mind that kshetra, which is almost inert, becomes sanctified by the residence of kshetragna, which is Gnana Swarupa.

When somebody says that he is God, we expect him to be above all other human beings. When God does anything wrong, we wonder if he is God and if he could do that, because we think of God as One, Who always does right. Even in the case of a human being, when we consider him to be gentle by temperament, even if he is once motivated by anger, then we begin to doubt. Could we call him sathwic? Then, we condemn him and think that if he is really good, he would not have done this at all. Will you ever take to bad deeds, when you feel that God resides in this body? When you recognise the sacred principle dwelling within you, you will always do good and take to good actions. You must also recognise this body as a temple and feel that God resides in that temple. It is said that this body is your temple and within this body God, the Eternal Principle, dwells. But today, this body has unfortunately degenerated into a dwelling place of the devil. You must understand the difference between the dwelling place of God and the dwelling place of the devil. In the house of God, there will always be an eternal flame, shining forever. Where there is light, you will find no bats. Where there is darkness, you will find bats befouling the place. If you do not kindle the flame of pure thoughts in the temple of your body, then bats will befoul it and it will be densely dark. You must see that this sacred flame burns eternally. Kindle the flame of love, the flame of knowledge, and the flame of devotion in your hearts. So long as a bright light burns in that shrine, the bats or evil tendencies will not cross the threshold of the shrine.

We have accepted the Nama Sankirtan as one of our main programmes of Sai activities. The name of the Lord must dance on your tongues forever. Nama Sankirtan and Nagar Sankirtan are given a prominent place in our activities. There are some amongst you, who ask why we should utter the name of God with our tongue. Is it not enough to think of God in our mind? The Lord's name is like an effulgent lamp. The form of the holy name can be compared to the great sacred cow that confers on us all that we desire. The form of God, with the help of the name which is like the rope, must be tied to your heart. The heart, which is like a pillar, is where it should be bound. Your mouth is the main entrance to the house of the body. When you have a lantern at the main gate, the light can be seen without and within. So, the sacred flame of the holy name sheds light inward and outward.

If we compare our life to a tree, like many birds perch on the branch of a tree, we can conceive of several birds perching on the branches of this tree of life. These birds come to eat food, to rest, or to foul the place. When we see a number of birds making noise on the tree in our courtyard, we go out, clap our hands, and shout to scare the birds away. The birds that perch on the tree of our life are the bad tendencies that wish to foul our thoughts. We should drive them away with the 'Nama' and the 'Tala'. But, in doing this, what do we gain? When the birds remain on the tree, the shade below the tree is befouled. When the birds go away, the precincts become pure and clean. Probably, you may be wondering what you should do if the birds come again. If you continue to make the sound with your hands and with your mouth, the birds will not return to the tree at all. To purify your minds and to prevent these bad tendencies from entering your thoughts must be the aim of your life. You must continuously chant the name of the Lord, so that these birds may not return. The tongue of man is the holiest instrument, because it can utter the sweet and delicate name of God. Therefore, you must never feed this tongue with impure sounds, because the tongue by itself is sacred and holy. It is one of the most sacred and holy things for you to learn from the summer classes that you should feed your tongue with sacred sounds and words. You must also not use your eyes to look at harmful things. You should look at good and useful things only.

Many may be familiar with the story of Suradas. He was blind. In His infinite mercy, Lord Krishna asked him if he wanted vision, so that he could look at Him. Suradas said, "Though people have eyes, they are filled with ignorance and are not able to recognise Your grand form. Though people have ears, they are deaf and cannot appreciate the sweetness of Your holy name. Many people have eyes and ears, but they do not use them to look at Your scintillating form and listen to Your name, but I want eyes, which will always visualise Your grand form and ears, which will always listen to the harmony of Your song." Prahlada used to say, "What is the use of these ears, if they are like the caves in the mountain of the human body? What is the use of eyes being always wide open like the goat's eyes, if they do not have light of knowledge and eagerness to know the real truth of the world?" We should not use our eyes for looking at things of a petty nature, but we should use them to look at our parents, at God, at our elders, and at all good things. But, today, the eyes of our young men are focussed on the banners and posters of film stars pasted on the walls in the street. If you focus your attention on such objects, you get lost. Thereby, your hearts will be devoid of humane qualities. If you give place to evil thoughts, if you degrade the temple of your body, then the very purpose of your life will be lost.

Dear students! When you return to your places, avoid bad friends and fill your minds with noble and elevating things. Chant the name of God and practise Nama Sankirtan in the early hours of the day and remember the name of God throughout the day. Though you have now developed the habit of getting up at 4 or 5'o'clock, you may relapse into the habit of getting up at 9'o'clock at home. Then, there is no person more idle than you. You will be humiliating yourself. When you get up in the morning, sit on your bed and think of the Lord. Think that your getting up from the bed is like rising from the womb. Therefore, you are just born. As soon as you get up, throw your troubles and burdens at the feet of the Lord and pray to Him to guide you through life and give you only good thoughts and noble ideas, which always serve as uplifting factors in life. When you go back to bed at night, imagine that to be a state of death. When you back to bed at night, tell yourself that during the day, you have acted according to the Lord's orders. Ask for forgiveness if there is anything wrong and ask to be led on the path of righteousness. In the morning, before entering the world of action, have implicit faith in God and be back in bed at night, requesting God to keep you in the right path and to help you. If you begin and end your day with such prayers, it will help you reach higher altitudes of living. Even during your bath, if you remember the name of God, it will be like bathing the form of God.

When you take food, all the evils are eliminated if you offer the first morsel to God. The food then becomes prasad of the Lord bestowed on man. Prasad is the very embodiment of elixir. It may not be possible to insist that the vessel be pure, that the man, who cooks the food, be pure, and that the food be pure, but if you offer the first morsel to God, it becomes utterly pure.

When you return to your homes, you may find Seva Samithis and Seva Dals in your places. Take active part in them. Always try to help those, who are in distress, those, who are suffering, and the poor. Once upon a time, there lived in Tamil Nadu a poet and holy man named Manika Vachi. He used to sit on a verandah in his house, in front of the Lord's picture and chant beautiful songs, songs which are like the shining gems after which he was named. He gave the message of service to mankind. One day, it was raining heavily and he sought shelter in another little verandah in the village. One other man came and asked him if he could also take shelter there. Manika Vachi said he could. He said, "There was place only for me to stretch out, but now that you are here, we will sit up." Later, another man came and asked for shelter. Manika Vachi consented, saying, "There was place for the two of us to sit. Now that you also have come, let us all stand." Manika Vachi taught this principle of helping one another and not send anyone away, who needed help. If you have three morsels of food and you find another man with no food, you must cultivate the spirit of serving and parting with one morsel of food for the other man. You must cultivate this attitude of sharing with others the good things you have. Then only can you put into practice the great principle of finding Ishwara in every creature. You must practise this principle in daily life. All of you have great love and adore Swami, but that love and adoration are of no use, if you ignore the teachings of Swami. Even if you do not adore, but if you believe in the truth of the word and enforce it in your daily life, Swami's grace will always be with you in your life. It is no use if you simple utter the name of the Lord and if you do not follow the good things that go with the Lord. It is just like uttering the name of penicillin, when you are running a high temperature. Only when you take in the penicillin will the temperature come down. When you are hungry, the hunger cannot be satisfied by uttering words, like potato and chapati. If you eat them, it will be satisfied. It is no use, if you only listen. You must try to remember the discourses you have listened to during this month, put them into practice, and judge for yourself how far you have acted according to the word. Your parents must be able to recognise the transformation in you. When you return home, try to give evidence of the changes that have come about in you and make your people realise that you uphold the great culture of India.

21.

Learning And Humility

India is a sacred land and in this sacred land, tolerance has always been the cardinal virtue. Of all the 'vratas', or the acceptance of codes of conduct, the vrata of truth plays a high role. The highest and sweetest of all emotions is that of maternal love. People in India always considered honour greater than life. Alas, today, we have let all those laudable ideas slip away and we have begun to ape the cult of the west. We have reached a stage, where we have lost the sense of our own greatness like the elephant, who does not know its own strength.

In the front line are seated the wise elders, who have striven all through the month to inculcate into the minds of the young students gathered here, knowledge of the soul. They have been expounding our sacred texts, the shastras and the vedas, reminding you about the glory of ancient India. Today, there is a feeling of a possible separation, but there is also a feeling of oneness between the teacher and the taught. Today, we think of wealth as consisting of buildings, property, material goods and we have lost ourselves in the mad pursuit of temporal values. These do not constitute real wealth, which is capable of giving us abounding joy. Character is our wealth and good conduct is our treasure. Knowledge of God is the foundation for both. We should not lose that abiding, precious, and eternal wealth, which is knowledge of God, for fleeting and temporary things, which are like the passing clouds. We should also know that in our country, many Rajas, who were very rich at one time, are today reduced to the level of the common people and on the other hand, some of the common people have come up to the position of kings, enjoying greater material wealth; therefore, we should not equate lasting happiness with changing material wealth.

When the pond is full of water in the rainy season, there are a million frogs in it; but when the water runs dry, the frogs jump out of it. In the same way, when one has power and wealth, people gather around him in this world, but as soon as he falls upon evil days and adversity stares him in the face, all his best friends leave him. It is the paramount duty of man to know what will not leave him and to gain that wealth, which will always be with him. The history of India has always given us examples of great incidents and illustrious people. We remember people like Ravana, Hiranyakasipu, and others, who had all material wealth, but forgot the values of life and started insulting others. They ultimately had a great downfall.

Today, those, who are proud of their material prosperity and ignore the higher values of life, must know that the same ruin awaits them. Viswamitra felt proud of his physical strength and the strength of his tapas. He even challenged Vasishta, but realised that Vasishta had something he did not possess and that was the strength of God, which is superior to all other kinds of strength.

There is an incident in our tradition, which every student should know and bear in mind. Krishna posed a question to Arjuna and Duryodhana. He said, "Duryodhana, there are two things, namely the army and Myself. Which of the two do you want?" He asked the same question of Arjuna, too. Because Duryodhana was ignorant, he had foolishly thought that all the physical prowess of the army would make for him a stronger support than Krishna, Who was only one individual. He, therefore, asked for the army and not for Krishna. But, Arjuna realised that if he had Krishna by his side, he would have everything. So, he said, "Lord, be the charioteer of my chariot and not only of my chariot, but the charioteer of my life. Your proximity is my eternal treasure." Arjuna cared for quality and Duryodhana cared for quantity.

Today, we must focus our attention on the higher values of life and we must not lose sight thereof in mad pursuit of the baser values, which would mislead us. In God's creation, man is the most precious of all creatures. Man today is behaving in such a way that there is no trace of Divinity in him. He behaves like a monkey, exhibiting his baser instincts, losing sight of the higher values of life. The four wheels of the chariot that lead man safely to his destination are character, truth, sacrifice, and tolerance. Man, today, loses sight of the fact that he is an eternal spirit and lives only for the present moment, losing sight of the sublime values of life. Good education is only that, which unfolds all the hidden powers in man. Today, people are wasting their lives just by reading many books. They do not try to understand the spirit, nor do they implement that, which they read. Today, book knowledge has increased and experience has not correspondingly increased. If we look at the records in any college, we see more remarks on students than marks for each one of them. The real marks we should aim at are such as to get rid of remarks.

Real education requires the cultivation of a sense of humility. Great learning brings great humility. Without humility, there is no education. This is wanting in the youth of today. Several differences are cropping up between the teacher and the taught. There are several differences developing between students and the centres of learning. When we look at this problem and try to understand what is at the back of all this, how these sad situations have developed and where the responsibility lies, the answer comes that it is generally not the teacher, nor the student, but it is the politician, who has much to do with it. Students are pure, their minds are pure and are selfless. The white dress, which they have put on as a uniform this day, is the emblem of the innate purity of the young. They have been living for the past one month in Whitefield. The white uniform is in tune with the spirit of Whitefield. Your heart is the field, which is the Kshetra. It is not enough for you to remain pure only as long as you are in Brindavan, but your hearts must be pure wherever you may be.

There are a number of people, who approach the youth, pervert them, mislead them, use them as instruments to be provoked while whipping up their emotions. Students should not let such people ruin their future. They should not become pawns in the hands of the selfish people and be exploited by politicians. You must first of all work for yourself and enjoy happiness for your own sake. In the beginning, you must try for self-satisfaction. Only after attaining self-satisfaction can you be self-confident. As students, you must spend all your time in studying and later, serve your country when you leave the portals of your institution. When your heart is not pure and your powers are not developed, you cannot become a leader of your country. Only when a tank is full of water, it can be made to flow into the taps. Only when you fill your hearts with noble thoughts, powerful ideals and, sublime emotions will you be able to distribute them to the country, just as water is distributed through taps.

When there are any differences between students and the centres of learning, it is up to the students to make a peaceful and gentle representation to the authorities. Then, the authorities will also be in a gentle mood to consider the representation. On the other hand, if the students indulge in violent demonstrations, they are forgetting their natural role in life. If the student is a seeker of vidya, he should not behave in a manner that tells us that he is a student, who is going on the path of ignorance.

Even if you win your point through violent agitation and by creating trouble for others, such gains will not be permanent gains for the student body. Therefore, students must always cultivate the habit of representing their grievances in a peaceful and gentle manner, so that the elders may pay heed to them.

Several people want to whip up a revolution, but do not know what they want to achieve. On the other hand, what we can achieve through love, tolerance, and peace is always greater and more lasting than what we can achieve through a violent revolution. What we gain through violence will be temporary and unholy. Indians achieved their freedom by adopting the technique of peaceful agitation and not through violent revolution. When we want to gain something good, naturally, we will be confronted with certain difficulties. We should not be deterred by these obstacles, but go ahead focussing on the goal that shines ahead of us. People pelt stones only at the tree, which bears good fruit. If the tree does not bear good fruit, nobody would care to fling a stone at it. We will be able to display the Divine in us, when we are able to put up with all these difficulties and offer the supreme fruit of such patience to others as well. During the period of your studies, you must realise your responsibility as students. You must show proper regard to the parents and teachers and thereby, fill your minds with happiness and peace. In the ancient Gurukula, the relationship, which existed between the teacher and the student, was as intimate as that, which should exist between a parent and his offspring. The student would always try to give mental and physical happiness to the

Learning And Humility

guru. That service pleased the guru and he would impart very vital secrets to the disciple and a very sacred, holy atmosphere prevailed in the precincts. Arjuna served Dronacharya in several ways. He was able to win the heart of Dronacharya through that service. Dronacharya loved Arjuna more than his own son and used to send his son away on some pretext and then, impart some vital secrets to Arjuna. In order to elicit the secrets from the guru, the first requisite of the student is that he must win the grace of the guru by pleasing him. Only after satisfying your guru can you get the secrets, which are of great importance, from him. If you do not give satisfaction to the guru, you will be put to a great loss.

You must try to give satisfaction to your parents as well. Your parents are the source of your physical body. Ancient Indian culture has offered us gems of wisdom in asking us to revere our parents and gurus as gods on Earth. Today, we rarely find such parents, such gurus, and such sons. It is very important that all the girl students be trained into good housewives and good mothers. Just as they have tasted the sweetness of the love of Sai Mata, so also they must taste by their actions of dedication, the love of Desa mata and train themselves into ideal mothers in future. I hope that you will all treasure these gems of wisdom you have extracted from the discourses, in the last month, preserve them in the casket of your heart and now and then bring them up as ornaments on your person.

At one time, there was a severe famine in Bihar. A family consisting of father, mother, and two children started from Bihar to find livelihood elsewhere. The father of the family being responsible to feed his family, underwent many difficulties and hardships. He even starved himself on some occasions and because of this frequent starvation, he died after sometime. The mother, having lost her husband, suffered from loneliness and had to bear the burden of keeping the family alive in this wide world. She went begging from house to house for food and if she got some and if it was not enough, she starved and let her children eat. In course of time, she became so debilitated that she found it difficult to walk from house to house and beg. The boy of twelve looked at the pitiable sight of his mother and sitting on her lap, said, "Oh mother, please take rest for some time. I shall beg and bring food for you." As she listened to the words of her son, her heart melted. She felt very miserable that she had to send her son to beg for food. No mother wants her child to become a beggar. But, because the boy insisted, the mother consented. From that day, the little boy was begging for food and giving it to his mother and the little brother and he himself would starve. After some days, he felt he could not walk and go out for begging. He went to a house and found the master of the house reading newspaper, sitting on an easy chair. In a feeble voice, he asked the master for food. The master replied that it would be useless to give him alms and said that he would give him food on a leaf. The boy, out of weakness, fainted. The master of the house lifted the boy and put him on his lap. The boy was mumbling some words. To be able to understand what he was saying, the master put his ear close to the mouth of the boy. The boy was inaudibly whispering, "The food that you wish to give, please give it first to my mother." After uttering those last words, he passed away.

We do not now find this kind of love, this intimate love existing between the members of a family. Here, we find that the head of the family starved himself to death for the sake of his family, the mother starved herself for the sake of her children, and the son starved and killed himself to save his mother from begging. Look at this noble example of affection that bound together the different members of the family. When these three are united together as father, mother, and child, they look like the Holy Trinity. Therefore, each member of the family must discharge his own responsibility. Only then will the family be in a state of prosperity and happiness. All the householders in ancient India tried to follow their duties of discharging all obligations and never claimed any rights for themselves. Wherever we go today, we find agitation for rights by people, who do not recognise their responsibilities. If you discharge your responsibility in the right spirit, that will give you real power from the well deserved authority. Our students must always remember the two great principles – work and worship – and follow them every minute of their life. Whatever job you take up, do it to the best of your ability and do your duty to the best and utmost satisfaction of everyone concerned. Even in your home, you must discharge all your obligations and responsibilities. If you are able to satisfy your parents today, by discharging your duty in the proper spirit, tomorrow your children will offer you similar satisfaction. If you aspire for a happy and secure life in the future, you must lead your present life in a conducive way by discharging all your obligations in the right spirit.

I have been talking to you these thirty days about several things. Today, I do not want to take time and talk about things that have already been spoken about and tax your patience, but I hope that you will follow the ideals that you have imbibed in the past one month. When you will be out of Brindavan, you should show the same sense of discipline and follow the same principles in any walk of life or in any place you may go to. In course of time, you may come back in a different role; in the role of teachers, who teach youngsters. The teachers of today hope that all their messages will be implemented in your daily practice and when you become teachers, you will hope the same from your students. If you try to live up to the expectations of your teachers, by implementing the advice they have offered, you can then hope that the students in the future will offer you similar satisfaction, by implementing your message in their lives. All the wise elders, who gave you messages during this course, were also students at one time. You must try to preserve in your mind and put into practice all these good things, which these wise elders, who had the benefit of wisdom of years of learning, have given you. There may be summer courses in several places, but they will not have the same kind of training that you get here and the type of atmosphere, in which you have been living. Those students, who have attended this summer course, are fortunate and this surely is the result of the merit, which they have accumulated through a number of births. They had the benefit of many wise teachers and their teachings should not be ignored. Every teacher, who has delivered lectures, has delivered not only lectures, but delivered drops of love that had emanated from his heart. You have seen how these teachers were touched to leave you and how they had broken down. This is the true quality of a guru. Where else can you find it, except in a summer couse of this kind? These gurus are feeling very much for the separation from you. You must also be feeling pained at the thought of getting separated from your gurus. You should not feel pained by the mere thought of separation. When you put into action the wise things that your gurus have taugth you, then they and also Swami will be with you. Only through action can you have the vital presence of the guru deep down in your heart. He will be a living presence within you.

www.ingramcontent.com/pod-product-compliance
Lightning Source LLC
Chambersburg PA
CBHW020922090426
42736CB00010B/1007